Container
Gardening
on
Balconies
and
Terraces

Susan Berry
and *Val Bradley*

COLLINS & BROWN

First published in Great Britain by
Collins & Brown Limited in 2001
London House, Great Eastern Wharf
Parkgate Road, London, SW11 4NQ

1 3 5 7 9 8 6 4 2

British Library Cataloguing in
Publication Data:
A catalogue record for this book is available
from the British Library.

ISBN 1 85585 8088

Designer **Ruth Hope**
Editor **Corinne Asghar**
Editorial assistant **Niamh Hatton**

Reproduction by Global Colour Separation,
Malaysia, Printed and bound in the
UK by Bath Press

Distributed in the United States and Canada by
Sterling Publishing Co,
387 Park Avenue South, New York,
NY10016, USA

Contents

Introduction

Small-space gardening makes particular demands on you the gardener. Dealing with such a limited space means that there is no room for plants that are not looking and performing at their best.

You need to select the best plants and then ensure that they are in good shape. With only a small space to play with, you are going to have to opt primarily for short-term results – bulbs and annuals – with the occasional backdrop of permanent planting.

Plant choices

Choosing the structural or feature plants has to be done with careful consideration, since ideally you want plants that look good all year round. Do not be seduced by a flowering shrub which looks good for ten days in summer, and has nothing to recommend it the rest of the year, unless you position it in a group with plants that perform well at other times. Camellias, for example, offer a fairly short-lived but breathtakingly beautiful display in spring only, but their evergreen foliage will act as a backdrop to other plants flowering later in spring and summer.

In towns, with just a window box or two, or a very narrow balcony, you might consider opting for a permanent, highly structured evergreen display, in which small-leaved foliage plants are clipped into formal shapes. You can

Japanese style (left)
Creating a theme for a balcony or roof terrace gives a feeling of space, enhanced by well-chosen plants. Pebbles, decking and reed screens are the key features for this theme.

Lofty plant perch (right)
Florists' buckets on a former chimney stack create a blue-mauve, pink and grey scheme with grasses, lavender, pinks and Convolvulus cneorum.

Formal balcony (above)

Here, an elegant, classically inspired balcony has an all-year-round display
of clipped box in pots which are lined against the railings, and staged
against one wall.

combine a few pots of flowering plants among them to add colour at the
different seasons, but to keep the formal effect you will need to go for a series
of single-theme pots rather than a mishmash of colours, shapes and sizes.

Display areas

Even the smallest space offers potential for plant displays; the top of a wall,
around a doorway, up a flight of steps, and of course the windowsills of the
house or apartment. In addition, you can hang containers on walls or suspend
them from brackets.

When choosing the containers and plants, you need to consider the setting
and situation, aiming to achieve an effect that complements the surrounding
architecture, since it provides the backdrop to the entire scheme. Different styles
of architecture, and differing materials, demand different treatments. Soft grey
stone walls can be cheered up with bright displays of colourful flowers. Pure
white walls look best with less garish displays as the effect of brilliant scarlet and
white, unless in a very hot climate, can be overpowering. Softer blues and
mauves, with silvery-green foliage, would look more harmonious, as would
simple displays of clipped formal evergreens.

Individual taste and preferences will play a very great part in your plant
choice, but try to resist a natural instinct to have 'a bit of everything' in order to
give the display greater unity and harmony. Cottage-style planting
looks wonderful in cottage gardens, and although there is a certain glamour in
having a riot of colour surrounding your house and balcony, you can tire of its

effect rather quickly. A scheme that is more low key is likely to appeal over a longer period of time.

It is always a good idea to include scented plants in small spaces. Being so close to them, you get the full advantage of their gloriously fragrant flowers and leaves, as the breeze wafts their perfume through open doors and windows. Plants that attract butterflies and insects are worth a try too, although you may decide, for obvious reasons, that you do not want the latter on windowsills when the windows are opened.

Climbing plants are a huge bonus because they take up such little ground space in return for providing you with yards of foliage and flower power. Trained up a house wall, or over a pergola or canopy by a door, they can be used to stunning effect. Try growing a sweetly scented semi-evergreen honeysuckle over a porch, a grape vine over a series of metal poles on a balcony (to cast marvellous dappled shade in summer) or a combination of roses and clematis against the walls of a house or flat.

Shelter and screening

Privacy and protection from strong winds are prime considerations when creating a planting scheme for a balcony or roof terrace. Some plants withstand cold winds better than others, and if you use these for windbreaks, you can then grow more tender plants, with their protection, than you would be able to do otherwise. Usually those plants that cope well with coastal conditions – evergreens like sea buckthorn, escallonia and griselinia – all fairly hardy and evergreen – are ideal. Some of the hardy bamboos make a similarly useful screen, grown in a deep trough. Alternatively, put up stout trellis made from sturdy timber and grow hardy climbers over it. Honeysuckle, for example, is not only tough but most varieties have the bonus of sweetly scented summer flowers. One honeysuckle, *Lonicera* x *purpusii*, has similarly fragrant flowers in winter.

Size counts (left)

Large pots do not have to house large plants. Here, a giant terracotta pot houses an informal display of daisies.

Tiered display (right)

A narrow shady terrace is enhanced with a tiered planting of topiary in raised urns and pots. A ribbon-like planting of busy lizzies flanks one side – ideal for adding colour to a shady area.

Gardening using pots and containers is not so very different from gardening generally, but you have to understand that the limited growing space and the lack of a natural cycle of decay for nutrients imposes certain conditions on you, the gardener. This chapter covers the basic techniques of gardening in containers, from choosing the type of pots and plants, planting, watering and feeding to increasing the stock and supporting the plants, as well as general container-plant maintenance throughout the year. A small section provides guidance on pests and diseases, but, if well cared for, container-grown plants should not have too many problems.

TECHNIQUES

Wire pot (right)

An ornate semi-circular wire basket makes a good choice for wall planting.

Choosing containers

Because you are gardening in a very confined place, you are limited to using containers of one sort or another, and the container is as much in evidence as the flowers or foliage it contains.

Choosing and displaying the containers themselves requires as much artistry as grouping the plants, and the size, shape and construction of the container makes a major contribution to the effect. As with all other elements of gardening, there are fashions in containers, too. The classic shapes – the Versailles tub (copied, as the name suggests, from the famous garden), the large simple terracotta pot, and the classical stone urn – never go out of fashion but they look better in some settings than others. If, for example, you have a modern penthouse or balcony flat with quite strong modern architecture, these classical containers would look totally out of place. Modern rectangular metal tubs or long troughs would be eminently more appropriate, as would slatted wooden containers, and both look equally good on decked surfaces, which have become increasingly popular for both balconies and terraces.

Terracotta pots (above)

Terracotta pots come in a wide range of sizes and colours. These elegantly simple 'Long Tom' pots are both modern and sophisticated.

Stone containers (below)

Real or imitation stone is often used for classical containers. Group them with other pots of a similar tone or texture.

Weight is always a consideration and you need to ensure that the construction of your balcony or terrace can support the containers you have in mind. If necessary, get advice from a structural engineer if you are planning a large or particularly heavy display.

It is a good idea, always, to group containers. Not only does it improve the effect of the display, it makes tending the plants easier and they benefit from mutual support, and you can stagger the heights and sizes to give variety to the planting. Generally it is better not to mix materials unless you can provide some other link – colour, perhaps, or texture. The colours of containers should be carefully considered too. Generally, the quieter, more subdued colours look best – well-weathered terracotta, grey stone, gunmetal or weathered wood provide the ideal backdrop for the plants. If, however, the plant itself is highly architectural (a yucca, or cordyline with spiky purple leaves) then you could opt for, say, a deep blue ceramic container.

Grouped pots (right)

It is best to group pots of a similar texture and colour together to unify the planting scheme. Here, terracotta pots in different sizes are used for a table-top display.

Stone trough (left)

Real or reconstituted stone is used to make handsome, classical-looking troughs which are ideal for window boxes or balconies.

Metal window boxes (above)

Elegant metal window boxes with a nineteenth-century embossed design suit a formal town house or apartment.

Versailles tub (right)

The wooden 'Versailles' tub is the ideal choice for small trees or formal standards.

INSTALLING AND FIXING CONTAINERS

On a roof garden, windowsill or balcony, safety is vital. Make sure containers on ledges or wall tops are fixed with a chain or there is a lip to prevent them being blown away in high winds. Put the heaviest containers in roof gardens closest to load-bearing walls. Use drip trays to prevent seepage of silt from containers, which can block drainage channels and gutters.

Hanging baskets need properly fixed brackets and supports. For wall fixing, a wrought-iron bracket is most attractive. You will need a drill with a

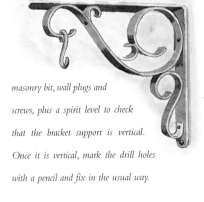

masonry bit, wall plugs and screws, plus a spirit level to check that the bracket support is vertical. Once it is vertical, mark the drill holes with a pencil and fix in the usual way.

Overhead hooks must be able to hold the weight of a hanging basket, which can be considerable when wet. The best kind has a hook and pulley, so you can lower the basket to water it. The metal holding plate is screwed to a supporting beam. If you are using a pulley, fix the stay to the wall using screws and wall plugs.

Decorating containers

Exercise your creativity by customizing containers to suit your planting scheme. Even old wallpaper troughs can be given a lick of paint to make successful window boxes.

Containers are expensive, and one way to make your budget go further is to decorate pots that are not intrinsically attractive in themselves. Old tomato tins could be recycled as plant containers with a coat of paint, a plain terracotta pot could be given a contrasting border, or an old metal tub given a verdigris effect using special paint finish techniques.

It is best to opt for fairly simple decorative techniques that weather well and do not look too gaudy. An equally useful trick is to weather the brash colour of new terracotta pots to a naturally aged and softened colour much faster than time would normally allow by applying a coat of yoghurt to the pot, which encourages green lichen to form.

Make sure that the colours of your chosen plants and containers complement each other. White daisies or yellow calendula would look good in bright blue containers, while brilliant pink and red zinnias could be put into scarlet pots for a hot-coloured display.

Verdigris pot (above)

The simple technique of verdigris suits classic-style plantings, as this little pot of ferns for a shady corner demonstrates.

HOW TO VERDIGRIS A POT

Copper, when left to weather, turns a wonderful bluish-green in colour. This effect can be imitated on a simple metal bucket.

1 *Clean the bucket and apply a coat of metal primer with a soft paintbrush, and allow to dry.*

2 *Apply a coat of mid- to dark brown emulsion to cover the surface of the bucket, and leave to dry.*

3 *Stipple light green and light blue emulsion on the bucket and leave to dry. Apply a coat of clear varnish.*

PAINTED TIN CANS

A large tin can makes a useful container. Given a coat of gloss paint to withstand the rain, these cans look best with a natural cottage-style planting.

1 *Turn the can upside down and use a hammer and nail to punch six holes in the base, as shown.*

2 *Make sure any cut edges of the can are not sharp. If they are, cover with masking tape which will be hidden when the can is painted.*

3 *Give the can a coat of gloss paint, and leave to dry before potting up your plants.*

Painted tomato tins (above) *Fill the tins with a repeating planting scheme – in this case white argyranthemums.*

Tools and equipment

A small selection of tools is essential. Keep them in a wooden box, and ensure that any blades are oiled and sharpened once a year.

shears

You need very little in the way of special tools if you are gardening in containers, but you will need a hand fork and trowel, a good garden knife, secateurs and shears. You will also need watering and spraying equipment. It is helpful to have a special storage place for the tools and materials (a small lean-to can often be constructed on a large balcony or roof garden).

hand trowel

Choosing tools

The better quality tools will have the handle fixed to the shaft with tang-and-ferrule construction. A dibber is a useful tool to have, but a sharpened stout stick will do the job. It can be used for making planting holes and for pushing the compost around the roots of the plant when potting on.

Secateurs are either of anvil construction – with a blade that chops against a flat plate – or with a double blade. The latter are more costly, but eliminate bruising and tearing because they tend to make a cleaner, sharper cut. A good watering can is well balanced. Modern watering cans tend to be oblong, but the old metal ones, in my opinion, do the job as well and look attractive enough to be left outside on display. A hand-held sprayer (1.5l/2½ pints upwards) is invaluable for foliar feeds and for misting plants in hot weather.

secateurs

hand fork

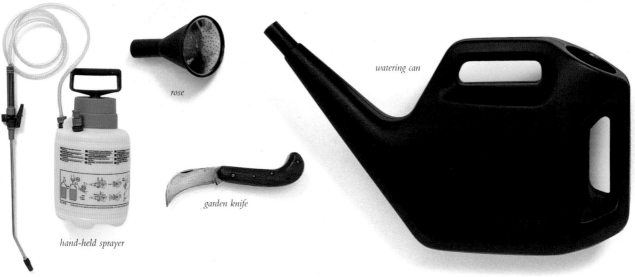

rose

watering can

hand-held sprayer

garden knife

Composts and potting mediums

Most plants need repotting every couple of years with fresh compost. Although the compost contains nutrients, these will eventually be leached out from the pots by rain, so you will need to add nutrients as necessary.

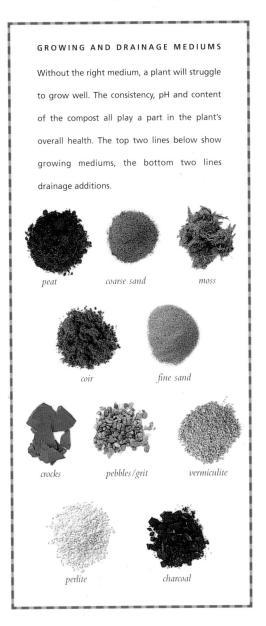

Those of us without a garden are obliged to buy some form of compost in which to grow our plants. In the old days, special formulas were created and you chose the best for a particular plant. Multi-purpose compost (made up of loam, sand and peat) suits most plants of average vigour, but if you are growing edibles such as tomatoes, you would be better off with a formula containing a greater amount of nutrients. Grow-bags, with specially formulated composts for edible plants, can be bought and the plants inserted into them through crosses cut in the plastic. As the bright yellow bags can be unsightly, construct a simple wooden container for them and cover the surface of the bags with compost.

Some plants have special requirements, preferring either acid or alkaline conditions in which to grow. You can buy purpose-made composts for these conditions. Check the plant label on purchase to find out what kind of conditions it requires. Acid-loving plants, such as rhododendrons and azaleas, for example, need an ericaceous (lime-free) compost. Many gardeners make their own compost with which to feed the plants, but as the space on a balcony or terrace is probably too limited to indulge any passion for composting, you will have to buy the necessary nutrients instead.

GROWING AND DRAINAGE MEDIUMS

Without the right medium, a plant will struggle to grow well. The consistency, pH and content of the compost all play a part in the plant's overall health. The top two lines below show growing mediums, the bottom two lines drainage additions.

peat

coarse sand

moss

coir

fine sand

crocks

pebbles/grit

vermiculite

perlite

charcoal

Potting bench (left)

It is a good idea to create a workspace for yourself (even a board that you slide on top of the kitchen table will do if you are short of space) where you can assemble your tools and potting equipment.

Choosing plants

Most planting schemes are more satisfying if you have chosen a mixture

of plants – trees, shrubs, climbers, perennials, bulbs and annuals – although

much obviously depends on the amount of space at your disposal.

Healthy shrub (below)
*When choosing a shrub
look for a well-branched
specimen, like this* Elaeagnus
commutata, *with a good
open shape, rather than a
shrub with one spindly shoot.
Check the leaves for signs
of pests or diseases. The
plant should come easily out
of the pot, with the rootball
and its soil intact.*

On a windowsill your choice will be limited to a few
dwarf shrubs, and principally perennials, annuals and
bulbs. On a medium-sized balcony, you also have the option to grow climbing
plants to cover the wall surfaces, and possibly trail over the railings of the
balcony itself, together with a few shrubs. Larger balconies, roof terraces and
verandahs give you the greatest opportunity to create a planting scheme with
varied heights and types.

It is important to buy healthy plants from a reliable source – whether this is
a nursery or garden centre. A well-run nursery will ensure that all the plants are
in good condition and are regularly potted on (moved into larger pots if unsold),
but the less scrupulous may well sell you plants that have languished too long in
their original containers, with the consequence that the roots have become
constricted and wound around the rootball. This will
eventually lead to the demise of the plant through slow
strangulation. If a plant you buy is found to be pot-bound,
to such an extent that the roots cannot be gently
disentangled, simply return the plant to the place it
was purchased from.

Healthy perennial (above)
*Perennials can be bought
either young (in their first
season) or older, like this
well-grown hosta above.
The price of the plant will
be determined by its size
and maturity.*

Checking a plant for signs of disease or distress

Get into the habit of checking the plants you buy for signs
of good health and vigour. Shrubs should be well-branched,
not leggy and spindly. Perennials should be compact, with a
good clump of basal leaves. A few eaten leaves are not the
mark of a problem plant, but too many yellowing or wilting
ones indicate potential problems and the plant is best left on
the shelf. Most young shrubs will benefit from being
pinched out or cut back by about one-third, either before
or after planting, to promote healthy new growth.

Remember that if you want the planting to look good
all year round, you will need a mixture of deciduous and

evergreen plants, so you should always check the labels of trees, shrubs and climbers when purchasing plants at the nursery. There are also a few evergreen perennials, so look out for these.

Growth rates and habit

If you are gardening in a limited space, you will either need to choose plants that have a naturally slow growth rate, or you will have to be prepared to prune and trim the plants (and possibly root prune them, see page 23) to prevent them outgrowing their containers. It is also important to make sure that the plants you choose have a more upward than outward growth, by and large, so that they do not spread too widely across the limited space. For this reason, climbers are particularly valuable, since they produce a great quantity of flowers while taking up relatively little ground space. Small fastigiate (narrow) and columnar trees are a better bet, generally, than those with wide-spreading branches, although ideally you need a variety of different forms to create an attractive display. Equally, small-leaved evergreens can be clipped into neater, less spreading shapes – rectangles, cones or spheres, as preferred.

Box (above)

*Slow-growing box (*Buxus sempervirens*) is an ideal container plant, as the leaves are small and evergreen and can be clipped into neat, geometric shapes.*

USEFUL PLANT SHAPES

Try to choose a varied range of plant shapes for your display. Those shown below are just a few of the best to choose from. Take care to match the form of the plant to the size and style of container, to create a harmonious balance between the two.

Trailers (left)

Plants with a lax habit can be grown to tumble down from high-level or tall containers, or to climb up supports.

Architectural plants (below)

Plants with dramatic foliage form, such as sword-shaped leaves, make good feature plants. Among these are cordylines, phormiums and irises.

Climbers (right)

Invaluable in small spaces, these will cover walls and fences with flowers and foliage while taking up minimal floor space.

Standards (above)

Plants trained with a clear stem with a mop-head of branches above allow more space lower down where it is most needed on narrow balconies.

Topiary (above)

Slow-growing evergreens can be clipped into neat formal shapes that add structure and solidity to more ephemeral flowering displays.

Planting and potting on

Nowadays, with plants grown in containers available from garden centres and nurseries, planting is seen by many simply as moving the plant from one pot to the next.

CLEANING A POT

All pots must be clean before use to prevent diseases.

Tip out the contents of the pot, scrub it with hot soapy water and then rinse it under the tap.

Any container-grown plant that you purchase will have grown accustomed to its pot, and transferring it to a new pot will cause it a certain amount of stress, which may have the effect of stopping it in its tracks for a longer or shorter time.

To give your plant the best start, aim to repot it into a container just a few inches bigger in diameter than the one it arrived in. If a plant is fast-growing, you will have to repot it once a year. Slower growing plants can be potted on every two years. Generally speaking, if a plant puts on 45cm (18 in) growth or more in a year, you can consider it fast-growing.

All plants should be given a pot of adequate depth to accommodate the rootball comfortably, with a few inches to spare at the base. All pots must be clean and should have a drainage hole, covered by a few shards of broken pot or pebbles, so that water will seep out and compost will not clog the hole. When planted, the top of the rootball should be covered with about 2.5cm (1in) of compost, which should finish about 2.5cm (1in) below the top of the pot. Plants will need to be planted up in the first place, and then repotted every so often with new compost. As they grow, they will need to be potted on into a larger container, to accommodate the growing rootball.

PLANTING A SINGLE-STEMMED PLANT

Tall plants with a single stem should be staked.

1 *Prepare a pot, covering the drainage hole with pebbles.*
2 *Insert the plant into the pot, add the stake and fill with compost, firming down well around stake and stem.*

3 *Tie the stake to the stem with ties (stout trees need expandable tree ties). Water in well to settle the compost around the roots.*

Choosing a compost

To obtain the best performance from your plant, you should take care to match the compost to its needs. The basic mixture devised by the John Innes Horticultural Institute consists of seven parts loam, three parts peat and two parts unwashed sand. The various strengths of John Innes compost (referred to as J.I.) are labelled 1, 2, and 3. The lowest number has the least amount of nutrients, and the highest the most. These composts have a small quantity of chalk added, so lime-hating plants will need a special lime free mix. Generally speaking, most trees, shrubs and perennials will do best with J.I. 2. In order to encourage fruiting, edible plants will need J.I. 3, which contains the most nutrients. Once you have planted the plants, close the plastic compost bag and keep it in a frost-free place.

Trees and shrubs

Trees will need to be given ample room for the roots to spread out and down, so make sure the pot is sufficiently deep to allow this to happen. The top of the rootball should end up just below the surface of the compost in the pot. If you have bought a tree or shrub mail-order, as a bare-rooted specimen (in other words, it comes without soil around it), it will need to be given a long, cool drink before planting. It is best to leave it to soak in a bucket of water for half a day before planting.

You need to make sure that the compost is appropriate for the plant. If it is an acid-lover, it will need specially formulated compost. Single-stemmed plants, such as trees and standard shrubs, will need staking to prevent the wind rocking the stem, which will in turn damage the roots. The thickness of the stake depends on the size and form of the plant; young plants can have a simple cane support; stouter stems will need a wooden stake. A normal 2cm (¾ in) diameter wooden stake will serve the purpose and a rubber tree tie allows you to adjust it as the tree grows and develops.

Climbers

Climbers will also need support, either within the pot itself or by placing the pot close enough to a supporting pillar or wall. The way in which the climber does its stuff – clinging on or twining – will determine the nature of the support and the degree of help needed. Self-clinging climbers like ivy and

PLANTING A CLIMBER

Climbers will usually need some form of support.

1 *Clean out the pot to reduce the risk of disease, then add the drainage layer of pebbles, and approximately 5cm (2in) of compost to the base of the pot. Insert the support.*

2 *Next, gently tease out the roots of the climber and insert the plant in the pot. Fill the container with compost to about 2.5cm (1in) from the brim.*

3 *Spread out the climber's shoots to form a fan-shape. Remove any stakes, and tie in the shoots of the plant loosely to the new support.*

Virginia creeper need little help from you (although they will need to be pointed in the right direction and tied in until they start to cling); twiners, like honeysuckle and clematis, need some kind of wire or wooden trellis support, with space in front and behind for the tendrils or the stems (according to type) to cling on. Vigorous clematis and honeysuckles will become very heavy when in full flower so make sure the support is adequate to take their weight.

Roses

Plants, such as roses, that have been grafted onto the rootstock of another plant, will need to be planted with more care, to ensure that the graft union (the knobbly bulge at the base of the stem) stays above the surface of the compost. If the compost is allowed to cover it, there is a danger that suckers will start to sprout from it. Roses also have deep-reaching roots, so it pays to plant them in a deeper-than-average pot, to give these roots a chance to reach downwards. They will benefit from a good feed of bone meal at planting time.

Climbing roses will need some kind of support. A fan trellis can be used to start them off. As the shoots grow, they can be trained against a series of wires nailed to the wall with galvanized vine eyes, or to a trellis fixed to the wall.

Perennials

Perennials with very fine roots, such as small alpine plants, will need to have grit added to the compost to make it more free-draining. Vigorous perennials, such as hostas, will need to be potted on every two to three years into a larger pot, at which time it may well be sensible to divide the plant, as herbaceous perennials grow from the centre out.

When to plant and pot on

The best time to plant up or pot on any plant is related to its flowering time. Spring-flowering evergreen shrubs and climbers are best dealt with in autumn, while the summer-flowering ones should be dealt with in spring. Deciduous trees and shrubs with spring or summer flowers should be planted or potted on in autumn, and the autumn-flowering ones in spring.

PLANTING A ROSE

It is important when planting a rose to ensure that the graft union (the knobbly bit on the base of the stem) is above the compost after planting, otherwise suckers may grow out from it at the expense of the grafted plant.

1 *Before you start, check that the pot intended for the rose is deep enough, as roses have deep roots that require plenty of space if the plant is to thrive.*

2 *Clean out the pot well, and incorporate drainage material – shards of pot or pebbles – to cover the drainage hole. Part fill the pot with compost.*

3 *Next, insert the rose into the pot and backfill with compost, positioning the plant so that the graft union is just above the surface of the compost. Water well.*

PRUNING A ROOTBALL

It is tempting to ignore the parts of the plant that you cannot see, but it is very important to keep an eye on the roots as well. A healthy root system is essential for healthy top growth: a plant which has become pot-bound cannot make the most of the nutrients in the soil, and will need repotting in a larger container. If the plant is becoming too big, and can no longer be potted on into a larger pot, you will have to trim the roots, which will, in turn, ensure that the top growth is checked (see steps 1–3 below).

Healthy rootball (left)

This plant has a healthy rootball, with room to spread its roots. Some plants have very fine roots, others are much stouter, but air must always be able to get to the fine roots.

Pot-bound plant (right)

This plant has remained too long in a small container and the roots have wound around themselves. Trim the roots out to leave a healthy core and replant in the usual way. Water well after planting.

1 *Firstly, tease out the roots gently, prising them away from the rootball with your fingers. Take care not to tug or damage the roots unnecessarily while you are doing this.*

2 *Using a sharp pair of secateurs, carefully trim off approximately one-third of the roots, leaving a balanced and more even root structure.*

3 *Trim off any top growth on the plant by one-third. Then sink the plant into a bucket of water for 30 minutes to give it a long drink before repotting it in the usual way.*

Planting bulbs

Unlike other plants, bulbs, corms and tubers need to be planted at different depths to

ensure the best flowering performance. They also need to be planted at

different times, depending on the season in which they flower.

Tulips (above)

Ideal for small containers, dwarf tulips should be planted roughly four months before flowering, at twice the depth of the bulb.

Bulb in cross-section (below)

The daffodil bulb shown here has been cut in half to demonstrate the way in which the flowering stem is encased in the outer leafy layers of the plant. The bulb itself is encased in a fine skin to protect the delicate storage layers within.

Bulbs are one of the best standbys for the container garden; they flower from spring through to late summer, depending on the type you have chosen, but you do need to ensure that you plant them at the right time of year, at the right depth of soil. Bulbous plants range from the tall and statuesque lilies, *Allium cristophii* and agapanthus of summer, to the tiny scillas, crocus and snowdrops of spring. The smaller ones are ideal for window boxes or table displays. The larger ones can become architectural features in their own right when several are planted in a large, deep pot. Most bulbs look best planted in groups of the same species or cultivar, rather than in mixed displays, although a grouped display of bulbs of different heights has considerable impact.

What is a bulb?

A true bulb, such as a daffodil, tulip or lily, is a self-contained plant in a small powerhouse. The emerging stems and flowers are packed within the fleshy scales of the bulb, which form the food supply for the whole plant; they are covered, in most plants, with a fine, papery skin, known as the tunic. Bulbs will propagate themselves by means of offsets, little bulbs that form from the parent plant.

Although not true bulbs, corms, tubers and rhizomes are treated similarly to bulbs. Corms look like squashed bulbs, and last only for one growing year. After that the corm shrivels, and a new corm forms on top or at the side of the old one. Crocus and gladiolus are corms. A tuber is similar to a corm in appearance, but is technically different. It is simply a swollen stem borne underground and it has no single growing point. Begonias and cyclamens are in this group. A rhizome is similar but grows by spreading along the surface of the soil – canna lilies are in this group. Yet another category is the tuberous root in which the storage organs are carried in a swollen root. Dahlias belong to this group.

Buying and storing bulbs

It is important to buy bulbs that are ready to flower if you want a display the same year. Very small offsets will not produce a flower for several years, so generally speaking, the bigger the bulbs the better. Bulbs are damaged by careless handling and if they are kept in unventilated, warm conditions. A healthy bulb has an unblemished tunic, a firm neck and feels solid and heavy. A damaged bulb will have mould marks on the outer tunic, feel light for its size and may be starting to sprout with a spindly shoot. You can buy bulbs from a garden centre or you can buy from mail-order catalogues, which generally offer good deals if you buy in bulk.

When to plant bulbs

Spring bulbs are planted before winter sets in and generally flower around six months after planting, summer-flowering bulbs about three months after planting. Corms, rhizomes and tubers of tender plants should be lifted after flowering, stored in a warm place, and replanted after the frosts have passed.

Depths at which to plant

Generally speaking most bulbs should be planted in a depth of soil to twice their own height, so a 5cm (2in) tall bulb is planted 10cm (4in) deep, while a 8cm (3in) tall bulb is planted 15cm (6in) deep. Corms and rhizomes are planted more or less on the surface of the soil, while tuberous roots should be planted slightly deeper in the pot.

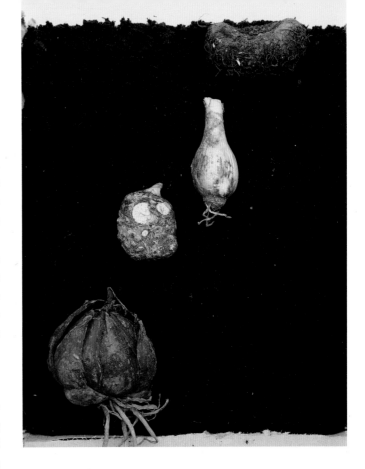

Planting depths (above)

Generally bulbs are planted at roughly twice their own depth, but some, such as those of lilies, benefit from deeper planting. From the left, a lily, a zantedeschia, canna lily and begonia.

PLANTING BULBS

Most bulbs prefer a well-drained compost. Taller bulbs like lilies need staking.

1 *Clean out the pot thoroughly, then cover the base with broken shards of pot or similar to ensure the drainage hole does not become blocked.*

2 *Add a layer of gravel or grit about 2.5cm/1in deep and then enough compost so that the base of the bulb sits twice its own depth deep in the pot.*

3 *Cover the bulb with compost to within 2.5cm (1in) of the rim, water well, and label. Provide cane supports for tall flowering bulbs.*

Watering

When you grow plants in containers, you will discover that they dry out with remarkable speed, particularly in hot,

sunny weather. To grasp the scale of the problem, a pot that is 1m (3ft) in diameter, fully covered with growing

plants, could lose up to 6l (1½ gallons) of water a day in hot, sunny, windy weather.

REVIVING A WILTED PLANT

In ideal circumstances, your plants should not wilt, but all of us occasionally forget or fail to water our plants adequately. If the leaves are still green and have not become crisp, a badly wilted plant can still be revived by plunging the pot in a bucket of water. Weight the top of the compost with a stone, and then wait for the air bubbles to stop rising, at which point the compost will be fully saturated. With luck, the plant will recover itself within 24 hours.

Your most laborious task, and often your most pressing one, as a container gardener, is watering your array of pots. The shape and structure of the container will determine how quickly it dries out. Terracotta, although attractive, is highly porous and will encourage the soil to dry out more quickly than a non-porous material like plastic. Containers with a wide top will dry out quicker, and it is often a good idea to put a layer of shingle over the top surface of the compost to reduce moisture loss.

Grouping the containers together makes them easier to water in one hit, and the plants give each other a certain amount of protection from moisture loss. Sitting the pots on a shallow driptray containing gravel will also help to keep them moist (and is a good solution when you go away for a few days).

HOW TO WATER

Container plants will benefit from ensuring that the water reaches to the basal roots of the plant.

1 *With a narrow stick or pencil, penetrate the compost around the plant at 5–7.5cm (2–3in) intervals. This will provide water channels down to the roots.*

2 *Water in the usual way with a watering can, until water emerges at the base. If the compost has become dry, water once and then water again half an hour later.*

WATERING A HANGING BASKET

Hanging baskets dry out in hot weather notoriously quickly, sometimes requiring twice-daily watering during spells of really hot summer weather.

Improving water retention (above)

Put a few water-retaining crystals in the compost when you plant.

Holiday care (above)

If you are away for a day or two in hot weather, stand the basket in water.

High-level watering (above)

To reach hanging baskets with the hose, you can create a homemade hose support by tying a long bamboo cane to the last few feet of the hose nearest the nozzle, fixing it with small plastic ties. This will then keep the hose rigid, enabling you to direct the water supply straight to the hanging basket.

Much depends on the amount of space you have at your disposal. On a terrace that is heavily planted, it would be helpful to have a hose with a spray attachment and this is useful for high-level hanging baskets as well, unless they have been mounted, as suggested, on pulleys. You do need to ensure that a roof terrace or balcony has an adequate drainage system to cope with surplus water.

It is important to ensure that the water gets to the base of the rootball of the plant. If you water too little, you will find that only the surface of the compost ever really gets wet, and the plant will suffer as a consequence. Inserting some form of drainage into a large pot is a good idea – it ensures that the water gets right to the bottom of the pot and soaks the whole of the rootball. In smaller pots, you can use a dibber or pencil to make a few holes around the rim of the pot to act as a mini drainage system.

Gravel pot holders (above)

A shallow tray filled with gravel and water will enable plants to survive longer without watering.

DEEP WATERING A LARGE SHRUB

Big plants in pots may need some additional help to ensure that water reaches the roots.

1 *Begin by inserting sawn-off sections of pipe or bamboo cane around the perimeter of the pot. You can either do this when you plant or later on.*

2 *Water the plant, using a funnel to direct the water through the pipes to the base of the pot. Then water the surface of the soil in the usual way.*

Feeding

Plants grown in containers will not get the opportunity that they do in natural surroundings to absorb the nutrients and minerals they normally take from decaying plant matter in the soil.

The plant's powerhouse lies primarily in its roots (and secondarily in its leaves). The soil or compost in which the roots are housed must provide sufficient nutrients and moisture for the roots to do their work and keep the plant healthy. It is your job, as a container gardener, to supply these nutrients in the form of fertilizer.

Forms of fertilizer

The issue is what sort of fertilizer, when and how much? Plants have differing needs. Those that are grown for their flowers need one kind of fertilizer, those for their fruit another. However, a multi-purpose fertilizer, with fairly balanced amounts of the different nutrients and minerals, will usually serve the purpose of most gardeners. Most proprietary fertilizers contain a mixture of the main nutrients – nitrogen (N), phosphorus (P) and potassium (K) and the amounts of each are normally indicated on the bag, so always read the instructions. To correct specific nutrient deficiencies, buy feeds that are based on these. Feeds with iron, for example, are useful for azaleas, which can be susceptible to iron deficiency when grown in containers. The nutrients can be delivered directly to the roots, via the soil, or via the leaves, which will pass the nutrients down the stems. Feeds which are delivered via the leaves are known as foliar feeds.

FORMS OF FEED

There are many different forms that plant food can take. Each feeding system has its merits, but it is usually a matter of personal choice which you prefer to use in your garden or container. The plant spikes, slow-release granules and slow-release pellets are all applied dry to the compost, and they become activated on contact with water. The liquid feed needs dilution with water (see below) as do the dissolvable crystals.

*plant spikes
(14–21 days)*

*slow-release granules
(14–21 days)*

*liquid feed
(5–7days)*

*dissolvable crystals
(5–7 days)*

*slow release pellets
(14–21 days)*

APPLYING LIQUID FEED

Liquid feeds are normally watered into the compost at the strength recommended in the manufacturer's instructions. Plants need most feeding during their active growing season.

1 *Pour the appropriate quantity of liquid feed into the watering can, and dilute as instructed. Stir the contents with a stick.*

2 *Water the plant in the usual way. If water tubes are used (see page 27) you will ensure that the feed reaches down to the base roots as well.*

Application methods

Fertilizers come in granular or in liquid form, for you to dilute with water and then apply to the leaves or soil as appropriate. One of the most popular new types is a slow-release fertilizer which delivers small quantities of concentrated nutrients over a long period of time. The benefit is that the plant gets a regular, accurately dosed supply of food which improves its general growth and health. Release rates for the different types of fertilizer vary. Slow-release fertilizers give out their nutrients over a two to three week period, quick-acting fertilizers take a week to ten days, general liquid feed five to seven days, and foliar feeds three to four days, so for plants in distress the foliar applied feeds are the best.

Plants have a natural cycle of dormancy and growth, so time feeding to coincide with the point when the plant is doing most of its work. This is generally when it is forming flowers or fruit. Nutrients leach out of containers rapidly during watering or heavy rainfall (up to one-third of the nutrients are lost in this way). It is important to be able to recognize when your plant is short of a nutrient. The table below lists some common nutrient deficiencies, their symptoms and their control.

Foliar feeds (above)

These can be used as a pick-me-up. They are best sprayed onto the plant in cool weather after dilution in the usual way.

COMMON NUTRIENT DEFICIENCIES

The disorders shown below are the most commonly found in plants; each can be corrected with the addition of certain minerals to the compost.

Nutrient	Nitrogen	Phosphate	Potassium	Magnesium	Manganese & iron
Symptom of deficiency	Reduced growth with spindly plant, pale green leaves with yellowish tinge.	Slow plant growth and yellowish young foliage.	Foliage turns purple or yellow with brown blotches or brown margins and tips. Leaves may curl down.	Discoloration, reddish or yellowish, between veins of leaves. Premature leaf fall.	Yellowing or browning of the leaf margins, that extends between the veins.
Control	*Add a high-nitrogen fertilizer, such as sulphate of ammonia or dried blood.*	*Add bone meal or superphosphate.*	*Add sulphate of potash or a high-potash fertilizer.*	*Add Epsom salts to watering can.*	*Apply trace elements or sequestered iron.*

Supports and screens

When you are gardening in a very limited space, it is vital that your plants look their best

at all times. Plants that have weak stems, or those that depend on supports for climbing,

demand ingenious methods of control and support that also look attractive.

Climbing plants (above)
Vigorous climbers, such as honeysuckle, need support during the growing season.

There is a wide range of supporting devices you can buy from garden centres for plants, but most of them are really only suited to plants in a large border, where the foliage of other plants disguises the staking mechanisms. On a balcony or terrace, it pays to be more inventive and to use natural materials, whenever possible, to create sympathetic support structures.

Supporting plants

Instead of using bamboo canes, try to find some twigs. They tend to blend in better with the plants and are less obvious. The tops of canes and sticks are dangerous to the eyes if left uncovered (it is all too easy to bend down and fail to spot one of them) so either buy specially made plastic caps or make your own out of adhesive putty.

By far the most attractive material to use is wood, either as hardwood or as greenwood (wood cut from young stems). Greenwood supports have

Soft-stemmed perennials (above)
Plants with floppy stems benefit from gentle support. A few greenwood twigs, pushed into the compost, will do the job, or use canes and string.

Willow cage (right)
Create a decorative support using willow stems, tied together at the top to create a supporting cage.

MAKING A WILLOW CAGE SUPPORT
You will need six to eight flexible young willow stems, together with a length of natural raffia.

1 *Plant up the bulbs or plants and cut an even number of willow canes to the same length – six canes roughly 60cm (24in) long are ideal for a 30cm (12in) diameter pot.*

2 *Insert the canes around the rim of the pot, one next to each plant. Push them well down into the compost so that they are firmly anchored.*

3 *Take an opposite pair of canes and twist them over each other at the top. Repeat with the remaining canes and secure with raffia at the top.*

GREENWOOD WIGWAMS

You will need stout stems for the upright, more flexible stems for the weaving and young whippy stems for binding.

1 *Insert the five supporting poles for the wigwam around the perimeter of a deep, sturdy pot, spacing them evenly apart and pushing them well down into the compost to anchor them.*

2 *Take a whippy stem and bind it around the top of the poles to draw the poles together into a traditional wigwam shape. Push the tail end of the stem down inside the binding to fasten it.*

3 *Bind the base of the wigwam, roughly 15cm (6in) from the bottom by weaving a couple of supple stems in and out of the poles. Create a similar woven binding halfway up between the base and the top.*

Finished wigwam

(below)

The wigwam can support a range of climbers, from clematis to runner beans.

become increasingly popular in the last couple of years, and whole classes are now taking place at shows and horticultural institutes demonstrating the ancient crafts of hazel and willow weaving. If you cannot be bothered to have a go yourself, you can buy the supports ready-made, but if you can manage to do it yourself, you will pay a fraction of the bought price.

Small perennials with weak stems will need some support. A flexible cage support made from pliable stems of willow or cornus, inserted around the edge of the pot, does the trick perfectly. Hyacinths, penstemons and other slightly floppy perennials will benefit from this treatment. Those that bush out higher up, but tend to be rather lax in form, such as the regal pelargoniums, fuchsias or the big hellebore, *Helleborus corsicus*, benefit from a ring-type support roughly one-third of the way up the stem, which will serve to hold the plant together at the base. Very tall plants, such as lilies, will need a similar support, but it will have to reach higher up the stems – to roughly two-thirds of the final height of the plant.

For climbers, you will need to construct some kind of lattice support, usually attached to a wall. The type of support will be determined by the nature of the climber – those that twine need sufficient space to twist themselves in and out of the support. It is a good idea when putting

trellis up against a painted wall to create a hinged support at the base and hook-and-eye fastenings at the top. When the time comes to paint the wall, the whole trellis, complete with its climber, can be demounted from the wall.

Screening plants

Another equally important element in balcony and terrace gardening is to provide screening for the plants. Ideally it should be wind-permeable, otherwise it takes off like a sail in high winds and for the same reason it needs to be extremely well anchored. You may also need to create your own dividing screen between your balcony and that of an adjoining apartment. Both your plants, and you, will enjoy the benefit of providing some sort of screening, particularly on a high-rise balcony or roof terrace.

You can create screens from sturdy trellising, either bought or made-to-measure, bamboo, reed, or any other fairly supple stem, which can be tied together to create a slightly open screen. Ideally, choose screening materials that are sympathetic in character to the architecture and the planting style. Alternatively, you can use living plants to make their own natural screen.

Trellis screen (above)

Stout trellis, well-anchored at the base, creates a permeable screen for a roof terrace, which helps protect both the occupants and the plants.

Hazel hurdles (left)

Woven hurdles make an attractive, inexpensive, natural-looking screen for balconies and terraces.

Propagation

It is unlikely that you will have the space to do more than grow a few plants on from seeds or cuttings, but the pleasure makes it well worth the trouble, and, of course, it is cost effective.

Some plants are easier to grow from seed or cuttings than others (see table below right), so unless you are fairly determined, stick to those that germinate easily or strike quickly from cuttings.

Sowing from seed

Seeds vary in size from fine as dust to the big pea-sized seeds of sweet peas or nasturtiums. To get any seed to germinate, you need to ensure that the conditions are appropriate. Adequate, even warmth and a sufficient supply of moisture are both critical, as is light in the later stages once germination has occurred, or the seedlings will end up tall and etiolated as they strive to find the light. Although some seed will stay viable for many years (poppies notoriously will flower from 70-year old seed), most will not, and the seed must also be kept in appropriate conditions – cool and dry. Some seeds are more likely to germinate if they have been exposed to low temperatures, and a plastic tub of seeds can be put in the freezer for ten days or so in those cases.

You will need a shallow seed tray or individual 'jiffy' pots into which the seed can be sown, together with a generous supply of seed-quality compost. Seed of summer-flowering annuals will be sown in early spring; seed of perennials in early summer. Annuals will race from germination to flowering in a space of about eight weeks, but perennials will simply grow into small plants and will not flower until the following year.

SOWING FINE SEED

Very fine seed is normally sown in shallow trays with a fine covering of compost. Adding sand to the seeds enables you to sprinkle them more evenly.

1 *Fill a pot or seed tray with seed and cutting compost. Level the surface by scraping a straight-edge across the rim.*
2 *Sprinkle seeds (held in a seed and sand mix) over the surface of the compost.*

3 *Cover the seed with a fine layer of sieved compost. Water by standing the tray inside a large container with about 2.5cm (1in) of water in the base. Cover and keep moist.*

SOWING LARGER SEED

Larger seeds can be sown about five or six to a pot in similar compost to fine seed.

1 *Fill the pot with seed compost and space the seeds evenly over the surface. Press them gently into the compost to a depth of approximately twice their own diameter.*

2 *Water with a fine spray and keep warm and moist. Remember to label the pots. Once the seedlings have grown large enough to handle, prick them out into individual pots.*

While the seeds are in their trays waiting to germinate, make sure the trays do not get baked. A windowsill is not a good place for them as the heat through the glass can become very intense. A slightly shaded spot outside on the balcony (once frosts have passed) or indoors on the floor or a low table are the best option.

Sowing from seed is the easiest and most reliable way to propagate annuals and many perennials. Seeds need some degree of warmth (about 18°C or 65°F) and adequate moisture in order to sprout shoots (germinate). If you purchase a heated propagator, it will ensure that the seeds are kept at a constant temperature, most likely to foster germination. Once the seeds start to shoot, they need adequate light, otherwise they will become pale and spindly. A moist environment is essential; the propagator conserves moisture, but if you do not have one, a sheet of glass or a plastic bag over the seed tray or pot will do the same job. The growing medium for sowing seeds must be fine and also sterile.

TAKING CUTTINGS FROM PELARGONIUMS

Some plants grow very easily from cuttings, pelargoniums included. All you need to do is to remove a short stem from the parent plant in late spring or early autumn.

Cuttings

Growing plants from cuttings is satisfying, because it involves relatively little effort and it is a great joy when the small cutting forms its own root system and starts to take on its own identity. It is also a reliable way of ensuring that you get the plant you want, since there is no doubt about the parentage. You can take cuttings at different times of year from different parts of the plant.

1 *Select a healthy non-flowering shoot and remove the top few inches, including the growing point, with a sharp knife.*

2 *Trim the shoot to below a leaf node and remove the lower leaves. Insert the base of of the cutting into fresh compost, and keep moist until it roots – normally about six weeks or so.*

EASILY PROPAGATED PLANTS

Fill the pots with seed-sowing compost. For cuttings, add a little sharp sand. Dip the base of the cutting in hormone rooting powder to encourage the roots.

Seed	Cuttings
Nasturtiums *(Tropaeolum majus)*	Box *(Buxus sempervirens)*
Sweet peas *(Lathyrus odorata)*	Rosemary *(Rosmarinus)*
Love-in-a-mist *(Nigella damascena)*	Pelargonium
Forget-me-nots *(Myosotis)*	Lavender *(Lavandula angustifolia)*
Foxgloves *(Digitalis purpurea)*	*Skimmia japonica*

Pruning

If you grow plants on balconies and terraces, you are unlikely to have to do much in the way of pruning, but it is important that you understand what you are doing, and why you are doing it.

Creating an open framework (above)
The main aim of pruning is to check vigorous growth and to keep the shape of the shrub open, which discourages pests and diseases.

P runing serves several purposes. Firstly, it keeps the plant's growth in check; secondly it can encourage a better framework of branches, so that the plant's habit and shape are improved; thirdly, it can promote health and vigour; and finally it can benefit flowering performance.

Any pruning needs to be done with really sharp secateurs, since the cleaner the cut, the less likely it is that disease will enter through the cut stems and branches. Torn branches are particularly susceptible. Where you cut is important, since the bud immediately below the cut you make will sprout the future branch and you want to make sure it sprouts in the appropriate direction – away from the plant, not in towards it. That is why you are always told to cut to an outward facing bud. If the plant has opposite buds (i.e. buds which are facing each other) you cut straight across the stem. If they are alternate (i.e. staggered up the branch) you should cut diagonally downwards, away from the bud.

There are whole books which are devoted to pruning, but the most important thing to remember is that if you prune too late in the year you will remove that year's flowering buds, so generally spring-flowering shrubs are pruned in autumn, before the new growth has formed, and summer-flowering plants are pruned in spring. Fruit trees need fairly diligent pruning to ensure that they make the maximum amount of flower from which fruit will form.

PRUNING FOR A BALANCED FRAMEWORK

You need to prune your shrubs to try to maintain a good branch structure. Ideally you need to remove any congested or weak stems and correct uneven growth.

1 *Remove congested stems to open up the shrub's centre.*
2 *Thin out weak or spindly stems, and leave only those that are growing strongly.*

3 *Check the overall shape of the shrub, and cut back any branches that are growing too strongly and distorting the shape, and trim back new shoots by about one-third.*

REJUVENATING A CLIMBER

Some vigorous climbers that have become straggly will benefit from hard pruning.

1 *After flowering, cut back the growing shoots to within 23cm (9in) of the base.*

2 *Water well and continue to feed and water in the growing season.*

3 *Train the new shoots over or against the support, tying them in as they grow.*

The aim is to pare the tree down to the strongest growing stems and buds and to create a strongly branching bushy framework in the plant's early years. To this end, the plant is quite severely pruned in the first three years of being established, with the aim of strengthening the potential fruiting branches and spacing the stems out sufficiently that air and light get to the buds.

For a general tidy up, most plants should have about 15cm (6in) of growth removed. For shrubs that have become old, it is often a good idea to give them a more drastic pruning. This involves taking out some of the old stems at the base of the plant to encourage new stems to form. This is particularly valuable with climbing roses, for example.

Evergreens tend to need less pruning than deciduous shrubs, and some need no pruning at all (*Fatsia*, *Choisya,* etc.). Small-leaved evergreens, such as box, bay or myrtle, can be trimmed into formal or exotic shapes (see Topiary pp. 90–93). Removing dead flowers (known as deadheading) will prolong the flowering season. This is because if you cut off the flowers before the plant produces seed, new flower buds will appear.

DEADHEADING

Deadheading your flowering plants improves their appearance and encourages a second growth of flowers. Geraniums in particular benefit from regular deadheading, and look more attractive, as do roses, especially those whose petals turn brown. Snip the dead flower and stalk off with scissors.

PRUNING A ROSE

Standards and bush roses need hard pruning after flowering, cutting back new growth by one-third. Climbing roses are best pruned by removing old wood from the base.

1 *To prune a standard or bush rose cut back the stems to leave a couple of buds at the base of each stem. Make the cut just above a bud.*

2 *To prune a climbing or bush rose, remove weak, crossing or inward growing shoots at the base, to leave a healthy framework.*

Maintenance

With only a tiny space in which to garden, both the area and the

plants are on show all of the time, so extra care is needed to keep

them looking good.

Since you do not have vast acres to care for, you can give your plants lots of attention. Maintenance will take you little more than an hour every fortnight, but it is an essential part of creating an attractive small-space garden.

Deadheading Ensure that you remove any dead flowers. This improves the appearance of the plant and, in most cases, encourages a second crop of flowers to form later on in the season. Snip off dead flowers at the base.

Staking and supporting Staking, supporting and tying in are regular maintenance chores which you should not neglect, if only because, with space at a premium, you do not want snaking branches, particularly those with thorns, invading your sitting space. New shoots can be tied in with plastic ties, making sure they are not so tight that they chafe the branches. Add more horizontal supporting wires, using vine eyes, as the plants grow.

General cleaning Surface areas need regular brushing and occasional cleaning. Decking will need to be scrubbed down at least twice a year with a wire brush and an algaecide to get rid of the green slime that tends to accumulate in rainy climates. Softwood will need an annual coat of a wood preservative, as will any unpainted softwood fence panels.

MAINTAINING WOODEN SURFACES

Some basic maintenance will help to keep your wood healthy and looking good.

1 *Remove any deposits of algae with a stiff brush and a proprietary algaecide to prevent the timbers becoming slippery. In wet climates, this will need to be done every couple of months; in drier climates, once a year.*

2 *In towns and cities, wooden decking will need scrubbing down every three or four months to remove any dirt or grime that has accumulated on the deck.*

3 *Untreated wood (for both surfaces and fences) will need an annual coat of timber preservative to prevent it rotting.*

Potting on Plants that are outgrowing their pots need to be removed and replanted in a pot at least one size larger (known as potting on). Large clump-forming herbaceous perennials can be divided every three years and planted into new pots. Failing to divide large clumps will lead to the centre dying out.

Pest and disease control Carry out regular checks for pests. Lily beetles, for example, will quickly ravage a plant and can quite easily be spotted and removed by hand. Watch out for aphid attacks on the first young shoots in spring, and deal with them quickly.

Container care Clean out discarded containers by washing thoroughly in soapy water and stack upside down to dry. Cracked terracotta containers can be repaired with strong multi-purpose glue or, if there is one clean break, you can wire the container just under the rim. Ensure that all containers have drainage holes in their base, and make sure when planting up a container that you have put shards of terracotta in the base or a layer of large pebbles, so that the drainage holes do not get blocked.

Tools and equipment Tools should be kept clean and sharp. Wrap them in a sacking roll when not in use, and make sure any blades are cleaned and oiled before being put away. Get secateurs and shears sharpened once a year. Make sure that you have a neatly organized supply of labels, string, vine eyes, nails and garden wire ready to hand when you need it, along with the tools such as scissors, secateurs, sharp garden knives, a pruning saw and so forth. Being able to find the appropriate equipment quickly makes it far more likely that you will get round to doing the jobs when needed.

Autumn and winter tasks If you live in a cold climate and you grow tender plants, you will need to protect them in the winter. Some plants that are marginally tender will survive if the pot and the base of the plant are wrapped in hessian or bubble-wrap. Before the first frosts set in, find an out of the way corner in a sheltered spot, and leave the plants there for the winter. Really tender plants must be brought indoors until the frosts have passed.

If you have to move a large plant, you can do it by rocking the pot onto a large piece of sacking, and then using the sacking to drag the plant along. Or make a platform from a piece of stout timber and insert metal dowels under the platform, rolling it across the metal dowels, which are removed from one end and inserted at the other, as it rolls. You need two people for both jobs.

In autumn, clear up fallen leaves; they harbour diseases and are slippery and dangerous to walk on when wet. Pick them out of the centres of any plants since if they are left there over winter the centre of the plant may well die back. Make sure no leaves are blocking drains and drainage holes. You can also cut down the dying heads of any perennials (although some people enjoy the effect, particularly that of plants like the big sedums).

Repairing pots (above)

Terracotta pots are expensive, and frost may damage them. Repair clean breaks with proprietary glue applied to each side of the break. Allow each piece to harden before dealing with the next.

Moving pots (above)

Slide the pot onto a board, then insert the dowels under the board, removing one at the front and putting it to the back as you roll it.

Pests and diseases

Unfortunately, gardening in a limited space is no guarantee of pest- or disease-free

gardening. If anything, you need to be even more vigilant, since the ravages of nature

are all too evident when your entire garden is within visual range at all times.

A few pests (and some diseases) do not make it at high-level, and one of the benefits of gardening on an apartment balcony or a roof terrace is that you do not have to worry about slugs or snails (unless a bird drops them by mistake). Many of the pests you are likely to find will have arrived with the plant that you

Earwig trap (above)

An earwig trap, consisting of an upturned pot stuffed with straw, will successfully trap crawling insects overnight, from which you can remove them each morning.

PESTS

DESCRIPTION	SYMPTOMS	PREVENTION	CONTROLS
Aphids Green, brown, pink, grey or black winged and wingless insects that suck sap.	*Distorted shoot tips and new leaves. Sticky coating on leaves, sometimes with black sooty mould.*	*Remove and burn badly infected plants.*	*Spray at regular intervals with a systemic insecticide such as heptenophos, as soon as the first aphids are seen in late spring.*
Caterpillars Butterfly and moth larvae with smooth or hairy tubular bodies and dark green or brown heads.	*Holes eaten in leaves, flowers and seed pods. Plant may be completely defoliated.*	*Small numbers of plants can be protected by removing the caterpillars by hand.*	*For large infestations, spray plants thoroughly with permethrin.*
Earwigs Fast-moving, small, shiny brown insects with a pincer-like gripper on the tail.	*Small circular notches or holes in leaves and flowers of plants and vegetables.*	*A small amount of damage may be acceptable as earwigs eat aphids.*	*Traps such as straw-filled pots will catch adult insects. Spray badly affected plants with HCH or malathion.*
Froghoppers Small green insects which suck sap from a wide range of plants.	*Clusters of easily removed frothy bubbles on stems and leaves. Damage is aesthetic rather than harmful.*	*Spray with a jet of water or pick off by hand as soon as they are spotted.*	*Spray at regular intervals with a systemic insecticide such as heptenophos as soon as the insects are seen.*
Leaf miners Very small insect larvae which tunnel around inside leaves as they feed, leaving wiggly lines.	*Pale green or white wiggly lines on leaves. Aesthetic nuisance rather than harmful.*	*Pull off affected leaves as soon as they are spotted.*	*Spray at regular intervals with a systemic insecticide such as heptenophos or malathion as soon as the insects are seen.*
Lily beetle Small, bright red beetles on lilies and fritillaries, followed by grubs in mid-summer.	*Holes eaten in leaves, flowers and seed pods. Plant can be completely defoliated.*	*Small crops can be protected by picking these pests off by hand.*	*Spray at regular intervals with a permethrin-based insecticide after seeing the first symptoms.*
Red spider mite Minute mites, sucking sap. A serious problem when their populations reach epidemic proportions.	*Yellow stunted growth, curled and mottled leaves covered with a fine webbing covering breeding colonies.*	*Spray the undersides of leaves with water, and maintain high humidity.*	*Spray with systemic insecticide as soon as spotted, or use asitic insect Phytoseiulus to control biologically.*
Scale insects Small, brown, blister-like bumps on stems and lower leaf surfaces. The insects suck sap, weakening the plant.	*Stunted growth and yellowing of leaves. Sticky coating on lower leaves, sometimes with black sooty mould.*	*Barrier glue around the stem stops the larval stage moving to new sections of the plant.*	*Introduce Metaphycus (predator) in mid-summer. Apply a systemic insecticide spray such as heptenophos, in late spring and early summer.*

DISEASES

DESCRIPTION	SYMPTOMS	PREVENTION	CONTROLS
Botrytis (grey mould) A fungus which infects flowers, leaves and stems. It usually enters through wounds.	*Discoloured, yellowing leaves which die slowly. Stems may rot at ground level. Plant becomes covered with a grey felt-like mould.*	*Prune out affected stems and burn. Maintain good air circulation.*	*Spray with thiophanate-methyl as soon as the disease symptoms are seen.*
Canker A fungal problem caused as spores infect wounds caused by pruning, frost damage or pests.	*Small sunken areas of bark, which enlarge, restricting growth, leading to stem die back.*	*Prune out affected branches or cut out affected area and treat with canker paint.*	*Spray the sunken wound lesions with mancozeb fungicide as soon as symptoms are spotted.*
Coral spot A fungus which commonly invades dead wood, but may also invade live tissue.	*Some branches wilt in summer, grey-brown staining may be under bark. In autumn branch is covered in small pink blisters.*	*Prune in summer when there are few spores. Clear away old prunings.*	*Remove and burn infected material as quickly as possible.*
Downy mildew A fungus which infects leaves and stems. It can overwinter in compost or plant debris.	*Discoloured, yellowing leaves with white patches on underside. Plants often die slowly in autumn.*	*Avoid overcrowding, use resistant cultivars. Maintain good air circulation.*	*Spray with mancozeb as soon as the disease symptoms are seen or remove and burn badly infected plants.*
Fireblight A bacterial disease which moves on a film of water, invading the soft tissue of plants. Eventually kills.	*Blackened, shrivelled flowers and young shoots. Leaves wilt and turn brown, shoots die back.*	*Grow as few susceptible plants as possible.*	*Remove and burn any plants with the above symptoms.*
Powdery mildew An asitic fungal disease. Invades soft leaf tissue.	*White floury patches on young leaves. Distorted shoots and premature leaf fall.*	*Prune out infected stems in autumn.*	*Spray carbendazim on the young leaves at the first signs of infection.*
Root rots Roots are attacked by spores that build up both in the compost and within infected plant remains.	*Foliage turns yellow, branches die back from the tips, affected roots usually turn black.*	*Avoid heavy watering and improve drainage. Never use unsterilized compost.*	*Dig up and burn affected plants. Choose varieties known to be tolerant or resistant.*
Rust Fungal disease which attacks many plants, including roses. Weakens growth, leads to premature leaf fall.	*Yellow blotches on leaf surface, bright orange or brown patches of spores on underside.*	*Wider plant spacing for good air circulation and increased ventilation.*	*Remove all affected areas. Affected plants should be thoroughly sprayed regularly with mancozeb.*
Silver leaf A fungus which enters the woody tissue of members of the cherry family (ornamental and fruiting).	*Leaves of infected trees adopt a silvery sheen. Branches die back. Brownish-purple brackets appear on stems.*	*Prune in summer when there are few fungal spores in the air.*	*Prune infected branches from healthy trees. Badly infected trees must be removed and burned.*
Virus Microscopic infection often carried by sap-feeding pests, such as aphids, and passed from plant to plant.	*Leaves (and shoots) are small, distorted, or grouped in rosettes. Yellow discoloured patterns on leaves.*	*Buy virus-free plants. Control potential carriers, and clear away weeds which may harbour virus.*	*Remove and burn affected plants as soon as possible. Do not propagate from them.*

bought from the garden centre, so it certainly pays to give all your plants a really thorough checking over before you take them home.

Good gardening practice will help to reduce pest and disease attacks. Make sure any pots and potting mixtures you use are sterile. Keep plants well fed and watered; those which are fed and watered irregularly become stressed, and more prone to disease.

Most of the proprietary remedies for pests and diseases contain chemicals that, while not overtly harmful to humans, probably do not do you much good either. Take great care when using them and always spray chemicals on a windless day after sunset, when any beneficial insects such as ladybirds have retired for the night. Make sure you wear both a mask and gloves when spraying, and keep children and pets out of harm's way while doing so.

Diseased leaves (above)

Remember to check the undersides of leaves for signs of pest and disease damage.

Even the smallest space offers you an opportunity for interesting planting, from narrow ledges to the tops of walls, from shady side passages to doorways. When planting up the space, you need to choose plants that look appropriate for the setting and which will cope with the aspect, be it full sun or shade. Where space is at a premium in the garden, you can use hanging baskets, suspended from stout hooks. Expanses of bare wall can be given a facelift with repeating pots of brightly coloured plants, hung on brackets or suspended from trellis.

PLACES TO PLANT

Planting for the place

The key to success lies in understanding the limitations of the situation, and working within its confines. Not only do you need to think about your actual space, but what lies behind and beyond it.

Your plants are not seen in a vacuum, they are framed by their setting. The size and scale of the planting will inevitably be governed by your surroundings. If you have only a tiny window ledge on which to exercise your design creativity, you clearly have different constraints than if you had a whole terrace, roof garden or large balcony at your disposal. Choosing plants that make an impact becomes important, so that the setting does not dwarf them and make them look silly. Equally, with limited space, you cannot afford to take up too much of it with the plant itself, or you would have nowhere to sit yourself. Achieving the right balance, as well as making creative use of the space available, is all part of the challenge. Don't forget odd corners, too, for planting: the top of a wall, a small alcove or on top of a piece of built-in furniture. A single, eye-catching plant in a handsome pot on top of a pillar, for example, lends an air of

Bright ideas (left)
In a hot sunny courtyard, a vibrantly coloured planting scheme is given a sense of unity with the repeated use of brilliant blue ceramic containers.

Vertical dimension (right)
On a balcony, a small flowering cherry tree adds vertical interest to the planting, and blends with the foliage beyond.

distinction to an otherwise unassuming front yard. The more unity the display has, the greater the impact, so aim to keep the colour palette limited, and ensure that the containers enhance it.

Displaying plants

There are various simple rules to follow when creating displays for small spaces. The most important thing to remember is that your plants and their containers are always front of stage. Unlike gardening in a larger space, where plants are not necessarily in focus right through the year, it is hard to avoid looking at a windowsill or small balcony. The demands on the plants, and on you as their keeper, are therefore much greater. Not only do you need to be a creative designer, but you also need to be a careful gardener, too. The objective is to get the most out of the least, and to ensure that the planting looks as good as possible for as much of the year as possible.

Unity

Firstly, you need to ensure that the display has a feeling of unity, which will increase its visual impact. Simple tricks can be employed to this end. Paint disparate containers the same colour so that they form a united whole. Equally, use a row of containers of the same height, material and colour. Go for a single colour theme in a flowering display of different plants, or you could employ a two-tone scheme matching the containers (or even contrasting them) with the chosen colours.

Making the most of the space

It is always worth remembering that you can garden on more than one level. Climbing plants are ideal for small spaces because they offer you the chance to have colour and interest at different heights. They can provide either an attractive all-year-round green backcloth, in the form of evergreen climbers like variegated ivies or *Clematis armandii*, or they can be chosen for more glamorous flowering abilities (which do not last as long). However, even on a small balcony you could choose four or five climbers with different flowering seasons – a jasmine for early spring, clematis for late spring, roses and honeysuckle for summer, and perhaps a vine for autumn colour. On high-level roof gardens, climbers can be grown up trelliswork to provide a protective screen for more tender plants beneath, and also to shield you and offer you more privacy, although you will be more limited in your choices, as those plants that do not like cold winds will not happily survive in these conditions. Ivy is always a good standby, as are most of the creepers because they will generally withstand a lot of punishment.

Grouping displays

Plants generally look better and are more comfortable when grouped together. Grouping helps prevent moisture loss and also makes it easier for you to look

Simple style (above)

The clean shapes of simple metal containers bring order to a mixture of flowering plants, as does the limited colour palette of pinks and grey-greens.

after the plants, for watering purposes. You will need to think quite carefully about plant form and shape when planning grouped plantings, and also about staggering heights to get the most from the display. Since the plants are essentially portable, you can change the construction of the group to bring those in flower to the forefront, and push those that are out of flower to a less conspicuous place. Staging or small tables are very useful for displaying small pots and plants, so that the flowers or scent can be better appreciated.

Focal points

Look at the setting to see if there is a place for a special display. A small window could be ideal for a tiny display of small foliage plants or some exquisite jewel-like bulbs in spring, or perhaps a single pelargonium of vibrant colour in summer. Big is not always best and the small-scale space can concentrate the eye on smaller treasures. Remember that the display not only gives pleasure to you, but also to those looking at it from the street. The architecture of the house or flat will almost certainly have a considerable effect on the kind of display you choose. A formal townhouse with white painted walls would make the ideal place for a series of neat topiary pots in a repeating display. A formal door can be enhanced by a pair of standard architectural plants either side of it, while a country cottage lends itself to a less structured, more gently flowering display.

Matching plant to pot

You will, at various times, look for containers for a specific plant, and at others, look for plants to fill a particular container (gardening being what it is, and losses of plants inevitable at some time, you may well have containers going begging). It is extremely important to consider the two together, and it is never good enough to simply grab a container of the right size and think it will do.

Contrary to what you might expect, you can break the rules with considerable success. Large pots do not always need large plants, although large plants do need large pots! Scale is a major consideration in planting design, and recently garden designers have created innovative schemes playing with texture, scale and form in very different ways, rather than concentrating solely on flower power to do the job. There used to be a golden rule in flower arranging that the pot was about a third of the final height of the arrangement, and this has been taken across into container gardening. Generally, it is a fairly satisfying proportion to opt for, but you can, at times, do something quite different and get away with it. The design will work if the composition as a whole creates an integrated visual picture. For example, grasses could be massed together to make a small topping on a very large container where tiny individual plants, separated out, would simply look lost and rather silly. It helps if you can see the creation in 'blocks' of either texture or colour. Bittiness, confusion and broken lines are the things to avoid.

You will find that certain textures and colours go particularly well with particular plants. Grey- and silver-leaved plants, blue, mauve or white flowers and blue-green foliage look particularly good in gunmetal or silver containers, because the whole scheme has a cool, classic sheen to it. Terracotta looks good with most things, but not generally as good with yellow, red or pink, which are all set off well with natural stone.

It is always worth while thinking of unusual forms of container for specific plants and maybe even converting household objects into plant containers. You do need to be careful to avoid anything that looks trite or inappropriate, but small modifications or even a bit of lateral thinking can convert a useless object (a pot that has lost its spout or handle) into an attractive plant holder.

Recycled containers (above)

A seaside balcony picks up on a nautical theme using pebbles and a rusty anchor chain to form a container for tough grasses.

Massed planting (below)

A single mass of one plant in a large pot creates a far greater impact than a mixture of colours. Here, argyranthemums are set off by a simple metal bucket.

Window displays

Window ledges require a succession of attractive planting schemes

throughout the year, from bulbs in spring to heathers in winter, and

small flowers benefit from being seen close up on a window ledge.

The window box gardener can start to find exciting planting material at the tail end of winter with hardy cyclamens, winter-flowering heathers, gaultheria and snowdrops. A month or so later, the dwarf narcissus, crocuses and then hyacinths and muscari come into bloom, with tulips following hard on their heels. Throughout this period, winter-flowering polyanthus, primulas and pansies, make good standby plants for window boxes.

Generally speaking, the waxy flowers of bulbs do not look good when combined with the soft petals of primulas and pansies, and the displays are much, much better if the two are not mixed. If you want to bulk up a flowering display of bulbs, then use the black-leaved *Primula* 'Guinevere' to go with white flowering bulbs, for example, which will have died down by the time the pink petals of the former are in flower. Look out for some of the more interesting ivies with dark neat leaves or maybe some bun-shaped fescue grasses. The very rigid forms of dwarf cypresses are sometimes too severe and simply look dull. The frequently used variegated ivies with splashes of white can look too fussy with the smartly regimented lines of spring bulbs, although they will come into their own with softer-petalled summer planting or the pansies and primulas.

It is important not to look solely at colour, but to look at texture and form, too, and a window display needs to be clear and sharp to compete with the formal shape of the architrave. To this end, square pots and neat rectangles generally look better in formal windows, whereas old stone windows are better set off with softer displays in more ornate terracotta troughs.

If you are planning to plant your own bulbs, remember that spring-flowering bulbs need to be planted roughly six months before flowering time – most are available in early autumn and are best planted shortly after they come on sale, before they dry out too

Foliage display (below)

Try to pick plants that have more than just flower power to recommend them. Interestingly shaped or coloured foliage, or an attractive growing habit, are equally important, as this pot of pelargoniums demonstrates.

Winter window box (above)

This simple wooden trough has been planted up for winter with purplish-pink-tinged ornamental cabbages and the pink spires of heather (Erica) and cyclamens.

Summer pots (below)

Recycled catering tins, painted electric blue, have been filled with bright daisies and lined up on a windowsill to great effect.

much. (See information on pages 24–25 for bulb planting.) Once they have flowered, remove them and put them in a plastic pot in good quality compost and keep well watered. If they dry out, they will fail to flower next season.

Later in the season, you can opt for more exuberant plantings with a profusion of flowers and much more relaxed foliage. Pelargoniums are the obvious choice for window boxes or pots on window ledges, and there is now a truly amazing array of types. Among the most attractive are the slightly smaller flowered ivy-leaved trailing pelargoniums, with their waxy leaves, or the miniature pelargoniums, such as 'angels'. Displays of pelargoniums look best when unmixed with other plants, as the strong colour then creates the most impact. They come in a range of colours from white to deep carmine pink and red. If you want blue-flowering displays though, you will need to find another candidate – brachyscome, forget-me-nots, *Convolvulus sabatius*, pansies and lobelia are all good candidates for this, although they lack the sheer force of character that pelargoniums offer, which are also extremely forgiving of neglect and poor treatment, but they dislike being overwatered – the leaves will turn yellow very rapidly.

As the days get longer and the sun is lower in the sky, the deep reds and golds tend to come into their own.

Classic display (above)
A profusion of petunias and pelargoniums, set in a stone trough, shines out in jewel-like fashion from its surround of deep green foliage.

Table displays

There is no better place to display small treasures than

on a table set in front of a window, as the charms of your plants

are raised up closer to eye-level for you to enjoy.

Drosanthemum hispidum

Geranium cinereum

On a balcony or terrace, it is particularly satisfying to have a small table with a seasonally changing display of plants. If it is positioned in front of a window, you get the satisfaction of a continually changing scene to look out on. Provided the display is changed every few weeks, the aspect is not that important. Most plants will survive for a relatively short space of time in less than ideal light conditions.

You can alter the planting from one particularly fine specimen plant in the centre of the table to a grouped display of smaller plants, and you can vary your colour theme and the style of the planting as and when it suits you to do so. If you want to use the table for eating, you can simply group the plants on the floor when necessary.

It is often a good idea to have one central foliage plant – such as a neatly clipped small box ball – around which other plants can be displayed to create a small formal arrangement. Individual pots with pansies alternately in dusky purple-black or white look very smart, as do small pots of little yellow narcissi like 'Tete-a-Tete'. You can follow this up slightly later with *Bellis perennis*, the little pompon-shaped daisy in pink and white, or perhaps brilliant orange ranunculus or primulas. Later in the summer, you could have small pots of

Co-ordinated colours

(left)

An array of interesting
dark-leaved foliage plants
in matching silvery-grey
pots creates an attractive
foil to the central planting of
pink pansies and black
Ophiopogon *grass.*

Sisyrinchium bellum

Dianthus 'Nyewood Cream'

Miniature trough (left)

A small alpine-style trough takes pride of place on a wooden table. Mound-forming plants, such as miniature dianthus and saxifrages, are ideal for this purpose, making a texturally interesting surface, surmounted with bright flowers in early summer.

black-leaved grass (*Ophiopogon*) and silver cineraria for a foliage display. Miniature plants are ideal for table-top displays, and succulents or alpines are ideally suited. You could plant them up in interesting shallow containers – shells, clay seed trays or inverted clay tiles for example. Sedums and sempervivums, with their curious, fleshy green leaves, sometimes tinged with maroon, look terrific, although they need a sunny spot to perform well. Other good alpines are the dwarf mound-shaped forms of dianthus contrasting with the more strappy leaves of tiny irises and dwarf sisyrinchium, with delicate little rock roses (*Helianthemum*), for example, softening the planting.

Accent on foliage (right)

Small pots of sedums and saxifrages, which require only minimum watering, are ideal for a low-maintenance all-year-round display on a table.

Doorways and steps

Symmetrical arrangements make the ideal planting design for doorways and steps. Matched pairs of geometric evergreens, flowering standards or large pots of flowers are ideal in this setting.

Doorways and steps make a naturally theatrical setting for plants. Obviously, the architecture and style of the setting will influence the nature of the planting. Formal doorways demand a similarly precise and elegant planting display, set in suitable containers, whereas two large tubs playing host to a pair of neatly clipped standard evergreens make ideal partners for a traditional Adam doorway.

Smart standards (above)

Flowering or foliage standards make ideal doorway companions.

Matched pairs (left)

Elegant, modern pots of cannas line a path and flank the steps to great effect.

You do not have to stick to traditional containers and traditional plants, but they must have some resonance with the architecture. If you want to go down the modern route, two tall metal florists' buckets holding singularly beautiful grasses, such as *Milium effusum* 'Aureum' would have the same simplicity and elegance of style, but in a much more modern idiom.

If you own an old stone building with cottage-style doors, then a much softer planting style would look right, as would climbing plants trained to frame the doorway. Scented ones, such as honeysuckle or one of the perfumed jasmines, are ideal, but make sure they have an adequate support. Some honeysuckles are extremely vigorous and, if not checked regularly, will rapidly threaten to keep you (and visitors) out of the house!

Topiary (below)

Clipped evergreens, such as box or privet, in balls or cones make good flanking plants for doorways.

Steps provide a chance to create regimented displays of a single pot per step, each bearing the same plant. Pelargoniums are great favourites, but some of the strappy grasses look equally good, as could neat pots of auricula primroses in spring. Wider steps provide an opportunity for larger, grouped displays. Steps also make an excellent setting for scented small plants, such as hyacinths and narcissus in spring, or aromatic herbs in summer.

Colour planning will enhance the overall impact of your planting, so choose plants that tone well with any painted surfaces.

Hanging baskets and wall pots

Devotees of hanging baskets most enjoy the way in which the sheer exuberance of the planting makes such an eye-catching display, particularly in high summer as the trailing pelargoniums and petunias so often planted in them fill out to create a literal explosion of colour.

It is the sheer vulgarity of hanging basket planting that usually attracts the most criticism, but if colour and impact are what you are striving for, the fact that the planting is at head height or above gives you a better than average chance of catching the eye. Unfortunately, the exposed position of any hanging basket also draws attention to any shortcomings in the condition of the plants or the state of the basket; the worst cases reveal a large expanse of browning moss or, worse, green foam and a few puny plants. If you are going to go for big and brash, you have to do it in style. If you look after the plants well, they will fill out quite rapidly over a three week period. To plant up a 30cm (12in) diameter basket you will need six to nine plants, depending on their size. Plants raised in jiffy (biodegradable) pots are ideal as you can push the whole pot into the basket when you plant up, avoiding damage to the roots.

Cool tones (right)

For a subtle effect, pick toning colours in shades of blue, silver and grey. Here blue pansies, Salvia farinacea, Senecio maritima *and silvery-grey* Helichrysum *create an attractive mix of flowers and foliage.*

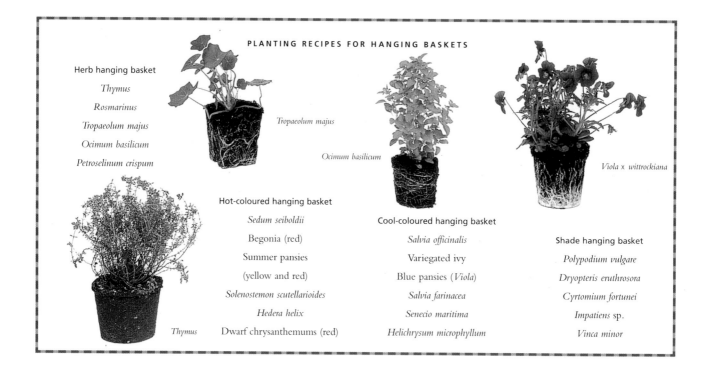

PLANTING RECIPES FOR HANGING BASKETS

Herb hanging basket
Thymus
Rosmarinus
Tropaeolum majus
Ocimum basilicum
Petroselinum crispum

Tropaeolum majus

Ocimum basilicum

Viola x wittrockiana

Hot-coloured hanging basket
Sedum seiboldii
Begonia (red)
Summer pansies
(yellow and red)
Solenostemon scutellarioides
Hedera helix
Thymus   Dwarf chrysanthemums (red)

Cool-coloured hanging basket
Salvia officinalis
Variegated ivy
Blue pansies (*Viola*)
Salvia farinacea
Senecio maritima
Helichrysum microphyllum

Shade hanging basket
Polypodium vulgare
Dryopteris eruthrosora
Cyrtomium fortunei
Impatiens sp.
Vinca minor

PLANTING UP A HANGING BASKET

You will need a wire or cane basket, a basket liner and compost, plus the plants, together with a stout hook and chains.

1 *Rest the basket on a bucket for stability. Cover the base with a layer of moss 2cm (¾in) thick. Line with plastic and pierce holes in the base.*

2 *Cut holes in the plastic and push trailing plants though the lower sides of the basket.*

3 *Fill with compost and continue to plant around the basket. Complete the central area with the tallest plants. Trim the trailing plants if necessary.*

It is important that you look after your basket properly. Exposure to the elements – drying winds and scorching sun – demand that the plants are watered well and frequently. Add water-retaining gel to the planting medium to help ensure that the baskets stay as moist as possible.

If your tastes do not run to brilliant colours, you can create more restrained but eye-catching plantings using a single colour theme or toning colours, with ivy, senecio and silver-leaved cineraria to create an elegant colour scheme. The main point of any hanging basket planting, however, is that it must contain enough plants with a lax habit to mask the base of the basket, and for this reason trailing plants – both for foliage and flowers – are predominantly used. The plants should ideally be able to withstand drought fairly well.

Although most hanging baskets are destined for sunny areas, if your balcony or terrace is north-facing or in part shade, you can create attractive baskets using ferns, ivies and other foliage plants. Busy lizzies are also good plants for semi-shade. Remember that by and large shade-loving plants tend not to have brilliantly coloured flowers, so opt for schemes for these situations that are predominantly white and green. They look more appropriate, and tend to gleam out from the more shadowy light. Bright colours simply look wrong and, in all probability, the plants chosen are inappropriate for these conditions and will rapidly become weak and sickly looking.

Supporting and maintaining hanging baskets

The weight of a fully planted, watered hanging basket is considerable, so make sure that you use stout hooks and chains, and that the supporting hook is fastened to a weight-bearing beam, support or bracket. Feed the plants once a fortnight with a proprietary fertilizer, and ensure you water the basket often enough and thoroughly enough for the compost to stay moist.

Kitchen colanders (above)

An inventive and witty use for old metal kitchen colanders sees them doing duty as kitchen herb containers, filled with a mixture of useful herbs, such as dill, rocket and chervil.

Sutera diffusa

Ballota acetabulosa

USEFUL TRAILING PLANTS

A few trailing plants are essential to flesh out the planting for a hanging basket · or wall pot. In addition to the foliage plants shown here, consider using *Convolvulus sabatius* with blue flowers, *Tropaeolum majus* (with orange, yellow or red flowers) and *Helichrysum petiolare* (with silver, green or gold foliage).

Diascia vigilis

Sphaeralcea sp.

Glechoma hederacea 'Variegata'

Wall mask (left)

In addition to the commonly found semi-circular wall pots, you can create wall pots from interesting sculptures with a hollow top, or even found objects, such as drain pipe covers.

Roof tile (left)

A clay roof tile has been nailed to the wall and a terracotta pot filled with succulents attached to it, to make a sculptural wall hanging. Place a wire around the rim of the pot, and create a hook to attach it to the tile.

Wall pots

These are very similar to hanging baskets, but are semi-circular in shape, and are attached, as the name implies, to a wall or fence. They can be made of different kinds of material – wire, metal or terracotta are all attractive materials and therefore the best ones to choose since the container is more visible. Because most walls offer a fairly large expanse, it is usually a good idea to create a repeating display of pots, either in a row or staggered to create a diamond-shaped pattern. This has the most impact when the planting in each pot is the same (or at least uses similar colours) as those in the other pots. You can either hang the pots directly on the wall, or use trellis from which they can be suspended with hooks or wires.

PLANTING A WALL POT

You will need four or five plants with sufficient compost to fill the pot.

1 *Half fill the pot with compost, and then insert the backing plants.*

2 *Arrange the front plants last, and arrange the foliage so it drapes attractively over the pot. Fix the pot to the wall.*

Scaling the heights
(above)

*When space is at a premium,
do not forget that you can use
the tops of walls for planting
displays. Here repeating pots
of lavender add a flourish to
a boundary wall. Make sure
the pots are secured to the wall.*

Wall tops

In a small space, any area for potential planting should not be ignored. On roof terraces, or where there are varied heights of buildings around a balcony, for example, you can make use of the space on top of a wall to create eye-catching plant displays. The surrounding architecture will dictate the style of the display. In a small town apartment, for example, with plaster or brick walls, formal schemes, with neatly clipped evergreens and attractive rectangular terracotta or metal containers, may well look appropriate, but in a country setting with soft golden stone, you may find cascades of small-flowered cottage-garden favourites, like aubretia or dianthus, blend in better with the surroundings.

For more formal wall-top planting, you could create a small repeating herb pot scheme, in which you alternate neat small terracotta pots of well-rounded mounds of parsley, sage and marjoram. A larger scale herb planting could have pots of French lavender, interspersed with rosemary and artemisia.

Clipped box, trained into satisfying geometric shapes like balls or pyramids, also makes a good wall-top feature. You could alternate the container shapes between neat squares for the balls and round pots for the pyramids, to make a striking architectural feature. A backcloth of evergreen planting clothing the wall softens the effect. Virginia creeper, which turns a glorious scarlet in

Auricula theatre (right)

*Traditionally auricula
primroses were displayed in
small black theatres. Here the
idea is translated across to
shelves, painted matt black,
and used to display a small
collection of auriculas in
simple antique terracotta
pots. Other small plants,
such as pansies, would look
equally attractive.*

Metal sieve (above)
Recycling old pots and kitchen containers is always worthwhile. Here a metal sieve makes an attractive frame for a small saxifrage in a terracotta pot.

autumn, ivy or the golden-leaved hop, *Humulus lupus* 'Aurea' are all good candidates for this.

Tiered planting

In a very small area, it pays to make best use of what space there is by creating 'tiers' of planting. You can do this either in standing displays, like the traditional tiered Victorian jardinière, or by attaching shelves to an existing wall. The style will depend, to a great extent, on the situation and the surrounding architecture, as well as on your own, particular, planting preferences.

Small-flowered plants are ideally shown off on some form of shelving. The famous 'florists' flowers' for showing, such as tulips and pinks, with their great followings of dedicated growers were traditionally displayed in little 'theatres'. A similar arrangement of black shelving is ideal for small-flowered pansies or dianthus, although the best known of these are the auricula primroses, originally displayed in their own auricula theatres. The flower markings of auricula primroses deserve close inspection, and there is no better way to do this than by raising them from ground level.

Ornate wirework jardinières, in which the plants encircle a central structure with three levels of planting in a 'wedding-cake' arrangement, give you scope for varying the planting. Large specimens are displayed on the bottom tier, the plants diminishing in size on each tier. This kind of wirework looks its best when planted up with principally foliage plants, such as ivies and ferns.

Wire staging (above)
Double the number of plants can be displayed if you employ simple forms of shelving or staging. Here, antique wire shelves house a formal collection of box topiary.

Auricula primroses (left)
Two particularly attractive cultivars: 'Sirius' (far left) has bronze flowers: 'Walton' (left) has mauve flowers. Both have the typical slightly bloomed greyish-green leaves.

Railings

Most balconies have some form of railing as a security device, so it pays to try to make the most of this feature with appropriate planting.

Much will depend on the architectural style of the railings. Classic wrought-iron railings are a distinguished feature in their own right, so it would be a great shame to overwhelm their appearance with too many fussy flowers. Ideally, simple geometric shapes and handsome foliage plants make the ideal combination.

Less-attractive, more serviceable railings can perform the role of plant supports, so that you can grow a wide range of plants either up them or backed by them. Among the climbers to choose from would be small-flowered tough clematis like the viticellas, with their exquisite small flowers in shades of mauve, blue or white or the eye-catching passion flower with its curiously formed flowers in mauve, white and green. Fast-climbing annuals like nasturtiums, or the more tender morning glory (*Ipomaea*) with its magnificent large cerulean blue flowers, would be an equally good choice.

Small troughs can be fixed both at the base of the railings and suspended from the top rail, to increase the area of possible planting. Nowadays, metal mesh screening is often used to surround a balcony or divide one balcony from another. Its uncompromisingly modern nature demands a suitably modern style of planting, in which simple shapes and strong colours play a major role, although the very nature of its construction, with frequently spaced horizontal and vertical supports, makes it ideal for sweet peas.

In hot sunny climates, the bold statement made by canna lilies would be a good choice for your planting, as would other large-flowered perennials, such as lilies. Equally good in this kind of setting would be a trough of bamboos or attractive grasses. Some useful bamboos and grasses are listed on pages 88–89.

Ivies (above)

Climbing and trailing plants, such as different forms of ivy, help to soften the outline of railings.

Long troughs (below)

To complement the shape of the railings, create long, low plantings in terracotta troughs or wooden boxes.

Fancy primulas (above)

The delicate dark flowers of Primula 'Gold Lace' complement the form of the wrought-iron railings behind.

Summer ledge (right)

Glazed terracotta pots filled with the bright hot colours of ivy-leaved pelargoniums make a splash of colour against the dark railings behind.

Even in the smallest space, it is heart-warming and very encouraging to create planting schemes of seasonal flowers. Particularly in cities, where it can be hard to appreciate the changing moods and colours of the seasons, creating your own small area of seasonal change becomes particularly valuable. Underplanting any summer-flowering climbers with spring bulbs helps to make the most of any available space. Equally, choosing plants that perform over more than one season – spring flowers and brightly coloured autumn foliage – is another good idea. In autumn, fruiting plants are well worth growing, and provide food for wildlife as well.

SEASONAL DISPLAYS

Spring bulbs

While we are still in the grips of winter, a few bulbs will start to flower, bringing with them the unmistakable feeling that spring is just around the corner.

Snowdrops (*Galanthus* sp) are the earliest of all bulbs, and it is worth growing a small container of them to set on a table in front of a kitchen or living room window, surrounded by attractive variegated ivies. Less than a month later, the first crocuses will be in flower. Their delicate waxy petals and diffused colours, such as white (sometimes flecked with mauve), purple or creamy yellow, make excellent displays in modern aluminium containers, which seem to suit their uncompromising lines. Before they are over, the hyacinths

Spring bulbs (below and right)

A small windowsill makes the perfect frame for delicate small plants – in this case jewel-like Iris reticulata *and small-leaved ivies. Seen in close-up (right), their exquisite markings can be better appreciated.*

have come into flower, with their overpowering, almost cloying, scent. Since the heads of the double-flowered varieties are too heavy for their slender stems, it pays to give them a supporting cage of twigs (see pp. 30–31). Equally highly scented are some forms of narcissus, such as 'Paper White' or the orange-flowered, flat-trumpeted 'Pheasant's Eye'.

Since the flowers of most bulbs are small and jewel-like, it pays to raise them from the floor. They make ideal subjects for windows boxes, or for grouped displays on small tables, an old garden bench or a flight of steps. Two large matching pots could stand sentinel either side of the front door with a succession of scented bulbs, from spring through to summer.

The spring-flowering bulbs will need to be planted in early autumn. Most bulbs are planted at a depth of twice the height of the bulb itself, so tiny bulbs, such as snowdrops, are planted quite close to the soil surface, while larger bulbs, like daffodils, should be planted approximately 10cm (4in) deep in the soil. If you expect the bulbs to flower again the following spring, make sure you do not allow them to dry out after flowering, and let the leaves die down naturally – they provide the newly forming bulbs with food.

Scented narcissus (left)

Small pots of scented narcissus pack a surprising punch in terms of scent. To create more impact, line up several pots of narcissus along a windowsill.

Lily of the valley (right)

Equally perfumed, lilies of the valley are the ideal choice for a shady corner. A rustic bucket makes the ideal container for these delicate plants.

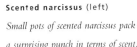

Summer plantings

As soon as the frosts have passed, your choice of plants widens

to include the summer-flowering perennials and bulbs, as well

as shrubs and tender annuals.

Canna lilies (above right)
These elegant plants with their glossy, strap-shaped leaves add a touch of class to a balcony in early summer.

Flowering profusion (below)
The roof of a barge has been planted with cascading summer-flowering annuals, such as verbena, in a vibrant display.

The best displays tend to come from containers of one type of plant, grouped with other containers containing single plantings. Although it was once popular to mass lots of different plants together in one colourful display, tastes have changed in recent years. 'Tiering' or 'blocking' the display, and the colours, adds to the impact, so you might, for example, have a long trough of *Primula* 'Guinevere' with small grasses, backed by large tubs of pink and red cosmos and, perhaps, a pink climbing rose behind.

The single colour theme, and massed groupings, lends solidity and strength to the overall design.

Flowering displays are short-lived, so use structural plants to flank or back up the display. Among the best complementary foliage plants in pots are hostas, whose large clusters of ribbed leaves are the ideal foil to more delicate flowers, particularly those with a waxy or well-formed appearance, similar to their own spires of slightly tubular bells. The smaller, softer flowers look good combined with pots of clipped box, or edged with a rim of parsley.

Some summer flowers – pelargoniums for example – look best alone. A single bushy pelargonium could sit framed on a window ledge, for example, but make sure the plant is healthy and well-grown when it has a prime position. (It pays to nip out the growing point of pelargoniums to get them to form side shoots, adding to the bushiness.)

If you want to combine colours, go for complementary colours – mid-blue and apricot-orange – for toning colours – shades of pink and mauve – or for clashing colours – strong blues, reds, oranges and purples. The secret when combining clashing colours is to get a similar degree of brightness in each shade – the strongest orange, the brightest red, the most brilliant blue and the most vibrant purple. A muddier or paler shade will unbalance the display.

Focal point (right)
Small flowers can make a bold statement if mass planted in a large container. Try lobelia, pansies and brachyscome.

Summer-flowering annuals

One of the greatest delights of small-space gardening is to grow a few plants yourself from seed. Nothing beats the speed of growth of tender annuals, which you plant in the warmth indoors in early spring to be rewarded by a stunning display in midsummer.

Two of the easiest seed plants to grow both have a climbing or trailing habit – sweet peas (*Lathyrus odorata*) and nasturtiums (*Tropaeolum majus*). The sweet peas have the bonus of wonderfully scented flowers (and are great for cutting and displaying indoors); you can buy the seeds in packs of mixed colours, or you can choose individual colours. The deep purplish-black ones look particularly smart. Nasturtiums have singularly beautiful leaves in a luminous, light-reflecting apple green (some have darker leaves and unusual, deep red flowers). The flowers and seeds are edible, too, and add a splash of colour to a summer salad.

Non-climbing summer annuals well worth growing from seed are the highly scented tobacco plants (*Nicotiana*). They, too, come in a mixed range of colours, from gleaming pale green to deep, dramatic maroon, but the most exotic of all are the impressively tall *Nicotiana sylvestris* which tower to a height of 1.5m (5ft), and make an eye-catching feature when planted in a large pot. They are, unfortunately, much loved by slugs and snails, so if you have a ground-level terrace use grit or broken egg shells on the surface of the compost to deter any marauders from attacking your plants.

Other good summer-flowering annuals and biennials include *Ageratum*, with powder-puff blue flowers, *Calendula* with bright orange flowers, and dwarf cosmos (in shades of pink, white and red). Tender perennials grown as annuals include begonias and *Canna indica*.

Cooking pot
(far left above)
A rusty barbecue has found a new lease of life planted up with bright nasturtiums.

Sweet pea supports
(far left: below and left)
Sweet peas demand a good support system and plenty of sun to flower profusely.

Small is beautiful (above)
These dwarf forms of cosmos in shades of bright pink make excellent windowsill plants.

PLANTING SWEET PEAS

You will need a 30cm (12in) pot and six supports.

1 *Grow the seed in spring in jiffy pots. Transplant in early summer into a suitable container.*

2 *Surround the pot with 90cm (3ft) twiggy supports.*
3 *Tie together at intervals with twine or wire.*

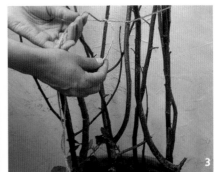

Summer climbers

Nobody can afford to be without a few really stunning summer-flowering climbers because they produce a truly amazing number of flowers while taking up next to no space on a balcony.

Roses and clematis are the two most popular summer climbers, and deservedly so. For a start, there are many varieties to choose from, with a range of flower types and colours, so that you can find something for almost any colour or style of display. Roses and clematis mingle surprisingly well together, which helps to extend the flowering season if you choose carefully. The smaller-flowered clematis, like the viticellas, with their little drooping heads of four-petalled flowers, have a delicate charm quite unlike the more flamboyant large-flowered hybrids, which simply clamour for attention, but they also tend to be fairly sturdy and relatively easy to grow. The toughest of the lot is *Clematis montana*, but it flowers earlier, in late spring, and is useful for a cool or slightly shady wall. Most roses and clematis prefer sun, although clematis roots are best shaded. Of the roses, there is little point growing those with hardly any scent, and of those that are scented, the old-fashioned roses have the most exotic perfume.

A good candidate for warmer climates is the vigorous bougainvillea. Its brilliant purple or crimson flowers are the trademark of any southern terrace. Hardier but no less showy is the glory vine (*Campsis* x *tagliabuana*) with its vast, deep orange trumpet-shaped flowers (and rather unpleasant thorns, so be careful where you site it). The smaller, more starry flowers of *Solanum crispum* 'Glasnevin' are a zinging blue with a yellow eye, and it rapidly makes a great deal of growth.

It always pays to include scented plants, and there is a good range of scented climbers, including the popular honeysuckle (*Lonicera*); many cultivars have good scent, including *L. periclymenum* 'Graham Thomas'. Equally perfumed is *Jasmine officinale,* with tiny white flowers that emit a powerful scent in summer, as does *Trachelospermum jasminoides*, which also has small white flowers.

Hot summer mix (below)

Hybrid large-flowered clematis, such as velvety 'The Vagabond', look stunning coupled with other climbers like the scented Trachelospermum diffusum.

Clashing colours (above)

Contrasting colours, like the bluish-purple of Solanum crispum 'Glasnevin' *with a yellow-flowered honey-suckle enlivens a patio wall.*

Romantic balcony (right)

Using the wrought-iron canopy of a balcony to support several clematis softens its appearance while adding welcome shade in late spring and summer.

Autumn and winter planting

As summer gives way to autumn, a different mood develops in the planting.

The foliage of deciduous trees and shrubs takes on rich warm tones of russets,

gold and even bright scarlet.

Autumn fruit starts to swell and ripen, bunches of grapes cluster on the vines, apples are ready for harvesting and the scarlet, orange and gold berries of pyracantha and the white and pink fruits of *Gaultheria procumbens* provide food for birds in the winter to come.

A few flowers appear at this time of year, among them those of the autumn-flowering bulbs, like *Crinum* x *powellii*, and some crocus. Later, as the frosts harden, you can find the cyclamen flowers, the frilled leaves of ornamental cabbages and the spires of heathers and heaths. Grouped together in window boxes, these plants create a cheerful, hardy display. *Elaegnus* x *ebbingei* has tiny flowers that produce wafts of heady scent in autumn. Grasses come into their own at this time of year, with seedheads in rich shades of gold and brown. Quite a few shrubs have winter flowers, some of them scented, including witch-hazel (*Hamamelis*) and Christmas box (*Sarcococca*) and some daphnes.

As winter moves towards spring, the very first harbingers of it are small clusters of snowdrops, and it is well worth growing a small pot of snowdrops, positioned on a patio table or windowsill, as a reminder that winter will not last for ever.

Discreet charm (far right)
The softer colours of autumn are emphasized here in a pretty blue glazed bowl of colchiums, heathers and cotrus.

Autumn gold (right)
Pots of chrysanthemums in bronzes, gold or russet colours are well worth including on a table-top display in front of a window. Match them with golden grasses or the variegated foliage of euonymus.

Winter delight (right)
Winter-flowering pansies are one of the best plants for this time of year, with a long flowering season when most other small perennials have ceased to put on a show.

Golden glow (left)
The leaves of many perennials, like those of Hosta sieboldiana, turn wonderful colours before they fall in autumn, and deserve to be brought into a prominent place at this time of year.

There is no shortage of interesting ideas for planting up balconies and terraces. Colour combinations are always important, and it pays to consider your colour schemes carefully, to gain the maximum impact from the flowers you choose. However, foliage, too, can play its part, whether in the form of slender grasses or neatly clipped small evergreens. Tiny water pots, displays of scented flowers and useful herbs and edibles all add to the variety and pleasure of balcony planting. Don't forget to add a few suitable plants to encourage wildlife to visit your garden.

SPECIAL EFFECTS

Warm colours

If you have a sunny terrace or balcony, you can make the most of

strong colours. Those in the 'hot' end of the spectrum are the bright

yellows, oranges, reds, pinks and purples with a tinge of red.

Brilliant mixture (left)

Among the best vibrant plants are pelargoniums and azaleas, which have a wide range of pinks and reds. Combine clashing colours for the strongest impact.

Stacking colour (below)

Shelves can be used to make a wall of colour. Here pelargoniums have been lined up on rustic shelves.

Certain shades of blue – those that contain some red – combine well with oranges and purples to create a vibrant colour scheme.

Plants from hotter climates – particularly those from South Africa or Australia – tend to have big, brightly coloured flowers. Planting schemes featuring brilliantly coloured flowers can look brash, so compose them in planters that redress the balance. Oversized terracotta pots or Italian-style urns give the design stability and 'weight'. To create a strong statement, plant deep blue ceramic pots with orange- and red-flowered displays – bulbs such as tulips or *Fritillaria imperialis* in spring or lilies for summer, or blood red anemones or salvias. The larger-petalled summer-flowering annuals and perennials are good for hot schemes – nasturtiums, zinnias and petunias. Smaller-petalled flowers will need to be massed to give the same dominance of colour.

Elegant lilies (above)

Canna lilies come in pinks and mauves, adding a gentler warm tone to the planting.

Silver or grey foliage makes a good foil for bright planting. Cineraria, senecio, lambs' ears (*Stachys byzantina*), lavender and santolina are all good foliage companions for these kinds of scheme, as are the silvery thistles.

Wall pots and small windowsills can be given a facelift with pots of scarlet pelargoniums set against soft, golden stone. Pelargoniums come in a range of colours, but the traditional bright red still has the greatest impact.

For a softer, but warm-toned, scheme mid-pinks are ideal. To give the natural prettiness of this more delicate colour some substance, choose flowers with architectural merit such as canna lilies, and combine them in ways that have strength of form – building a 'tower' of plants with the most striking at the centre, and smaller more flowing plants around them.

Cool colours

For a sense of tranquillity and timelessness,

cool colours – pale blues, lemon yellows, lime greens,

very pale pinks, pale mauves and whites – are the best choice.

Muscari window box
(above right)

These attractive small bulbs make a smart display in spring, particularly when massed together in a single specimen planting.

Cool colours look good seen against a backdrop of dark evergreen foliage or combined with soft, apple green leaves. The brilliant blue faces of pansies, with their centre eye of bright yellow, look particularly good in hanging baskets when surrounded by crisp curly-leaved parsley. Gentle cascades of pale pink diascia and white ivy-leaved pelargoniums, combined with silvery helichrysum, make subtle combinations for hanging baskets or loosely planted window boxes. Crisp, sharp plantings of small clipped evergreens, combined with waxy white dwarf narcissus make a clear statement on a town doorstep or window ledge or, in summer, small standards of clipped myrtle or ivy could be underplanted with a carpet of white pansies or osteospermums.

Lilies can be used to flank a doorway, and if you choose a scented variety like 'Regale' they will fill the space indoors with delicious scent in summer. White is an excellent choice for shady balconies, in part at least because many of the shade-tolerant plants have white flowers – busy lizzies have white and coloured forms, but the big *Zantedeschia aethiopica* is good in shade (provided you keep the containers moist) and looks architectural, as do large-leaved hostas with their white, ice blue or mauve flowers in early summer.

In winter, white cyclamens can be combined with evergreens to create stunning window box displays, to be replaced with snowdrops in early spring. In spring, you can use the blue flowers of *Muscari armeniacum*, either on their own or combined with blue iris and delicate small white-flowered narcissus.

Vertical display (left)

The cool blue flowers of the summer-flowering climber Plumbago auriculata *cover a wall with restrained colour.*

Steely trough (right)

The cool blue flowers of the mop-headed hydrangea make the perfect choice for an elegant metal trough.

Vibrant colours

The really vibrant colours of the garden palette – such as fully saturated oranges, purples and scarlets – can make a major impact in a small space.

The strongest colours in the gardener's palette look their best when used in either single colour displays or in those in which these vibrant colours clash. As they are so noticeable and strong, you should avoid using them as spot colours in more quietly coloured displays, as they tend to jump forward, unbalancing the rest of the display.

Some plants, in particular, have really brilliant coloured flowers. The verbena hybrids come in a mixture of pulsating vermilions, purples and shocking pinks, as do the multi-petalled daisy-like flowers of zinnias. In spring, papery ranunculus flowers in hot oranges and egg-yolk yellows combine well with some of the more brightly coloured primulas. These strong colours look good planted up in terracotta pots or troughs, or, for a truly bright effect, in deep blue glazed ceramic pots.

Individual pots with a mixture of orange, red and purple zinnias could be lined up on a window ledge, one plant to a pot. A blazing display of nasturtiums, trailing verbena and 'hot'-coloured petunias and pansies, backed with dark green ivy (*Hedera*) would make equally vibrant hanging baskets.

Hot orange (far left)
The orange flowers of French marigolds (Tagetes) make a bold statement combined with deep sapphire blue lobelia.

Brilliant purple
(left above)
The clustered heads of small verbena flowers make a vibrant mid-summer display.

Bright combination
(left below)
Papery ranunculus flowers combine with burnt orange primulas in a colourful spring display for a balcony.

Electric blues (left)
Lobelia comes in wonderfully vivid, sharp blues, which provide the perfect foil for bright orange and gold flowers, such as those of French marigolds.

Water pots

Water features have become increasingly popular in the last few years, in part at least because they offer an attractive counterbalance to expanses of hard surface.

Small water troughs, tubs and pots can be created for tiny spaces but make sure that the weight-bearing capacity of any raised area, such as a balcony or roof terrace, is able to take the weight of water. If in doubt, consult a surveyor.

Large ceramic pots (with the drainage hole effectively stopped with cork) can be converted into small water lily pools, for example. There are a number of smaller water lilies which do well in shallower water, their rounded leaves making an attractive feature in addition to their beautiful, sculptural flowers. These include *Nymphaea* 'Aurora' with yellowish-red flowers, *N.* 'Albida' with fragrant white flowers and *N.* 'Ellisiana' with scarlet, scented flowers. The water hawthorn (*Aponogeton distachyos*) also has floating leaves, but longer, more arrow shaped and white, scented flowers. Among the plants that enjoy their feet in water are the Japanese irises whose brilliant blue and yellow flowers and elegant strap-shaped leaves have a strong architectural quality and the marsh marigold (*Caltha palustris*) with bright gold buttercup-shaped flowers.

You can create an unplanted moving water feature as a living sculpture. You will need an outdoor electricity supply which must be cabled correctly for outdoor use (consult a qualified electrician). Water splashing from a small bubble fountain over stones creates a sound that is relaxing and reassuring.

Nautical feature (above right)
A simple pool can be made from a shallow pan, in which pebbles and water combine, here with a salvaged ship's anchor.

Watering can (centre right)
A bucket filled with pebbles, in which a watering can acts as a fountain, is relatively simple to construct. A hole drilled in the base of the can allows the water to circulate while the pump is hidden in the base.

Lily pond (above and far right)
A ceramic bowl makes an excellent water feature. Dwarf water lilies and irises make attractive planting choices.

Scented displays

Scented or aromatic flowers and foliage are an essential ingredient for any

small space, as they offer such great value, and help to create the feel of a real

garden on an otherwise hostile high-rise balcony, for example.

Flower power (above)
*Hyacinths are among the
most heavily scented of all
flowers. Grow them in pots
near an open window for
maximum benefit.*

Mixed scent (opposite)
*Shrubs also offer the bonus of
scent. Skimmia 'Kew Green'
has scented flowers in spring,
as does narcissus.*

There are many and varied scents and perfumes to choose from, but not all are enjoyed to the same extent. What one of us may regard as delightful, another may find unpleasantly strong. The perfume of lilies, for example, can be very cloying in a small space, and some flowers – such as those of *Choisya ternata* – have a 'foxy' aroma that is not always pleasant.

A few scents are widely regarded as 'special' and have formed the basis of many perfumes – roses and jasmine are two of the most popular, followed by lilies of the valley and narcissus. Some of the flowering shrubs offer really good scent, including several of the viburnums, honeysuckle (the winter-flowering form, *Lonicera x purpusii* is particularly good value) and lilac. Wisteria is also wonderfully scented, but is probably best grown as standards in pots, unless you want to spend a lot of time keeping it in check and pruning it to ensure it flowers where and how you want it too.

A small flight of steps is the ideal place for you to position a group of scented containers, as you can enjoy their perfume every time you pass. Hyacinths and narcissus in spring could be followed by lilies or tobacco plants in summer.

A few scented climbers are well worth growing if you possibly can. Of these, roses are always the most popular. The traditional old-fashioned roses smell exquisite, although their flowering season is relatively short. If you wish, you can extend the scented season of your garden by adding jasmine and *Trachelospermum jasminoides* to your group of climbing plants.

Scent over the seasons (left)
*Plan your planting so that you get scent in more
than one season. In this planting, when the hyacinths
are over, you get the scent of the standard lavenders.*

Foliage displays

No small space can afford to be without

at least one or two good foliage plants, if only

to provide a counterpoint to any flowering display.

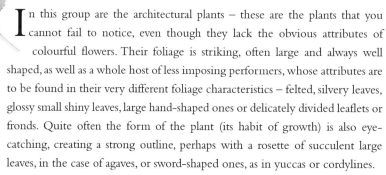

Grassy urn (far right)
Low-growing thyme is
surrounded with shrubs and
grasses, including a variegated
euonymus and a fescue grass.

Shady corner
(right above)
Hostas, Fatshedera x lizei
and ivies make a strong
statement on a balcony.

Foliage pots
(right below)
Here, a variegated hosta takes
centre stage. Ferns soften the
outlines of the pots.

In this group are the architectural plants – these are the plants that you cannot fail to notice, even though they lack the obvious attributes of colourful flowers. Their foliage is striking, often large and always well shaped, as well as a whole host of less imposing performers, whose attributes are to be found in their very different foliage characteristics – felted, silvery leaves, glossy small shiny leaves, large hand-shaped ones or delicately divided leaflets or fronds. Quite often the form of the plant (its habit of growth) is also eye-catching, creating a strong outline, perhaps with a rosette of succulent large leaves, in the case of agaves, or sword-shaped ones, as in yuccas or cordylines.

These plants lend a sensuous, textural quality to the planting, which gives it depth and, in the case of evergreen foliage, permanence. For a small space to remain furnished throughout the year, some evergreens are a must. Ideally, you should choose carefully so that you get maximum value from them (see pages 112–123 for good performers).

When composing a group of containers, it often pays to put the foliage plant in the centre of the display, slightly raised above it, and group the flowering plants (in a carefully composed symphony of toning colours) around your chosen foliage. For this kind of display, symmetry is important. You could create a circular display of small pots of the same plant in alternating colours. Another solution is to put the largest evergreen at the back, and then range the remaining pots down in size, creating a tiered arrangement. This works particularly well in the corner of a balcony or roof terrace, as the display fans out towards the front.

If you have unsightly walls they can be covered with evergreen climbers, such as ivy *Hedera helix* on a north-facing wall, or the vine, *Parthenocissus tricuspidata*, which turns brilliant scarlet in autumn. Some evergreen climbers also have the bonus of scented flowers – *Clematis armandii* is one such delight.

If foliage displays are to work, the leaves must be in peak condition, unmarred by blemishes and uneaten by scavenging insects. You need to give the plants regular foliar feeds and keep a watchful eye out for pests.

Grasses & grass-like plants

These elegant, slender-leaved plants have become deservedly popular

in recent times, in part at least because they are both versatile and

easy to look after, in the main.

Although they do not offer much in the way of a flowering display as such, the seedheads of grasses are good value, particularly when they catch low shafts of sunlight in the dying months of the year. Grasses make attractive candidates in their own right as specimen plants, have the bonus of good autumn colour in many cases, and also look particularly good in modern-style arrangements in metal containers. Some of the smaller ornamental grass-like plants, such as the black-leaved *Ophiopogon planiscapus* 'Nigrescens', make a good choice for combining with other dark-leaved plants, such as *Viola labradorica* and the attractive purplish-leaved primula, 'Guinevere'. Alternatively, plant it for shock effect in a silver and white scheme, with white pansies and cineraria.

Bamboos are particularly valuable as screening plants, since they create a natural windbreak, offering the plants in their lee a far better environment in which to flourish. There is a growing range to choose from, both small and large. Among the most attractive is the black-stemmed variety *Phyllostachys nigra*. Some are quite invasive, so they will need a reasonably large container to themselves, and will need fairly frequent dividing. The range of colour and form found in the grass family is surprising, ranging from the tiny, narrow-leaved fescues in surprisingly bright blues to the golden oat-like grasses, such as *Stipa gigantea*. Fascinating variegations, such as those of *Miscanthus sinensis* 'Zebrinus', colour the stems while plume-like seedheads in shades from oatmeal to bronze dance in the lightest breeze.

Simple contrast (left)

A fine-leaved black grass (Ophiopogon planiscapus 'Nigrescens') contrasts with this terracotta ball.

Hair-do (right)

A primitive sculpted head has been given a grassy wig (with a blue fescue grass), adding humour and textural contrast.

Topiary

Topiary is the art of clipping evergreen shrubs into formal shapes, but the term has widened

to include all kinds of shaping of plants, including the creation of flowering standards, and

'false' topiary, in which the geometric appearance is created using evergreen climbers.

Varied topiary (right
and below)
*Small, neatly clipped topiary
in different forms – spirals,
balls and pompon standards –
creates a centrepiece on a
terrace, the contrasts between
the forms giving a sensual
pleasure to an otherwise
subdued planting. The topiary,
right, is an embryonic peacock.*

The great benefit of evergreen topiary is that it looks good all the year round, so it can be used to make a really worthwhile contribution to the design of any planting, acting as a permanent anchor to the more fleeting displays of flowering plants, as well as being attractive in its own right.

Since its clearly defined shape and form is its principal claim to fame, it pays to remember this when devising a planting scheme around it. Nothing looks worse than a piece of formally clipped topiary surrounded by a sea of shapeless plants, although conversely, a neat frame of topiary can do sterling service when it constrains and confines a planting of exuberant perennials.

The shapes which you can devise for topiary are many and various, but unless you are an expert, you will get the best results by keeping to a relatively simple outline. Whatever you opt for, it is essential that the shrub in question is in prime condition, since the overall effect depends on the pristine uniformity of the small green leaves. (Large-leaved shrubs are useless because the cut marks show up and turn brown). Slow-growing shrubs are best because you have to clip them less frequently, and for this reason box, which is small-leaved, dense in habit and very slow-growing, is one of the most sought after. A clipped topiary plant will be expensive in a garden centre and it is not difficult to create your own.

Once you have created a topiary shape and it is in position, remember to turn it occasionally. Plants grow towards the light and one side of it will start to lean, or even die back, otherwise. A quarter turn every time you feed it will do the trick.

Standards

Although roses have long been grown as standards, the principle of creating a bush of flowers at the top of a clear stem has only recently become fashionable with other shrubs and perennials.

CREATING A STANDARD

In a standard shape a stem supports a bushy head of shoots

Many plants can be encouraged into a standard shape. Here Coprosma variegata *has been trained. To achieve this, the leading shoot is tied to a stake (1), the side shoots are snipped back to the main stem (2), the growing tip is pruned out when it reaches the right height (3), and the top allowed to bush out, nipped back as needed (4).*

Nowadays, standards are created from a whole host of plants – daisies, fuschias, wisteria, rosemary and lavender to name just a few of the more popular choices. Even pelargoniums can be trained into a standard shape, as indeed can anything which will make a strong enough 'trunk' to support the lollypop head of flowers or foliage. Those that do not have sufficient strength can be given some help in the form of a supporting cane.

False topiary

For a more instant effect, you can create topiary from quick-growing climbers such as ivy, or even from flowering climbers like clematis and *Solanum crispum* 'Glasnevin'. Use the same basic shapes – pyramids or hoops are the most effective – or you can also train the ivy over letters of the alphabet, for example, or any other fanciful structure that you might wish to use. It will take roughly one growing season to achieve a smallish pyramid or sphere, which you will have to clip fairly frequently to ensure it keeps its shape. You can combine them with traditional topiary in a grouped display, to give variety to the colour and form, or as a centrepiece to give structure to flowering displays.

A topiary pyramid

The best plants to use to make a pyramid are bay, privet or box. Privet will certainly work well but it is quite quick-growing, so needs lots of clipping. Bay looks smart but is prone to attacks by various pests. Box is ideal for this purpose, but you need to turn it frequently to keep your plant looking its best.

Classic pyramid (left)

This bay tree is being trained into a pyramid. Make a triangular frame out of canes, placed over the pot. Clip stray shoots which emerge beyond the frame.

False topiary (right)

An ivy sphere has been created as a wall hanging, with an underplanting of baby's tears (Soleirolia soleirolii) and other foliage plants.

MAKING A FALSE TOPIARY SPHERE

You will need a ball-shaped wire frame.

1 *You can purchase ready-made wire frames (which look quite attractive used on their own as sculpture!).*

2 *Plant up three or four container-grown trailing plants, such as ivies, around a 30cm (12in) pot and position the frame in the centre.*

3 *Train the stems up the topiary, tying in if necessary. Ivy will create a dense framework and can be clipped. Trim frequently.*

Herbs

Even a windowsill, provided it gets a reasonable amount of sunlight, will give you enough space to grow a few culinary herbs, ideal for adding to soups, stews and salads.

Nothing is nicer than to lean out of the window to snip off a few shoots of basil, rosemary, thyme or parsley, while you are cooking. You can plant the herbs up together in a mixed group in a window box or trough, or plant each different herb in its own pot. This is particularly useful for a herb like mint (*Mentha* sp) which tends to be invasive, and also needs more copious quantities of water than the more dry-loving thyme, marjoram or rosemary.

If space is at a premium, you could suspend a hanging basket planted up with herbs close to the back door. Make use of discarded kitchen utensils as planters. Old metal colanders or wooden sieves can be stacked to provide a useful, tiered herb garden. Parsley, with its tightly curled green leaves, makes an attractive edging for a container, and looks particularly good surrounding blue pansies, for example. Bay can be clipped into neat topiary shapes or into standards (see pages 90–93), as indeed can rosemary.

Some herbs have attractive foliage: look for variegated leaves splashed with gold or white, or cultivars in gold or purple. *Salvia officinalis* 'Purpurascens' makes an attractive foil for *Origanum vulgare* 'Aureum'. Basil also has a purple-leaved form (*Ocimum basilicum* 'Purpurascens'). A window box could be planted with a mixture of these herbs. Chives make a useful contrast with round-leaved herbs. Alternatively, make a planting of medicinal herbs – chamomile, tansy, artemisia and rue – for example.

Colourful companions (left)

A display of variegated sage and pinks in a metal trough makes an attractive contrast of colour and form.

Herb window box (right)

From the left, coriander, bay, thyme, rosemary and parsley fill a small window box, ideally placed on the kitchen windowsill.

Salad mixture (above)

Salad vegetables and herbs grown in small troughs on a roof
terrace, provide the cook with a range of ingredients.

Medicinal mix (above)

A combination of medici-
nal herbs, including tansy
and feverfew.

Balcony kitchen garden
(right)

Pots of herbs make a tiered
display on a narrow balcony.

Edible plants

With only the smallest space, you can still grow a few edible plants

– salad vegetables, tomatoes or perhaps strawberries in a pot – and

enjoy the benefits of picking your own fruit and vegetables.

Strawberry pot (above)
Grow your own strawberries
in a specially constructed pot
with planting pockets.

Roof terrace (right)
Keen cooks could devote the
entire area of their roof terrace
or balcony to edible plants.

Cut and come again
(below left)
Grow salad crops in several
square containers.

Keep it tight (below right)
Grow spring cabbages in
tight, neat rows and harvest
when they are still small.

Even on a small balcony it is possible to find space for a grow-bag of tomatoes or curly-leaved lettuce. Tomatoes, which have to be trained up canes, can be grown next to the fence or wall. A purpose-made strawberry pot, with pockets for planting, will produce a relatively large crop from a small area. Cucumbers and courgettes can be trained to grow upwards, rather than outwards. Lettuces make pretty edging plants for a flowering display, particularly if you choose the loose-leafed varieties which come in green and purple forms ('Lollo Rosso'). If you wish to grow fruit, you can buy dwarf stock (try family apple trees on which three different types of apple have been grafted), or you can grow the fruit espalier style (fanned out against a wall) or in cordons – narrow leading stems, set at an angle, trained against wires or a fence.

You will need to give the plants organic nutrients (tomato feed is excellent for most plants) in the growing season, and regular deep watering, to ensure a good crop. For cultivation for fruit and vegetables see pages 176–183).

Butterflies and bees

Even with a relatively small space, you can still do your bit for nature, by choosing plants that are visited by butterflies and bees for nectar and pollen.

Colourful visitor (above)
A swallowtail butterfly visits an inula flower in summer.

Come hither (below)
Brightly coloured flowers and foliage prove irresistible to all kinds of insects.

Bees are also pollinators of vegetables and fruit crops, so by growing these, you are also encouraging nature to flourish in your garden, provided you do not spray them with chemicals!

Among the shrubs most visited by butterflies is *Buddleia*, as its common name, butterfly bush, indicates. You will occasionally see hosts of butterflies on one bush. The flowers come in shades of white, blue, lilac, pinkish-mauve and deep purple ('Black Knight'). The white varieties need frequent deadheading. *Ceanothus* is another profusely flowering shrub with evergreen leaves and small light- or mid-blue flowers. It does best against a wall, and may need tying to prevent it from overtaking the space. Lavender is a great attraction for bees, as is rosemary. Both have evergreen aromatic leaves and, in the case of lavender, scented flowers. Both can be grown as standards, and rosemary makes an excellent culinary herb. Other herbs much loved by bees are marjoram (*Origanum*), with small mauve flowers, and thyme – one of the most decorative is *Thymus serpyllum*. Both are highly aromatic. All herbs need sunshine to thrive.

Of the perennials, *Achillea filipendulina* is much loved by butterflies. Grow it in a tall, wide pot to give the flowers more form. The variety that starts crimson and fades off to white is one of the most attractive, as is the pure white 'Mother of Pearl'. *Sedum spectabile*, known as the ice plant, is a great butterfly attractor, with its tiny star-shaped flowers in flat clusters from late summer onwards. Not only does it have noteworthy succulent foliage, but the flowerheads of some varieties, such as 'Joy' for example, look particularly attractive in the autumn too.

A large tub of *Helenium*, with its large daisy-like flowers in yellow, orange or copper, is another powerful attraction to bees and butterflies. *Helenium* 'Moorheim Beauty' is particularly attractive with deep burnt orange flowers.

Flag flightpath (right)
The markings on the falls of an iris provide a landing strip for bees.

Allium feast (left)

The multi-headed flowers of allium provide a rich source of nectar for visiting insects.

Ancient bee-skep (right)

Although no longer in use, an antique bee-skep makes an attractive ornament on a terrace or patio.

Birds and other wildlife

Most of us would feel that any garden is the poorer without at least a few birds and animals to visit it. Gardening in a restricted space does not prevent you from encouraging local wildlife.

A surprising variety of birds have accustomed themselves to breeding in relatively hostile urban environments, and more will probably be encouraged if there is a regular food supply provided.

You can buy a wide range of birdfeeders or you can make your own. A friend's grandmother, I recollect, had a paint can fixed just below the kitchen windowsill into which a sort of compost of peelings, fat and other kitchen scraps were regularly piled. Some birds are much less shy than others about approaching a house, and if the food is there over a long period of time, even the more naturally wary will make use of it. Almost every bird in the neighbourhood visited this, and whoever stood at the kitchen sink doing the washing up was often diverted by the antics of the visitors. A small bird recognition book stood nearby, and was often consulted. Great was the excitement when a flycatcher (a relative rarity in that part of the world) visited for the first time.

You will find, however, that most bird feeding tables also provide a very popular banquet for other small mammals that can climb, particularly squirrels. If you do not want to encourage these other visitors to your feeding table, then you need to buy a purpose-made squirrel-proof bird feeder, or, like my grandmother used to do, site the feeder on a window ledge high above the squirrels' normal reach.

MAKING A LANTERN BIRD FEEDER

A simple wooden, purpose-made lantern with removable glass panels can be converted into a bird feeder. Simply remove the glass panels, and then use the sharp edge of the candleholder to provide a secure base for a piece or fruit, or even a large piece of fat.

1 *First, insert the fruit or piece of fat through the sides of the lantern.*

2 *Position the food over the candleholder and press down firmly to secure it in place. This should prevent the food being dislodged.*

3 *Hang the lantern from your chosen branch. Make sure that it is positioned so that cats and other unwanted visitors cannot jump up.*

Nutty snacks (left)

A selection of nuts in terracotta pots can be suspended from a tree. A few decorative seedheads and some raffia create an attractive tie.

Metallic feeder (below)

Hazelnuts are particularly loved by blue-tits. The bird-feeder shown here is a heavy-duty metal one, with perching arms for the birds. However, squirrels will dangle from the top to help themselves as well if you hang the feeder from a tree.

If you have space, try to include a selection of berrying or fruiting plants as these will encourage birds to visit your garden. They particularly enjoy pyracantha berries, and will, of course, help themselves to fruit such as blackberries or raspberries that you are growing for yourself.

It is worth remembering that the local wildlife will need water during dry months, or when the ground is frozen, as much as they need food in winter. A shallow terracotta dish filled with water will give them an opportunity to perch and drink, or indeed to bathe. If you have a ground-level terrace or patio, consider incorporating a small shallow pool which will allow wildlife to drink, providing there is an accessible ledge for them.

Do take care, generally, not to use insecticides which will harm the local wildlife population. If you must use these chemicals, then try to do so in the evening after flying insects which are beneficial to the garden, such as bees, have returned to their nest or hive. Obviously, you must be very careful not to leave any chemicals lying around in the garden.

Choosing appropriate plants is a key factor in successful container gardening on balconies and terraces. The plants must be able to withstand a variety of demanding conditions and, to make the best use of limited space, should ideally offer more than one attractive attribute. This section lists a wide selection of both foliage and flowering plants. Their hardiness is indicated with zonal ratings (see page 192 for temperature guides) and with ratings from fully hardy to frost tender.

PLANTS A–Z

Nerium oleander

Trees and shrubs
Trees and shrubs provide the planting with permanent structure. This section has been divided into deciduous trees and shrubs (which lose their leaves in winter) and evergreens. Trees have a single stem, and shrubs are multi-stemmed, but many shrubs can be trained as standards (see pages 90–93) to have a single stem and a tree-like leaf canopy.

Deciduous trees and shrubs

Generally speaking, deciduous trees and shrubs have more interesting foliage than evergreens and many of them also offer an exciting display of flowers for a short period of the year. The magnolia is a prime example of this, with a whole range of exquisite flower forms and colours to choose from, some of them scented too. When the weather begins to cool after the summer, a process is set off whereby the leaves often change colour before they fall, so deciduous trees and shrubs often provide two seasons of principal interest. The Japanese maples (*Acer palmatum*) offer some truly eye-catching autumn effects in a range of colours from gold through scarlet to deep plum. Some have the advantage of attractive fruits as well (which may be a great draw for birds). In a limited space, you need to make a careful selection of those that offer the greatest benefit, and you will almost certainly need to have a mixture of both deciduous and evergreen trees and shrubs, so that there is some backdrop of foliage colour and form all year round. Single-stemmed trees will need staking when they are young to prevent wind-rock. To prevent them outgrowing their pots, they may need root pruning (see page 23) after a few years.

ACERACEAE
Acer
H Up to 3m (10ft)

ZONES 5–9

Acer griseum (Paper-bark maple) has cinnamon bark which peels to reveal orange-brown bark. Propagation is by seed sown in autumn. *Acer negundo* has ash-like leaves, bright green in summer, turning yellow. In spring, golden flowers are produced. The most popular cultivar for containers is *A. n.* 'Flamingo'. Propagation is by budding in summer. *A. palmatum* var *dissectum* is grown for its feathery leaves. Most forms produce autumn colours, and some have coloured bark. Propagate from seed in early spring or soft-wood cuttings in mid-summer.

hardiness Fully hardy
flowering Spring
position Partial shade. Thin, delicate leaves are prone to wind damage and scorch, so avoid open or exposed positions.
cultivation Loam-based compost (J.I. 3) or moist, free-draining soil. Prune in late autumn to mid-winter (cuts will 'bleed' profusely at other times). Water freely in summer, sparingly in winter.
overwintering Do not allow to become waterlogged.
pests & diseases Susceptible to aphids, scale insects, caterpillars, mites, coral spot and honey fungus
special features Watch for attack by coral spot fungus, and prune out affected shoots.
decorative ideas Dark-leaved varieties look good in metal or stone pots.

Acer palmatum var dissectum

LEGUMINOSAE/MIMOSACEAE
Albizia julibrissin
H 4m (12ft)   S Up to 4m (12ft)

ZONES 7–9

This large shrub or small tree, commonly known as the silk tree, has a domed shape, and fern-like foliage. The light to mid-green leaves are made of tiny sickle-shaped leaflets. In summer, clusters of fluffy-looking, spherical, lime green flowers are produced at the ends of the shoots, each about 3.5cm (1½in.) across. The form *A.j. rosea* has candy-pink flowers. This plant produces flowers after only a few years, and makes a beautiful specimen tree. Propagation is by semi-ripe cuttings which should be taken in summer or by root cuttings in winter.

hardiness Frost hardy
flowering Summer
position Full sun
cultivation Loam-based compost (J.I. 2) or poor to moderately-fertile, well-drained soil. Water freely in summer, sparingly in winter. Feed monthly with a balanced liquid fertilizer. May need pruning in spring to control growth.
overwintering In frost-prone areas, move into a cool greenhouse.
pests & diseases Whitefly and red spider mite can be a problem while the plant is under glass. Prone to vascular wilt.
special features Protect new foliage from damaging late spring frosts.
decorative ideas Underplant with blue or purple-flowered violas (including dark-leaved *Viola labradorica*) or *Campanula porscharskyana*.

Albizia julibrissin

LEGUMINOSAE/PAPILIONACEAE

Caragana arborescens

H Up to 3m (10ft), depending on variety

ZONES 3–8

The 'pea tree' is an upright, thorny, deciduous shrub with light green, pinnate leaves with up to 12 oval-shaped leaflets. It bears pretty, pale yellow flowers, either singly or in clusters, in late spring, followed by brown seed pods in autumn. Forms include: *C. a.* 'Lorbergii', which has longer leaves with up to 14 lance-shaped leaflets and small flowers; and *C. a.* 'Nana', which is smaller, with tightly packed branches and contorted shoots. *C. a.* 'Pendula' has stiff, weeping shoots and is often available as a grafted standard plant (at 1 or 1.5m/3 or 5ft tall) which is ideal for growing as a specimen in an attractive container. Propagation is by soft-tip cuttings taken in early summer.

hardiness Fully hardy
flowering Late spring
position Full sun
cultivation Loam-based compost (J.I. 2) or well-drained soil. Water moderately in summer, sparingly in winter, and feed monthly with a balanced liquid fertilizer.
overwintering Do not allow to become waterlogged.
pests & diseases None
special features This hardy plant will tolerate an exposed or windy position.
decorative ideas Underplant with cyclamen or snowdrops (*Galanthus nivalis*) for a winter/early spring display.

Caragana arborescens

Fuchsia

ONAGRACEA

Fuchsia

H 30–100cm (12–39in) depending on variety

ZONES 7–9

A genus of deciduous and evergreen shrubs, with more than 8,000 hybrids and cultivars. They flower during summer and autumn, and there is a fuchsia for almost every garden situation. Flowers are usually pendulous, with distinct sepals and petals, which can be single, semi-double, double or members of the *Triphylla* Group (which have a long perianth tube). Propagation of named varieties is by soft-tip cuttings, taken in spring and summer. *F.* 'Annabel' has pink-flushed white semi-double flowers; *F.* 'Thalia' is a *Triphylla* type with purple-tinted leaves and orange-scarlet flowers; trailing *F.* 'Golden Marinka' has yellow-variegated leaves and single, red flowers; *F.* 'Ballet Girl' has large, double flowers of cerise and white; *F.* 'Lady Thumb' has small, pink and white semi-double flowers.

hardiness Generally tender, although some varieties are hardy
flowering Summer to autumn
position Full sun to partial shade
cultivation Loam-based compost (J.I. 2), loamless compost or well-drained soil. Water freely in summer, sparingly in winter, and feed every two weeks with a balanced liquid fertilizer at half strength. Pinch out growing tips in spring to encourage the plant to bush.
overwintering In frost-prone areas, move the plant indoors.
pests & diseases Whitefly and grey mould
special features Shelter from cold winds.
decorative ideas Plant in a large handsome pot or grow as a standard.

MALVACEAE
Hibiscus syriacus
H 2m (6ft)

ZONE 10

This is a long-lived, deciduous shrub, with diamond-shaped, three-lobed leaves and single, five-petalled flowers in late summer and autumn. These are funnel-shaped, 6cm (2½in) across, and dark pink with yellow-anthered white stamens. Many forms have been bred with single or double flowers, in red, pink, blue and white. Propagation of named varieties is by rooting soft-tip cuttings in late spring, semi-ripe cuttings in summer or layering in summer. *H. s.* 'Diana' has large flowers up to 12cm (5in) across, with wavy-edged petals; *H. s.*

'Oiseau Bleu' has bright blue flowers up to 8cm (3in) across; and *H. s.* 'Red Heart' has white flowers with red centres.

hardiness Fully hardy
flowering Late summer to autumn
position Full sun
cultivation Loam-based compost (J. I. 2) or well-drained, neutral to alkaline soil. Water freely in summer, sparingly in winter, and feed monthly with a liquid fertilizer.
overwintering Do not allow to become waterlogged. In fr overwinter.
pests & diseases Aphids and mildew
special features Hibiscus flower best during a hot summer and will tolerate a hot paved area if they have sufficient water.
decorative ideas Good feature plant

Hibiscus 'Royal Orange'

Hortensia hydrangea

HYDRANGEACEAE
Hydrangea macrophylla
H 1m (3ft)

ZONES 5–9

A deciduous shrub with large oval-shaped leaves. It is grown for its flowers and divided into hortensia and lacecap types, according to the shape of the flowerhead. Hortensia group have large, mop-head blooms of sterile flowers. Forms include: *H. m.* 'Ami Pasquier', slow-growing with crimson flowers; and *H. m.* 'Europa', dark pink to purplish flowers. The lacecap group have flattened clusters of small, fertile flowers surrounded by larger, sterile ones. Forms include: *H. m.* 'Lanarth White' with pink to blue flowers surrounded by white ones; and *H. m.* 'Mariesii Perfecta' which has rich blue/mauve or dark pink/pink flowers. Propagation is by 10cm (4in) semi-ripe tip cuttings taken in summer.

hardiness Fully hardy
flowering Summer
position Full sun to partial shade
cultivation Loam-based compost (J.I. 2) or moist, well-drained soil. Flower colour is influenced by soil acidity. Blues need to be kept in an acid compost, or they will change to pink or red. Water freely in summer, sparingly in winter, and feed monthly with a balanced liquid fertilizer. Prune back to healthy buds in spring.
overwintering No special care
pests & diseases Scale insects, aphids, grey mould and mildew
special features Deadhead in the winter after the frosts (use the old flowerheads for frost protection through the winter).
decorative ideas Plant a matching pair to flank a doorway or steps.

MAGNOLIACEAE
Magnolia
H Up to 4m (13ft) S 1.2m (4ft)

ZONES 4–8

Originating in Asia or the American continent, there are deciduous and evergreen forms of these showy trees and shrubs. The flowers are generally large, waxy and scented, in shades of white, pink and purple, and are either cup- or goblet-shaped, or occasionally star-shaped. Those of deciduous magnolias appear before the leaves in spring, while those of evergreen magnolias are usually summer-flowering. The smaller magnolias, such as the starry-flowered *M. stellata* or the fragrant goblet-flowered *M.* 'Susan' are good choices for growing in containers. *M.* 'Susan' is upright, so takes up less space.

hardiness Fully hardy
flowering Spring for deciduous forms
position Full sun
cultivation Loam-based compost (J.I. 3) or fertile soil. Feed in spring with a balanced liquid fertilizer. Prune out any misplaced or crossing shoots in late winter.
overwintering No special needs.
pests and diseases Trouble-free
special features Ensure container is moved to a feature position in spring.
display ideas Underplant white magnolias with white crocuses or narcissus.

Magnolia stellata

Philadelphus

HYDRANGEACEAE/PHILADELPHACEAE
Philadelphus
H 1–2m (3–6ft)

ZONES 5–9

The 'mock orange' is a highly fragrant shrub, producing a mass of beautiful white blooms in summer. There are many hybrids available, sharing characteristics such as their rough, oval-shaped leaves, but differing in their flowers, which may be a single cross shape, semi-double or fully double. They are grown primarily for their scent, which is deliciously reminiscent of orange blossom. 'Beauclerk' has large, single, pink-flushed white flowers; 'Belle Etoile' has large, single flowers with a purple blotch at the base of each petal; 'Manteau d'Hermine' has double, creamy-white flowers; and 'Virginal' has double, pure white flowers. Propagate by taking soft-tip cuttings in summer or hardwood cuttings in autumn.

hardiness Fully hardy
flowering Late spring to mid-summer
position Full sun to partial shade
cultivation Loam-based compost (J.I. 3) or well-drained soil. Water freely in summer, sparingly in winter, and feed monthly with a balanced liquid fertilizer. Remove flowering shoots when flowers fade.
overwintering No special care
pests & diseases Aphids and mildew
special features These are tolerant shrubs which will grow in almost any conditions.
decorative ideas Use as a screening or background plant when not in flower.

Potentilla fruticosa 'Glenroy Pinkie'

ROSACEAE
Potentilla fruticosa
H 75cm (30in)

ZONES 7–9

This deciduous shrub has pinnate leaves and saucer-shaped, five-petalled flowers. The mid-green leaves have 5–7 leaflets, and are arranged in dense clusters over the shoots. The thin, spindly branches have orange bark which turns brown, flaking with age. Bright-yellow flowers are borne in loose clusters on the tips of the shoots, from late spring to late autumn. Numerous named cultivars are available in shades of white, orange, pink and red, including the low-growing 'Red Robin' with brick red flowers; and 'Snowbird', which has dark green foliage and double, white flowers.

Propagation is by semi-ripe cuttings taken in the autumn.

hardiness Fully hardy
flowering Late spring to autumn
position Full sun to partial shade
cultivation Loam-based compost (J.I. 2) or well-drained soil. Water freely in summer, sparingly in winter, and apply a balanced liquid fertilizer monthly. Prune by removing thin, spindly growths or old non-flowering stems in the spring.
overwintering Protect during severe frost, and do not allow to become waterlogged.
pests & diseases None
special features Red-flowered forms hold their colour better if grown in partial shade.
decorative ideas Use in mixed displays with a single colour scheme.

ROSACEAE
Prunus
H Up to 2m (6ft)

ZONES 2–7

Ornamental cherries are grown for both their attractive white, pink or red single, semi-double or double flowers, and their often spectacular range of autumn colour. Many smaller varieties will grow in containers, including *P.* 'Amanogawa', a small, upright tree with dense clusters of fragrant, semi-double pink flowers in spring and a glorious display of autumn colour, often with red, orange and green leaves on the tree together. *P. tenella* 'Firehill' is a bushy shrub with glossy, dark green foliage and dark pink, bowl-shaped flowers. *P. triloba* is a shrub with saucer-shaped, pink flowers, singly or in pairs, in early to mid-spring. Propagation is by budding or grafting onto a rootstock. Remove dead or diseased wood in summer.

hardiness Fully hardy
flowering Spring
position Full sun to partial shade
cultivation Loam-based compost (J.I. 3) or moist, well-drained soil. Water freely in summer, sparingly in winter, and feed monthly with a balanced liquid fertilizer.
overwintering No special care
pests & diseases Caterpillars, birds, silver leaf
special features Prunus will flower better if the roots are slightly restricted in the container.
decorative ideas Group small pots of spring-flowering bulbs around the plant. Grow autumn-flowering bulbs under it to complement the foliage in autumn.

Prunus triloba

ERICACEAE
Rhododendron
H Up to 1.5m (5ft)

ZONES 5–9

Rhododendrons include evergreen and deciduous shrubs. Deciduous ones are classified as the *Azalea* group within the genus *Rhododendron*. They have glorious autumn colour, and bell-shaped flowers in purple, red, orange, yellow and white. Ghent (A) hybrids have funnel-shaped, fragrant flowers, often double; Knap Hill-Exbury (K) hybrids have large trusses of trumpet-shaped flowers in bright colours; Mollis hybrids (M) produce funnel-shaped flowers before the leaves; and Rustica (R) hybrids have fragrant, double flowers on compact bushes. 'Berryrose' (K) has bright apricot flowers; 'Homebush' (R) has compact, semi-double pink flowers; 'Klondyke' (K) has golden-orange flowers with red reverse; 'Narcissiflorum' (G) has compact, semi-double, fragrant, yellow flowers. Propagation can be done by layering, or taking semi-ripe cuttings after flowering.

hardiness Fully hardy
flowering Spring to summer
position Full sun to partial shade
cultivation Loam-based compost (J.I. Ericaceous) or moist acid soil. Keep moist at all times and feed monthly with ericaceous fertilizer. Deadhead after flowering.
overwintering Mulch around the roots to protect them during periods of severe frost.
pests & diseases Vine weevil, scale insects, bud blast
special features Protect from cold winds for the best flowers and autumn colour.
decorative ideas Use the summer foliage as a backdrop for displays of smaller flowers.

Rhododendron 'Gilbert Mullier'

Ribes sanguineum

GROSSULARIACEAE/SAXIFRAGACEAE
Ribes
H Up to 2.5m (8ft)

ZONES 6–9

The flowering current is also grown for its edible fruits (as black and red currants and gooseberries) but it is also a very pretty ornamental plant in early spring, with its light to mid-green leaves and dangling racemes of flowers (in most species). The toughest species is *R. sanguineum* and there are white, pink, scarlet and wine-coloured flowers. Propagate from hardwood cuttings in winter.

hardiness Fully hard to frost hardy
position Full sun to light shade

Flowering Early spring
cultivation Grow in multi-purpose compost. Water freely in growth; sparingly in winter. Feed with a liquid fertilizer in growing season. Prune after flowering (ornamental currants).
overwintering No special care
pests and diseases Prone to aphid attacks and mildew
special features Aromatic leaves
decorative ideas Grow with camellias and magnolias for a spring display.

Rosa 'Orange Sunblaze'

Rosa 'Chamaeleon'

Rosa 'Ballerina'

ROSACEAE
Rosa
Shrub roses H 30–40cm (12–16in)
Bush roses H 1.5m (5ft)

ZONES 7–9

Bush roses and specially formed patio and miniature roses make excellent flowering shrubs for containers, giving colour and fragrance throughout the summer. The flowers can be single, semi-double or fully double, in a range of colours including red, pink, yellow and white. They can also be grown as standards, with a single clear stem, giving extra height to a grouping of plants. The following are all good patio or miniature roses: *R.* 'Baby Masquerade' (Min.) (double, yellow-pink flowers); *R.* 'Ballerina' (Min.)

(pink flowers); *R.* 'Chamaeleon' (Min.) (double orange flowers); *R.* 'Darling Flame' (Min.) (double, orange-red flowers); *R.* 'Little Artist' (Min.) (semi-double, red flowers with white markings); *R.* 'Orange Sunblaze' (Min.) (full double bright orange flowers); *R.* 'Queen Mother' (Patio) (semi-double, pale pink flowers); and *R.* 'Sweet Magic' (Min/ patio) (double, apricot and yellow flowers). Propagate by taking 5cm (2in) tip cuttings in spring, using a rooting hormone.

hardiness Fully hardy
flowering Summer to autumn
position Full sun
cultivation Loam-based compost (J.I. 3). Water freely in summer, sparingly in winter, and feed every two weeks during spring and summer with a balanced liquid fertilizer.

Prune to outward-facing buds to shorten each stem by half in spring.
overwintering Protect during severe frost, and do not allow to become waterlogged.
pests & diseases Aphids, caterpillars, black spot, rust and mildew
special features Roses are usually grafted onto a rootstock. Any shoots originating from the rootstock are 'suckers' and need removing at their bases or they will outgrow the top variety.
decorative ideas Plant a pair of standard roses either side of a doorway, or use a pair of miniature or patio roses to flank either end of a display of summer flowers in a long trough.

Evergreen trees and shrubs

Trees and shrubs that retain their leaves throughout the year are termed evergreen, for obvious reasons. The foliage of evergreens is often dark green in colour and highly glossy and, more often than not, fairly small-leaved. The smallest-leaved evergreens make excellent subjects for clipping into formal shapes (Topiary, see pages 90–93), adding interesting form to their visual appeal and giving you the opportunity to unleash your creativity. In general, evergreens have less exotic-looking flowers than their deciduous counterparts, although there are notable exceptions to this rule, such as *Magnolia grandiflora*.

As a result of the dense nature of the foliage, they are best used to disguise unattractive walls or fences, act as a screen or provide a pleasant-looking backdrop to more intensely coloured perennials which have a short flowering season.

The tough nature of the leaves of evergreens makes them less prone to insect damage than deciduous plants, making them a good choice for most situations. However, certain plants, such as bay (*Laurus nobilis*) are nonetheless often affected by scale insects (see page 40–41), so remember to check your plants for pest damage.

Acacia cultriformis

COBAEACEAE
Acacia
H Up to 3m (10ft)

ZONES 8–10

A genus of over 1,000 species of deciduous and evergreen plants. They have alternate leaves, often pinnate, but sometimes modified to flattened leaf stalks which resemble entire leaves. The tiny flowers are produced in round heads or spikes and are usually sweetly fragrant, with long stamens. Varieties include: *A. baileyana* with silver-grey foliage and yellow flowers; *A. dealbata* (mimosa) which has ferny foliage and fragrant yellow flowers; *A. cultriformis* is smaller (3m/10ft) with bright yellow flowerheads on the tips of the stems. Propagate by semi-ripe cuttings in summer.

hardiness Half hardy to frost tender
flowering Winter to spring
position Full sun
cultivation Loam-based compost (J.I. 2) or well-drained neutral to acid soil. Water freely in summer, sparingly in winter and feed monthly with a balanced liquid fertilizer. Acacias resent hard pruning, so light-prune regularly to maintain the shape.
overwintering Move indoors until danger of frost has passed. May be left in place in frost-free areas.
pests & diseases Generally trouble-free
special features Spiny varieties are useful as a deterrent to unwanted trespassers. Most varieties can be wall-trained.
decorative ideas Underplant the acacia with a yellow-flowered display of crocus and narcissus.

Agave americana 'Marginata'

AGAVACEAE
Agave americana
H 1m (3ft)

ZONES 9–10

A rosette-forming succulent which makes a spectacular specimen plant. It has long, fleshy, rigid, grey-green leaves, with sharp-toothed edges and spiny tips. The funnel-shaped, greenish-yellow flowers have six tepals, and are produced in clusters on smooth stems from the centre of the rosette. Cultivars include: *A. a.* 'Marginata', with an attractive yellow edge to the leaves which pales as it ages; and 'Mediopicta', with a central yellow stripe to each leaf. Propagation is by seed sown in spring, or offsets lifted in spring or autumn (rooted offsets can be treated as

established plants, unrooted ones can be potted in a sandy compost until roots form).

hardiness Frost tender
flowering Summer
position Full sun
cultivation Loam-based compost (J.I. 2) or well-drained soil. Water freely in summer, very sparingly in winter (keep barely moist).
overwintering In frost-prone areas, move indoors.
pests & diseases Scale insects
special features Each rosette flowers just once, then dies off, leaving new offsets to replace it.
decorative ideas These handsome architectural plants look good seen in isolation. Mount them on a plinth for maximum impact.

SOLAMACEAE
Brugmansia
H 1.2–1.8m (4–6ft)

ZONES 9–10

The angel's trumpets (previously known as *Datura*) are evergreen shrubs which thrive in a protected position away from frost. *B. x candida* and *B. suaveolens* have large, mid-green leaves with wavy edges, sometimes toothed, and up to 60cm (2ft) long. The spectacular flowers are fragrant (particularly during the evening), trumpet-shaped and up to 30cm (12in) long in white, yellow or pink. Forms include *B. x c.* 'Grand Marnier' with apricot-coloured flowers, and the double *B. x c.* 'Knightii'. Propagation is by semi-ripe cuttings in summer (easier with some base heat).

hardiness Frost tender
flowering Summer to autumn
position Full sun to partial shade
cultivation Loam-based compost (J.I. 2) with extra grit. Water freely in summer, sparingly in winter and feed monthly with a balanced liquid fertiliser. Prune shoots back to within 15cm (6in) of the stem in early spring.
overwintering Take indoors until the danger of frost has passed.
pests & diseases Aphids and whitefly. Virus may cause yellowing on the leaves.
special features All of the plant is poisonous, particularly the seeds. Do not ingest.
decorative ideas Plant as a single feature.

Brugmansia aurea

BUXACEAE
Buxus
H Up to 2m (6 ft)

ZONES 6–9

A hardy, slow-growing, bushy evergreen plant which is useful as a foil to brightly coloured plants, or can be easily clipped to form different topiary shapes as specimens. It has small, tough, oval-shaped, glossy, dark green leaves and masses of tiny, star-shaped yellowish-green flowers in spring. There are several species, some with variegated forms, including *B. sempervirens* 'Elegantissima' with white-edged leaves; 'Latifolia Maculata' is compact, with yellow foliage which matures to dark green with yellow markings; and 'Marginata' which has yellow-edged dark green leaves.

Leaf colour is better in full sun, but beware scorching. *B. s.* 'Suffruticosa' is slow-growing and compact, making it good for topiary. Propagate by semi-ripe cuttings in summer.

hardiness Fully hardy
flowering Spring
position Full sun to partial shade
cultivation Loam-based compost (J.I. 2) or moist, well-drained soil. Water freely in summer, sparingly in winter, and feed monthly with a balanced liquid fertilizer.
overwintering No special care
pests & diseases Red spider mite
special features Tolerant of hard pruning, but prefers little-and-often.
decorative ideas Clip into geometric shapes in formal displays or use as a central plant in a window box.

Buxus semperivens 'Suffruticosa'

MYRTACEAE
Callistemon citrinus
H 1.5–5m (5–15ft)   S Up to 2–2.5m (6–8ft) wide

ZONES 8–10

The crimson bottlebrush plant hails from Australia, where it grows in both open and woodland areas. The leathery leaves are lance-shaped, and young shoots are tinted pink. The clusters of flowers are 5–15 cm (2–6in) long, and produced at the tips of shoots, although the growth then continues beyond them. Individual flowers are tiny, with long stamens, in shades of red, pink, purple, white, yellow or green. *C. c.* 'Splendens' has carmine-red flowers; *C. c.* 'White Anzac' has white flowers; and *C. c.* 'Mauve Mist' is a more compact form with spikes of mauve-pink flowers.

Propagate by sowing seed in spring or taking semi-ripe cuttings in summer.

hardiness Half hardy
flowering Spring to summer
position Full sun
cultivation Loam-based compost (J.I. 2) or moist, well-drained soil with a neutral to acid pH. Water freely in summer, sparingly in winter, and feed monthly with a balanced liquid fertiliser.
overwintering Move half-hardy species outdoors in summer, but keep in a frost-free greenhouse all winter.
pests & diseases Look for red spider mites, scale insects and mealy bugs under glass.
special features In frost-free areas, may be grown against a sunny wall.
decorative ideas Grow as a single feature.

Callistemon citrinus 'Western Glory'

THEACEAE
Camellia
H 1–2m (3–6ft)

ZONES 6–8

Shrubs with glossy foliage and flowers
in white, pink, or red, or a combination
of these. Flower shapes include single,
semi-double, double, anemone-form,
peony-form or rose-form. They are ideal
for containers, but need acid conditions.
C. japonica has many hybrids, with a variety
of shapes and colours, including 'Adolphe
Audusson' (compact, with semi-double red
flowers) and 'Nuccio's Gem' (double white
flowers). *C. sasanqua* hybrids include
'Narumigata' (small, fragrant, single white
flowers). *C. × williamsii* hybrids include
'Donation' (semi-double pink flowers) and
'Water Lily' (double, deep pink flowers).
Propagation is by semi-ripe cuttings taken
in summer. They need rooting hormone
and bottom heat.

hardiness Fully hardy to frost tender
flowering Early spring to mid-summer
depending on variety.
position Partial shade. They benefit from the
shelter and warmth of a wall.
cultivation Lime-free loam-based compost
(J.I. Ericaceous). Water moderately at all
times, as drought causes the buds to be shed.
Feed with a standard liquid fertilizer every
two weeks from spring to summer
overwintering No special care
pests & diseases Aphids, sooty mould
and virus
special features Avoid an east-facing
position, as early sun spoils frosted blooms.
decorative ideas May be briefly moved
indoors to a cool spot whilst in flower.

Camellia japonica 'Contessa'

Ceanothus impressus 'Puget's Blue'

RHAMNACEAE
Ceanothus
H 2m (6ft)

ZONES 7–9

The 'Californian lilacs' are bushy evergreen
shrubs which respond well to light pruning
to keep them in shape. They are ideal against
a warm wall, where they give year-round
coverage, although there are prostrate forms,
such as *C.* 'Blue Mound', which spill from
the container like a wave. The leaves are
usually glossy dark green, with toothed edges,
and the blue flowers are produced in fluffy-
looking spikes of varying sizes. There are
many hybrids, including *C.* 'Burkwoodii',
which has bright blue flowers; 'Concha', with
dark blue flowers; and *C. impressus* 'Puget's

Blue', with profuse, blue flowers. Propagation
is by semi-ripe cuttings in summer.

hardiness Frost hardy
flowering Late spring to mid-summer
position Full sun with shelter from winds
cultivation Loam-based compost (J.I. 3) or
well-drained soil. Water freely in summer,
sparingly in winter, and feed monthly with a
balanced liquid fertilizer.
overwintering Protect from severe frost and
waterlogging.
pests & diseases None
special features Established plants can offer
support to a small, late-flowering clematis for
added interest.
decorative ideas Plant with other blue-
flowered plants, such as muscari, blue pansies
and agapanthus.

CUPRESSACEAE
Chamaecyparis
H Up to 3m (10ft)

ZONES 6–9

These are attractive, densely leafy conifers which grow slowly to form architectural shapes, giving structure throughout the year. There are several shapes and colours available which will not quickly grow too large for containers, including *C. lawsoniana* 'Ellwoodii' (conical in shape, with upright branches and blue-green new growth); 'Gnome' (rounded, with blue-green foliage); 'Minima' (very dwarf, rounded, with blue-green foliage); 'Pottenii' (taller and narrower, with feathery green foliage); and 'Stardust' (taller, with ferny, golden-yellow foliage).

C. obtusa 'Nana Gracilis' is a good dwarf conifer, with dark green needle-like leaves. Propagation is by semi-ripe cuttings taken in summer.

hardiness Fully hardy
flowering Cones, in spring
position Full sun to partial shade.
cultivation Loam-based compost (J.I. 3) or moist, well-drained soil. Water moderately at all times, and feed monthly with a balanced liquid fertilizer.
overwintering Do not allow to dry out.
pests & diseases Generally trouble-free
special features Trim as necessary, but do not cut into old wood, as it will not regrow.
decorative ideas Use dwarf forms as a central feature in a window box. Use pairs to act as a full stop at either end of a long display.

Chamaecyparis obtusa 'Nana Gracilis'

RUTACEAE
Choisya ternata
H 2m (6ft)

ZONES 7–9

The Mexican orange blossom is a compact, dome-shaped shrub with glossy, aromatic, palmate leaves produced on green, woody stems. It produces clusters of small, white, musk-scented, star-shaped flowers in late spring and again in late summer and autumn. *C. t.* 'Sundance' rarely flowers, and has bright yellow foliage (although this may scorch in intense sunlight and turns lime green in partial shade). The cultivar *C.* 'Aztec Pearl' is compact, with long, thin, dark green leaflets and pink-tinted white flowers. Propagation is by semi-ripe cuttings taken in late summer.

hardiness Fully hardy
flowering Late spring, then again late summer to autumn
position Full sun, sheltered from cold winds.
cultivation Loam-based compost (J.I. 3) or well-drained soil. Water freely in summer, sparingly in winter, and feed monthly with a balanced liquid fertilizer.
overwintering Do not allow to become waterlogged. Protect from severe frost with insulation material.
pests & diseases None
special features This plant needs no regular pruning but young shoots may be damaged by frost.
decorative ideas This plant can provide useful background foliage planting for flowering displays, or position twin tubs either side of a doorway..

Choisya ternata

RUTACEAE
Citrus
H 1.2m (4ft)

ZONES 9–10

A group of species which include oranges, lemons and grapefruit. Smaller varieties are available for containers. x *Citrofortunella microcarpa* (formerly *Citrus mitis*) has small, white flowers are followed by small, round oranges. x *C. m.* 'Tiger' has leaves streaked white. *Citrus limon* (lemon) grows into a small tree or large shrub. Flowers open in spring and summer, followed by fruit. *C.* x *meyeri* 'Meyer' (syn. *C. l.* 'Meyer') is a more compact lemon. Clementine, mandarin and tangerine fall under *Citrus reticulata* . Fruit are produced after flowering. Propagate by taking

10cm (4in) tip cuttings (semi-ripe with a heel) in summer. Plants from seed are unlikely to fruit regularly, but have attractive foliage.

hardiness Tender
flowering Spring to summer
position Full sun
cultivation Loam-based compost (J.I. 2) or moist, well-drained soil, neutral to slightly acid. Water freely in summer, sparingly in winter, and feed monthly with a balanced liquid fertilizer.
overwintering Should be moved indoors in frost-prone areas.
pests & diseases Red spider mite, scale
special features Stand on a tray of moist pebbles to increase humidity.
decorative ideas Raise the pot on a pedestal or small table to create a feature.

x *Citrofortunella microcarpa*

Cordyline australis 'Purpurea'

AGAVACEAE
Cordyline australis
H Up to 4m (13ft)

ZONES 8–10

The New Zealand cabbage palm is an
evergreen palm-like tree, with arching
lance-shaped leaves that can be up to 90cm
(3ft) long, growing in a tuft on top of a
woody-stemmed trunk. Grown primarily
for its architectural foliage, the cabbage palm
produces fragrant cup-shaped flowers in
long clusters in mid-summer, followed by
round white berries. There are various
cultivars with attractively coloured leaves;
'Albertii' has green leaves with red midribs,
striped cream and pink; 'Purpurea' has
purple-flushed leaves; 'Variegata' has leaves
with cream stripes that run lengthwise.

hardiness Half hardy
flowering Mid-summer
position Full sun.
cultivation Loam-based compost (J.I. 2).
Grow variegated cultivars in sunlight; green-
leaved ones will cope with part shade. Water
moderately in summer, less frequently in
winter. Feed every couple of months with a
balanced fertilizer.
overwintering Bubble-wrap pot in cold
areas; move indoors in very cold regions.
pests and diseases None when grown
outdoors
special features Remove dying leaves from
base with sharp secateurs every few months.
decorative ideas Use as a focal point or
feature plant.

ROSACEAE
Cotoneaster
H 30cm (12in) unless grown as a standard

ZONES 4–6

Attractive evergreen shrubs with glossy
foliage, small creamy-white or pink flowers
and showy, bright red, orange or yellow
berries. They range from large, upright bushes
to prostrate ground cover. *C. horizontalis*
has small leaves and bright red fruit.
C. cashmiriensis (compact, prostrate, with pink
buds opening into white flowers); *C. congestus*
(also low-growing, pale green foliage); *C.*
dammeri (prostrate, spreading); 'Hybridus
Pendulus' (prostrate, but often sold as a standard, when it makes an attractive small 'tree');
and *C.* x *suecicus* 'Coral Beauty' (arching

branches, orange fruit) and *C.* x *s.* 'Skogholm'
(prostrate, spreading). These will spill from a
container, covering it in a green curtain.
Propagation is by seed sown in autumn, or
semi-ripe cuttings in late summer.

hardiness Fully hardy
flowering Summer
position Full sun to partial shade
cultivation Loam-based compost (J.I. 2) or
well-drained soil. Water freely in summer,
sparingly in winter, and feed monthly with a
balanced liquid fertilizer.
overwintering No special care.
pests & diseases Aphids and fireblight
special features The flowers and berries
give a long period of interest.
decorative ideas Raise the container and
allow foliage to spill down a wall.

Cotoneaster horizontalis

CYCADACEAE
Cycas revoluta
H 1–2m (3–6ft) with s similar spread

ZONE 9
The Japanese sago palm belongs to a group
of plants which is believed to date back to
the dinosaurs, the cycads. It has an upright,
columnar stem, scarred by leaf bases, which
sometimes branches as it ages. Long, arching,
pinnate leaves are dark green, often with over
100 sickle-shaped leaflets. They harden as
they age, and may be up to 1.5m (5ft) long.
The inflorescence is ovoid in shape, and
golden-brown, with male and female borne
on separate plants. The male cone is 40cm
(16in) long, rusty-yellow and pineapple-
scented; the female is 20cm (8in) and results
in ovoid yellow seeds. Propagate by removing
suckers or sowing seed in spring.

hardiness Frost tender
flowering Summer
position Full sun
cultivation Loam-based compost (J.I. 3)
with additional grit and a slow-release
fertilizer, or moist, well-drained soil. Water
moderately in summer, sparingly in winter.
overwintering Move indoors. If the plant is
outdoors, it will need good protection from
any frosts (wrapping in fleece).
pests & diseases Red spider mite, mealy
bugs and scale insects
special features Makes a wonderful
specimen plant in a container or border. No
pruning is needed.
decorative ideas Eye-catching on its own,
raised on a pedestal or table.

Cycas revoluta

ELAEGNACEAE
Elaeagnus
H 3m (10ft)

ZONES 6–7
A group of hardy, reliable evergreen shrubs
with a spreading habit and tough, leathery,
broadly lance-shaped leaves. In autumn and
winter, small, fragrant, white flowers are
produced beneath the leaves. The fragrance is
often noticed before the flowers are spotted.
E. x *ebbingei* has scaly golden-bronze shoots
bearing leaves which are metallic green above
and silvery-green beneath. Its cultivars
include 'Gilt Edge' (golden-edged dark green
leaves), and 'Limelight' (leaves marked yellow
and pale green). *E. pungens* has slightly smaller
leaves and spiny shoots, and the form *E. p.*

'Maculata' has glossy leaves with a bright
golden splash in the centre. Propagation is by
semi-ripe cuttings taken in late summer.

hardiness Fully hardy
flowering Autumn to early winter
position Full sun (especially variegateds)
cultivation Loam-based compost (J.I. 3) or
moist, well-drained soil. Water freely in
summer, sparingly in winter, and feed
monthly with a balanced liquid fertilizer.
overwintering No special care
pests & diseases None
special features Remove any shoots which
revert to green on a variegated plant, or they
will take over. Prune any wayward shoots as
they appear.
decorative ideas Position where autumn
scent drifts through a doorway or window.

Elaeagnus pungens 'Maculata'

Erica x darleyensis

ERICACEAE
Erica
H 30–45cm (12–18in)

ZONES 5–9

These low-growing evergreen shrubs are popular because you can achieve a year-round effect when different cultivars are planted. Many have attractive foliage as well as small, white, pink, red or mauve bell-shaped flowers. The leaves are small and thin, and may be green or golden. *E. carnea* and its forms flower in winter; *E.* x *darleyensis* types flower winter to spring; *E. cinerea* types flower early summer to autumn; and *E. ciliaris*, *E. tetralix* and *E. vagans* types flower mid-summer to mid-autumn. Propagation is by hardwood cuttings taken in late summer.

hardiness Fully hardy
flowering All year round if a range of cultivars are selected
position Full sun
cultivation Acid loamless or loam-based compost (J.I. Ericaceous), although some species (e.g. *E. vagans*) will tolerate neutral conditions. Water moderately in summer and feed monthly with balanced liquid fertilizer at half strength.
overwintering Avoid waterlogging.
pests & diseases Fungal rots
special features Pruning immediately after flowering, by removing the old flowers with shears, keeps the plants healthy and much more compact.
decorative ideas Excellent autumn and winter window box plant, with cyclamens and ornamental cabbages.

CELASTRACEAE
Euonymus fortunei
H Up to 1.5m (5ft)

ZONES 5–9

A group of low-growing evergreen shrubs which produce insignificant greenish-white flowers, but have spectacularly colourful foliage. The stems trail as ground cover, but will become a scrambling climber if given some support, and these plants thrive in poor conditions and full sun. The leaves of *E. fortunei* are oval, leathery and dark green, but there are many cultivars with coloured foliage, including: 'Emerald Gaiety' (bright green leaves with white-edged leaves); 'Emerald 'n' Gold' (green leaves with a broad, bright yellow edge); and 'Silver Queen' (deep green leaves, with a broad silver edge). The leaves flush pink in winter. Propagation is by semi-ripe cuttings taken in late summer.

hardiness Fully hardy
flowering Summer
position Full sun to partial shade (colour may be affected in shade)
cultivation Loam-based compost (J.I. 2) or any well-drained soil. Water freely in summer (especially in full sun), sparingly in winter.
overwintering Protect from cold, drying winds and excess water.
pests & diseases Aphids on young shoots, mildew
special features Valuable plants for covering a shady wall.
decorative ideas A useful flower-arranging foliage plant. A good foil for bright colours.

Euonymus fortunei

Gaultheria mucronata 'Mulberry Wine'

ERICACEAE
Gaultheria
H Up to 3m (10ft) S 3m (10ft)

ZONES 6–9

A genus of evergreen shrubs that prefer shady and acid conditions. They have leathery oval leaves and bell-shaped flowers borne singly or in clusters, followed by rounded berries in white, pink, red or purple. *G. shallon* is compact and bushy with pink-tinted white flowers followed by purple fruits. *G. mucronata* has spine-tipped leaves and white flowers. Grow both male and female plants to obtain fruit. *G.m.* 'Pink Pearl' has bright pink fruit. Propagation is by semi-ripe cuttings taken in summer, or rooted suckers removed in spring.

hardiness Fully hardy
flowering Summer
position Partial shade
cultivation Acid loam-based compost (J.I. Ericaceous) or moist acid soil. Water moderately at all times.
overwintering No special care
pests and diseases None
special features Useful for a shady corner where other plants might struggle. No pruning is usually needed.
decorative ideas Good winter window box plant, with cyclamens and heather and winter pansies.

Griselinia littoralis

CORNACEAE/GRISELINIACEAE

Griselinia littoralis

H 3m (9ft)   s Up to 1.5m (5ft).

ZONES 7–9

An attractive shrub with rounded, leathery leaves. It is tolerant of wind, even salt-laden coastal winds, and is useful as a windbreak in coastal positions. Yellow-green male and female flowers are borne on separate plants, so both are needed to produce the purple fruits. Many forms have striking variegations, including *G. l.* 'Bantry Bay' (bright yellow), *G. l.* 'Dixon's Cream' (creamy-white) and *G. l.* 'Variegata' (creamy-yellow margins), all of which have markings which produce an interesting marbled effect. Propagate by taking semi-ripe cuttings in summer.

hardiness Fully hardy, although may suffer in periods of intense cold
flowering Late spring
position Full sun through to moderate shade, although the variegations will fade if the light levels are low.
cultivation Loam-based compost (J.I. 3) with added sand or grit, or moist, well-drained soil. Water freely in summer, sparingly in winter, and feed monthly with a balanced liquid fertilizer.
overwintering Protect from cold, drying winds, as the leaves will scorch.
pests & diseases Fungal leaf spot
special features The succulent-looking leaves make this a dramatic specimen plant, as well as a wind filter in coastal gardens.
decorative ideas Good shelter plant for balconies to protect more tender specimens.

SCROPHULARIACEAE

Hebe

H Up to 1m (3ft) depending on variety

ZONES 6–9

Low-growing, decorative, evergreen shrubs grown for their attractive foliage and long period of flowering. Small flowers are borne in large, densely packed clusters on the tips of shoots, in colours ranging from white to blue, pink and red. *H.* x *franciscana* has fleshy, dark green leaves and purple flowers; the form *H.* x *f.* 'Variegata' has leaves edged creamy-white. *H. speciosa* 'Tricolor' is silver-variegated with its young growths tipped rosy-pink in autumn. The white-flowered *H. ochracea* 'James Stirling' is conifer-like, with arching shoots and scale-like leaves of deep yellow. Propagation is by cuttings taken in late summer.

hardiness Fully hardy
flowering Summer to autumn
position Full sun to partial shade
cultivation Loam-based compost (J.I. 2) or moist, well-drained soil. Water moderately in summer, sparingly in winter, and feed monthly with a balanced liquid fertilizer.
overwintering Protect from cold, drying winds and excess water.
pests & diseases Aphids and mildew
special features Ideal plants for containers, tolerating some pollution, and thriving in mild areas, particularly near the coast. Prune any shoots that die back.
decorative ideas Useful evergreen 'filler' for flowering displays.

Mixed hebes

Ilex aquifolium

AQUIFOLIACEAE

Ilex

H Up to 2m (6ft)

ZONES 6–9

Holly is a tolerant shrub, grown for its attractive, often sharply spiny leaves and bright berries in winter. Some forms have almost spine-free leaves, including *I.* x *altaclarensis* 'Lawsoniana' (dark green leaves splashed yellow and pale green, red berries). Others are spined on top of the leaf as well as the edges; *I. aquifolium* 'Ferox Argentea' has cream-edged green leaves and is male. Both male and female plants are necessary for berries to be produced. *I.* x *meservae* 'Blue Maid' is female, with red berries and dark blue-green leaves. *I. crenata* 'Golden Gem' is compact and low-growing, female, with small, spine-free golden-yellow leaves and black fruits. Propagation is by seed sown in autumn (may take 2-3 years) or semi-ripe cuttings taken in late summer.

hardiness Fully hardy
flowering Early summer
position Full sun to partial shade
cultivation Loam-based compost (J.I. 3) or moist, well-drained soil. Water moderately at all times.
overwintering No special care
pests & diseases Aphids and leaf miners
special features Spiny-leaved varieties are useful on a boundary to ward off any unwelcome visitors.
decorative ideas Good shelter plant or can be made into a standard; looks good in pairs.

Laurus nobilis

LAURACEAE
Laurus nobilis

H 2m (6ft) or more

ZONES 8–10

As well as being useful in cooking, bay makes an attractive specimen plant. Left to its own devices, it forms a large, straggling shrub, but it responds well to pruning, and can be shaped as it grows into a pyramid, ball or standard. The aromatic leaves are long-oval in shape, and glossy mid-green in colour. Small, greenish-yellow flowers are produced in spring, with male and female borne on separate plants. It needs a sunny or partially shaded position away from cold winds, and \in colder areas will need some protection against harsh winter weather. *L. n.* 'Aurea'

has golden-yellow foliage. Propagation is by seed sown in autumn or semi-ripe cuttings taken in summer.

hardiness Frost hardy
flowering Spring
position Full sun to partial shade
cultivation Loam-based compost (J.I. 2) or well-drained soil. Water moderately in summer, sparingly in winter.
overwintering Protect from severe cold, drying winds and excess water.
pests & diseases Scale insects, caterpillars and mildew
special features Tolerant of a hot position where other plants might struggle. Pinch-out growing tips to make bushy.
decorative ideas Train as a standard for all-year-round appeal.

Lavandula stoechas

COBAEACEAE
Lavandula

H Up to 1m (3ft)

ZONES 5–8

Lavenders are aromatic, evergreen shrubs with long, narrow, silvery-green leaves covered with fine hairs which are effective at preventing moisture loss in the hot areas where it originates. Small, tube-like, purple, blue, pink or white flowers are carried in narrow clusters (spikes) on long, tough, square stems. *L. angustifolia* 'Hidcote' is more bushy and compact, with strongly-scented, deep purple-blue flowers; 'Alba' and 'Nana Alba' have white flowers; 'Lodden Pink' and 'Rosea' both have pink flowers; French lavender (*L. stoechas*) has deep purple flower

spires. Propagation is by semi-ripe cuttings taken with a heel in August.

hardiness Fully hardy
flowering Summer
position Full sun
cultivation Loam-based compost (J.I. 2) or well-drained soil. Water moderately through the summer, sparingly in winter, and feed monthly with a balanced liquid fertilizer. Prefers a hot position with shelter from winds.
overwintering Protect from severe frost and cold winds.
pests & diseases Froghoppers
special features Prune lightly after flowering. The flowers may be picked and dried for use indoors in pot-pourri.
decorative ideas Can be trained as a standard. Plant pairs to flank steps or a door.

Leptospermum scoparium 'Burgundy Queen'

MYRTACEAE
Leptospermum scoparium

H Eventually reaching 2m (6ft)   S 1.5m (5ft)

ZONES 8–9

Commonly known as the tea-tree, this native of New Zealand forms a compact shrub with small, evergreen, spear-shaped leaves which are strongly aromatic, carried on tough woody stems. The white, or pink-tinged, saucer-shaped flowers are about 1.5cm (½in) across and carried singly or in clusters of up to three along the stem. The hybrid *L.s.* 'Kiwi' produces dark crimson flowers and bronze-tinted foliage and has a dwarf habit, making it ideal for growing in containers or confined places. The red- and pink-flowered forms are more attractive but are less hardy

than the white-flowered forms. Propagate by sowing seed in spring or rooting semi-ripe cuttings in summer.

hardiness Frost hardy
flowering Late spring to early summer
position Full sun to partial shade
cultivation Loam-based compost (J.I. 3) or well-drained soil. Water freely in summer, sparingly in winter, and feed monthly with a balanced liquid fertilizer.
overwintering Protect the base of the plant with mulch in periods of low temperatures.
pests & diseases Usually trouble-free
special features In colder areas, this plant can be grown as a wall shrub to provide extra frost protection.
decorative ideas Use as a feature plant. Underplant with pink pansies and primulas.

Myrtus communis

MYRTACEAE
Myrtus communis
H Up to 2m (6ft)

ZONES 8–10

The myrtle is a pretty evergreen shrub with small, pointed, aromatic leaves of a glossy dark green. It will thrive in the protection of a warm wall, and can be clipped to maintain its shape. Throughout the summer and early autumn, it produces clouds of small, fragrant, creamy-white flowers with prominent stamens forming a fluffy-looking central tuft. These are followed in a hot summer by oval-shaped, blackish fruit. *M. c.* subsp. *tarentina* is more compact, with pink-tinted flowers and white fruit. *M. c.* 'Variegata' has a narrow cream edge to the leaves. Propagate by taking semi-ripe cuttings in late summer or sowing seed in autumn.

hardiness Frost tender
flowering Summer to autumn
position Full sun
cultivation Loam-based compost (J.I. 2) or moist, well-drained soil. Water moderately in summer, sparingly in winter, and feed monthly with a balanced liquid fertilizer. Protect from cold winds.
overwintering Move indoors in frost-prone areas.
pests & diseases None
special features The flowers of this plant are traditionally used in a bridal bouquet to bring good luck.
decorative ideas Well-shaped shrub for a specimen plant or clipped into formal shapes.

Nerium oleander

APOCYNACEAE
Nerium oleander
H Up to 2m (6–7ft)

ZONES 9–10

The oleander is a large, evergreen shrub with leathery, dark green leaves, grown for its display of beautiful, often fragrant, funnel-shaped flowers. These are produced in terminal clusters, and can be single, semi-double or fully double, according to the variety, in shades of white, cream, yellow, apricot, salmon, copper, pink, red, carmine and purple. Individual flowers can be up to 5cm (2in) across, and they are borne in groups of six to eight. Propagation is by tip-cuttings, taken in summer, and rooted in either compost or water. Prune only to maintain shape.

hardiness Half hardy
flowering Summer
position Full sun
cultivation Loam-based compost (J.I. 2) or moist, well-drained soil. Keep thoroughly moist in summer and feed monthly with a balanced liquid fertilizer. In winter, keep barely moist. If the plant is allowed to dry out as the flowers form the buds will be shed.
overwintering Protect from frost and cold winds.
pests & diseases Scale insects
special features The plant is poisonous (sap, flowers and seeds), so handle with caution, and wash thoroughly after contact.
decorative ideas Plant against a wall for protection and surround with hot-coloured flowers – cosmos, pelargoniums and verbena – in summer.

Phormium 'Maori Sunrise'

AGAVACEAE/PHORMIACEAE
Phormium
H 1.2m (4ft)

ZONES 8–10

Clump-forming evergreen perennials, grown for their long, sword-like foliage. Ideal for milder coastal districts, they are tolerant of pollution. *P. cookianum* has arching, light green leaves and tubular, yellowish-green flowers on tall stems. Its forms include: 'Cream Delight' (cream-striped leaves); and 'Tricolor' (leaves edged yellow and red). *P. tenax* produces small, matt, red, tubular flowers on 1m (3ft) long spikes from June to September. Forms include: 'Purpureum' (maroon-purple leaves), and 'Variegatum' (leaves striped green and yellow). The hybrid 'Maori Sunrise' has pink-apricot, bronze-tinged leaves. Propagate by division in spring, each division should have at least three or four leaves.

hardiness Frost hardy
flowering Summer
position Full sun or partial shade
cultivation Loam-based compost (J.I. 2) or well-drained soil. Water moderately in summer, sparingly in winter.
overwintering It is hardy in all but the coldest areas, and can be left outdoors, although it may be killed in a severe winter. Protect the crown by covering with straw.
pests & diseases None
special features Makes a dramatic specimen plant.
decorative ideas Good feature plant.

Picea mariana 'Nana'

PINACEAE
Picea mariana 'Nana'
H 50cm (1½ft) with a similar spread

ZONES 2–7
This is a pretty little conifer which grows
slowly into a rounded, bushy shape with
short, densely packed branches. The tiny,
blunt leaves are needle-shaped and blue-grey
in colour with a whitish stripe underneath.
As it ages, the plant will produce oval female
cones which change in colour from a purplish-
green to brown, and remain on the plant for
2–3 years. Smaller, oval, yellowish male cones
appear in spring. This conifer grows about
3cm (1½in) a year, so is ideal for a confined
space or container where it will mix well
with small alpine plants or heathers, giving

all-year colour and interest. Propagation is by
semi-ripe cuttings taken in late summer.

hardiness Fully hardy
flowering None
position Full sun to partial shade
cultivation Loam-based compost (J.I. 3) or
moist, well-drained soil. Water freely in
summer, sparingly in winter, and feed
monthly with a balanced liquid fertilizer.
overwintering No special care
pests & diseases Aphids, adelgids, red
spider mite. Susceptible to honey fungus.
special features A tolerant and generally
trouble-free conifer, which remains attractive
throughout the year.
decorative ideas Makes an attractive
shape around which to group small
flowering plants.

PINACEAE
Pinus
H 3m (9ft) with a similar spread

ZONES 3–7
There are many forms of pine. The dwarf
mountain pine (*P. mugo*) forms a rounded
shrub with spreading, ascending branches.
The branches turn from green, through
brown to a scaly grey, and the new buds are
covered in sticky resin. Mid-green, needle-
like leaves are borne in pairs, and the female
cones are dark brown. Growing it in a
container will mean that this conifer will
grow only slowly, particularly if the roots are
kept slightly restricted, and is unlikely to
reach the size it would attain in the ground.
It is a useful plant for providing colour, shape
and interest throughout the year. Even more
compact forms include *P. m.* 'Mops', which is
almost spherical in shape and grows only
6cm (2½in) a year to an ultimate 1.5 x 1.5m
(5 x 5ft). *P. m.* 'Gnom' is broadly pyramidal
and reaches 2 x 2m (6 x 6ft). *P. parviflora*, the
Japanese white pine, is conical and much
larger, although it can be kept in check in
containers. Propagation is by seed sown in
spring. Cultivars have to be grafted in winter.

hardiness Fully hardy
flowering None
position Full sun
cultivation Loam-based compost (J.I. 3) or
moist, well-drained soil. Water freely in
summer, sparingly in winter, and feed
monthly with a balanced liquid fertilizer.
overwintering No special care
pests & diseases Aphids and adelgids.
Susceptible to honey fungus.
decorative ideas Use for a foliage display,
Japanese style, with bamboos and choisya.

Pinus parviflora

PHOSPHORACEAE
Pittosporum tenuifolium
H Up to 3m (10ft)

ZONES 9–10

A shrub, grown for its attractive, wavy-edged, glossy foliage, borne on grey-black stems. Unusual, sweetly fragrant, bell-shaped, red-black flowers are produced in small clusters in the leaf axils in spring and early summer, followed by dark grey fruits. Forms include: 'Abbotsbury Gold' (yellow leaves with green edges); 'Purpureum' (deep bronze leaves); 'Tom Thumb' (compact, with bronze-purple leaves); and 'Warnham Gold' (golden foliage). *P. tobira* is a smaller plant, with larger, smooth, leathery leaves. *P. t.* 'Nanum' is a compact form. Pittosporum thrives in coastal areas, where it makes a good windbreak, or it can be grown as a specimen in its own right. Propagation is by semi-ripe cuttings taken in summer, or air-layering in spring.

hardiness Frost hardy
flowering Late spring to early summer
position Full sun
cultivation Loam-based compost (J.I. 3) or well-drained soil. Water moderately in summer, sparingly in winter, and feed monthly with a balanced liquid fertilizer.
overwintering Protect from severe frost and excess water.
pests & diseases Mildew
special features The foliage is much prized by flower arrangers.
decorative ideas Good foliage plant as a foil to more spectacular flowering plants.

Pittosporum tobira 'Nanum'

RUTACEAE
Skimmia japonica
H 1m (3ft)

ZONES 7–9

Slow-growing, compact, aromatic shrubs with thick, leathery, oval- to lance-shaped, dark green leaves, carried on stocky green stems. Small, star-shaped, fragrant flowers open from buds, borne in spikes on the tips of the shoots, followed by long-lasting, crimson-red berries on female plants. Both male and female plants are necessary for berries. Female forms include: 'Veitchii' (upright and vigorous); 'Rogersii' (clusters of red berries); and 'Wakehurst White' (green flower buds and white berries). Male forms have more showy flowers, and include: 'Fragrans' (free-flowering with the scent of lily of the valley); and 'Rubella' (compact, with red-edged leaves and large panicles of buds, opening into pinkish-red flowers). Propagation is by semi-ripe cuttings taken in summer.

hardiness Fully hardy
flowering Winter to spring
position Partial to full shade
cultivation Loam-based compost (J.I. 2) or well-drained soil. Water moderately in summer, sparingly in winter.
overwintering Do not allow to become waterlogged.
pests & diseases None
special features Skimmias are very tolerant of atmospheric pollution.
decorative ideas Makes a neat, rounded shape to contrast with spiky foliage, such as irises or phormiums.

Skimmia japonica

AGAVACEAE
Yucca
H 60–90cm (2–3ft)

ZONES 7–9

A clump-forming shrub with long, stiff, lance-shaped, dark blue-green leaves, often dry and brown at the tip, forming a sharp, spine-like point. Tall, red-brown flower spikes are produced in summer, covered with drooping, white, bell-shaped flowers. Both *Y. filamentosa* and *Y. gloriosa* flower from a young age and produce the best displays during hot, dry summers. They are tolerant of exposed, windy sites, especially near the coast. Variegated forms of *Y. filamentosa* include: 'Bright Edge', with a bright butter yellow edge to the leaves, and 'Variegata', with creamy leaf edges, becoming pink-tinted in winter. Propagation is by division in spring; rooted suckers are removed and potted on.

hardiness Fully hardy
flowering Late summer
position Full sun
cultivation Loam-based compost (J.I. 2) or well-drained soil. Water moderately in summer, sparingly in winter, and feed monthly with a balanced liquid fertilizer. Remove faded flowers.
overwintering Cover the crown of the plant with straw as protection from frost.
pests & diseases Leaf spot
special features Good for creating an architectural feature, or a tropical effect.
decorative ideas Outstanding feature plant. Raise on a pedestal for maximum effect.

Yucca gloriosa

Trachelospermum jasminoides

Climbers and wall shrubs In any small space, climbers and wall shrubs

are an excellent choice as they offer a great wealth of blossom while taking up limited ground space. Those

with evergreen foliage will also help disguise unattractive walls. If possible, plant several different species

to extend the flowering season from spring to autumn.

While true climbers will support themselves with only a little help, either by twining around a pole or wire or using suckers, wall shrubs are simply shrubs with a tall, narrow habit that do best with the support and protection of a wall or fence. It pays to choose a variety of climbers and wall shrubs, selecting some with evergreen leaves (such as ivies and schizophragma, for example) or interesting foliage (the golden hop), some with good autumn colour (such as vines and parthenocissus) and others with flowers in spring (akebia, clematis and jasmine), summer (some clematis, roses and honeysuckle) or autumn (abutilon or bougainvillea). Even those climbers that are self-clinging or twining will need some help in the early stages to point them in the right direction, and wayward shoots will need to be tied in occasionally. A system of wires attached to the wall or fence with vine eyes makes a useful, multi-purpose support for climbers. Some climbers will thrive happily together. The less vigorous clematis, such as the viticellas, are ideal for growing through a climbing rose for example, and the combination of colours makes the display more exciting.

Make sure your climbers have an adequately sized container to allow the roots to develop. More vigorous climbers will need root-pruning every few years or they will outgrow their pots.

MALUACEAE
Abutilon
H Up to 3m (10ft)

ZONES 8–10
Usually evergreen, with mid-green leaves which may be entire or up to five-lobed. Some varieties have variegated foliage. Flowers are bell- or bowl-shaped, often with brightly coloured calyces and stamens. Varieties include: *A.* 'Canary Bird' with yellow flowers; *A. megapotamicum* which has a red calyx, yellow petals and purple stamens, and *A. m.* 'Variegatum' with yellow-speckled leaves; *A. pictum* 'Thompsonii' with yellow-flecked leaves and salmon orange flowers; and *A. vitifolium* 'Veronica Tennant' which is deciduous, with grey-green, slightly hairy shoots and leaves and 9cm (3½in) saucer-shaped mauve flowers with long stamens. Propagate by taking tip cuttings in summer.

hardiness Frost tender
flowering Spring to autumn
position Full sun
cultivation Loam-based compost (J.I. 2) or well-drained soil. Water freely in summer, sparingly in winter and feed monthly with a balanced liquid fertilizer.
overwintering Take indoors to avoid frost. May be left in place in frost-free areas.
pests & diseases Aphids, whitefly and red spider mites
special features Will grow well against a warm wall.
decorative ideas A good backdrop plant for less permanent displays.

Abutilon megapotamicum 'Kentish Belle'

LARDIZABALACEAE
Akebia quinata
H 5m (15ft)

ZONES 5–8
A semi-evergreen twining climber grown for both its leaves and flowers. Leaves are palmate, with 3–7 mid-green, separate leaflets often tinted bronze when they first emerge. This plant is known as the 'chocolate vine' because of the rich maroon-chocolate-brown, vanilla-scented flowers which appear in spring. Male and female flowers are borne separately within the same cluster, male ones at the tip, and the larger, female ones at the base. The long, purple, sausage-shaped fruits will only be produced if there is a second plant nearby to pollinate. Propagation is by layering in spring, semi-ripe cuttings in summer or seed sown as soon as it is ripe.

hardiness Fully hardy
flowering Spring
position Sun to partial shade
cultivation Loam-based compost (J.I. 2) or moist, well-drained soil. Water freely in summer, sparingly in winter, and feed monthly with a balanced liquid fertiliser. Prune after flowering, if necessary, to maintain the shape.
overwintering No special protection is needed, although late spring frosts may damage early flowers.
pests & diseases None
special features This plant needs a warm spring and long, hot summer to fruit well.
decorative ideas Plant two together if you want to produce fruit.

Akebia quinata

Aristolchia gigantea

ARISTOLOCHIACEAE
Aristolochia
H 3–10m (10–30ft)

ZONES 8–10

There are 300 shrubs, perennials and climbers in the genus, some evergreen, others deciduous, with lobed or entire leaves. The climbing plants can cover a structure quickly. Strange-looking flowers with no petals are found in maroon, brownish-purple or greenish-white, often with several colour combinations mottled together. *Aristolochia macrophylla* is a hardy, vigorous, deciduous climber. The large leaves are heart-shaped and mid-green in colour. The small, curiously shaped flowers, are yellow, brown and green in colour and appear in mid-summer. This plant is suitable for a wall, trellis or arbour. Provides a good wall covering when given support, but the leaves may suffer from wind scorch in exposed areas. *A. gigantea* is frost tender with large, wing-tailed brownish flowers. Propagation is by softwood tip cuttings in mid summer, layering in autumn or seed sown in spring.

hardiness Half hardy to frost tender
cultivation Prefers a well-drained soil and partial shade in the summer. Prune early in spring. Remove spindly stems and reduce vigorous growth by one third.
special features The plant can be placed outdoors during the summer months in a position which receives some direct sunlight every day.
display ideas The foliage makes a good screen.

Bougainvillea glabra

NYCTAGINACEAE
Bougainvillea glabra
H Up to 5m (15ft)

ZONES 9–10

An evergreen scrambler with oval, mid-green leaves. The common name, 'paper flower', describes the three paper-thin, wavy-edged bracts which surround the flowers, in shades from white to magenta. The flowers are small, creamy-white and tubular, borne in clusters of three. Some forms have sharp thorns on the stems. *B. g.* 'Sanderiana' has white margins to grey-green leaves and bright purple bracts. *B. g.* 'Snow White' has pure white flowers. Many colourful hybrids have been raised with *B. glabra* as parents Propagate by taking soft-tip cuttings in spring, semi-ripe cuttings in summer, hardwood cuttings in autumn, or layering in spring.

hardiness Frost tender
flowering Summer–autumn
position Full sun
cultivation Loam-based potting compost (J.I. 3) or well-drained soil. Water freely in summer, sparingly in winter, and feed monthly with a balanced liquid fertilizer. Prune in spring, if required.
overwintering Move indoors. Protect from frost. Survives cold better if kept slightly dry.
pests & diseases Under glass, red spider mite, aphids and mealy bugs
special features Responds well to hard pruning if it outgrows its situation.
decorative ideas Good for clothing railings on warm balconies.

Campsis x *tagliabuana* 'Mme Galen'

BIGNONIACEAE
Campsis
H 3m ′(10ft)

ZONES 5–9

The trumpet vine grows well when positioned against a sunny wall or fence, where it supports itself using aerial roots. It produces pinnate, mid- to dark green leaves, which turn golden-yellow in autumn. Trumpet-shaped flowers open, from mid-summer until the frosts, in clusters on the shoot tips. *C. grandiflora* has hanging clusters of six or more orange-red flowers; *C. radicans flava* has slender, yellow flowers in clusters of four or more; *C.* x *tagliabuana* 'Mme Galen' is vigorous, with showy salmon red flowers in clusters of up to 12. Propagate by taking semi-ripe cuttings in late summer or root cuttings in early spring.

hardiness Frost hardy
flowering Summer to autumn
position Full sun
cultivation Loam-based compost (J.I. 3) or well-drained soil. Water freely in summer, sparingly in winter, and feed monthly with a balanced liquid fertilizer. Tie young shoots to the support until the aerial roots take hold.
overwintering In colder areas, protect during periods of frost.
pests & diseases Mealy bugs, scale insects, and powdery mildew
special features It may take 2–3 years for this plant to establish itself in position.
decorative ideas A good feature plant near a gateway.

Clematis

Woody, climbing plants with both evergreen and deciduous species, grown for their attractive flowers and silky seedheads. They support themselves using their leaf stalks and are ideal for growing through other plants and against walls, fences and trellises. The 'flower' is actually four or more sepals, usually brightly coloured and varying from 1cm (½in) to 15cm (6in).

Clematis armandii

H Up to 4m (12ft)

ZONES 4–8

This evergreen species clematis has slender dark green leaves and pure white fragrant flowers in spring.

Clematis montana var. rubens

H Up to 8m (25ft)

ZONES 4–8

This vigorous, reliable plant is one of the easiest climbers to grow. The four-petalled flowers are pale pink and emerge from late spring into early summer.. No regular pruning is required.

Clematis 'Silver Moon'

H Up to 2m (6ft)

ZONES 5-8

This is a compact, early flowering hybrid clematis. From late spring, large silvery-mauve flowers with cream centres are produced on the new shoots. Pruning consists of cutting the plants down to 30cm (12in) each spring, and the plant can be increased by cuttings in summer.

Clematis texensis

H Up to 2.1m (7ft)

ZONES 4–8

This is one of the less vigorous members of the family and is ideal for growing into trees, bushy shrubs or hedges. The blue-green leaves comprise of up to eight oval leaflets. The leaf stalk twines to give the grey-green stems support. In late summer single scarlet tulip-shaped flowers are produced on thin graceful stalks. Propagation is by semi-ripe cuttings in mid-summer.

Clematis viticella

H Up to 4m (12ft)

ZONES 4–8

This species has a large number of cultivars covering a whole range of colours while retaining the charm of their bell-like blooms

Clematis hybrid

from summer to early autumn. It is ideal for growing on trellises and pergolas.

cultivation Prefers full sun but roots must be shaded in a well-drained, moist, slightly alkaline soil. Pruning is best linked to flowering time. For plants that flower before summer don't prune unless you have to.
flowering Early to late summer – trim back the shoots by one-third in late winter or early spring. Flowering late summer to autumn – cut back to 15cm (6in) in late winter.
propagation For large-flowered hybrids, take semi-ripe cuttings 10cm (4in) long in mid-summer. Herbaceous species should be divided in early spring.
pests and diseases Aphids may cause distorted growth if present in large numbers, and earwigs often eat holes in the flowers. Slugs may eat the young shoots as they emerge. Powdery mildew is often worse if the plants are grown against a wall; wilt is a particular problem.
special features Needs protection from frost and a sunny wall. Deadhead regularly. Support on wires or trellis.
display ideas Use balcony railings or wires on a terrace pillar to support.

Clematis armandii

Clematis 'Silver Moon'

ROSACEAE
Chaenomeles
H 1.5m (5ft)

ZONES 5–9

The flowering quince is a deciduous, spiny
shrub with glossy, toothed leaves. It is grown
for its colourful, cup-shaped flowers
produced early in the year as the foliage
opens. There are a number of hybrids, with
single or double flowers, produced singly or
in clusters. The flowers are followed by
edible, apple-like, yellowish fruit in autumn.
C. speciosa 'Geisha Girl' has apricot flowers;
'Moerloosei' has large, white flowers, flushed
pink; and 'Simonii' has double, dark red
flowers. *C.* x *superba* 'Crimson and Gold' has
red flowers with golden anthers; 'Knap Hill

Scarlet' has large, red flowers; and 'Pink Lady'
has dark pink flowers. Propagate by taking
semi-ripe cuttings in summer or layering
in early spring.

hardiness Fully hardy
flowering Early to mid-spring
position Full sun to partial shade
cultivation Loam-based compost (J.I. 3) or
moist, well-drained soil. Water moderately at
all times and feed monthly with a balanced
liquid fertilizer. Prune to maintain shape.
overwintering Do not allow the plant to
become waterlogged.
pests & diseases Aphids and canker
special features The warmer the position,
the better the fruit will be.
decorative ideas Grow in a fan shape
under an east-facing window.

Chaenomeles speciosa

Cobaea scandens f. 'Alba'

COBAEACEAE
Cobaea scandens
H Up to 3m (10ft)

ZONES 9–10

The cup-and-saucer vine is an evergreen,
half-hardy perennial climber normally grown
as an annual, which supports itself by means
of tendrils. The mid-green leaves are divided
into 4–6 pairs of leaflets, and the bell-shaped,
honey-scented flowers are creamy-green,
turning purple as they age. *C. s. f.* Alba has
greenish-white flowers which age to cream,
and is less hardy than the type. In frost-free
areas, grow against a sunny wall or pergola;
where frosts are a problem, grow as an annual
or in a cool greenhouse. Propagation is by
seed sown under protection in spring.

hardiness Frost tender
flowering Summer to mid-autumn
position Full sun with some shelter
cultivation Loam-based compost (J.I. 2),
loamless compost (if treated as an annual) or
well-drained soil. Water freely in summer,
sparingly in winter. Repot in spring. Prune
straggly or frosted growths in early spring,
and deadhead for a succession of flowers.
overwintering Protect from frosts.
pests & diseases None
special features Do not feed regularly or
the plant will grow, but not flower.
decorative ideas Grow with other
greenish-white flowers, such as hellebores
and euphorbias.

LEGUMINOSAE/PAPILIONACEAE
Cytisus
H 3m (10ft)

ZONES 5–9

There are many species in this genus, some
evergreen, some deciduous. The pineapple
broom with its pineapple-scented, yellow,
pea-like flowers in spring and silvery-green
leaves (*C. battandieri*) is half hardy and
vigorous, but prefers the protection of a wall.
C. praecox is much smaller (1.5m/5ft) with
masses of pale yellow flowers. Propagate from
semi-ripe cuttings in late summer.

hardiness Half hardy to fully hardy
flowering Early to late spring
position Full sun

cultivation Water freely in the growing
season; sparingly in winter and feed
monthly from winter to flowering. Prune
after flowering, but not into old wood.
overwintering No special care
pests & diseases Generally trouble-free
special features Plant the scented varieties
near doors and windows.
decorative ideas Underplant with yellow
crocuses and narcissus.

Cytisus praecox 'All Gold'

AVALIACEAE
Hedera
H Up to 3m (10ft)

ZONES 5–8

Ivy is an evergreen, self-clinging climber with aerial roots. Its leaves change with age, and many cultivars are noted for variegation. Young growth has three- to five-lobed leaves and adult growth has diamond-shaped leaves on the same plant. *Hedera canariensis* has reddish stems, three-lobed mid-green leaves and prefers some shelter. *H. c.* 'Gloire de Marengo' has light green leaves, edged and splashed white. *Hedera helix* has smaller, dark green leaves and has many cultivars with colourful foliage, including 'Buttercup' (gold), 'Atropurpurea' (dark purple) and 'Glacier'

(white-variegated). Propagation is by layering or taking tip cuttings as adventitious roots are produced.

hardiness Fully hardy
flowering Autumn (on mature plants only)
position Full sun to partial shade (variegated forms need bright light to maintain colour)
cultivation Loam-based compost (J.I. 2) or moist, well-drained soil. Water freely in summer, moderately in winter.
overwintering Do not allow to become waterlogged.
pests & diseases Scale insects
special features Small-leaved varieties will cover containers and trail forwards.
decorative ideas Ivy can be used to create imitation topiary to flesh out window boxes and hanging baskets and to cover walls.

Hedera helix cv.

Humulus lupulus 'Aureus'

CANNABIDACEAE
Humulus lupulus
H Up to 3m (10ft)

ZONES 5–9

The hop is a self-supporting, hardy, herbaceous perennial climber with thin, bristly, twining stems. The equally bristly, deeply lobed leaves have toothed edges. In summer, green flowers are produced, followed in autumn by clusters of fruit (hops). The cultivated forms are usually grown for their colourful or variegated foliage. These include: *H. l.* 'Aureus' has leaves, stems and fruits of a soft, golden-yellow; and *H. l.* 'Taff's Variegated' which is a less vigorous form, with creamy-white and green-variegated leaves. The dried stems and flowers can be

used for indoor arrangements. Propagation is by semi-ripe cuttings taken in June and July.

hardiness Fully hardy
flowering Spring and summer
position Full sun to partial shade (golden form turns greenish in shade)
cultivation Loam-based compost (J.I. 2) or well-drained soil. Water freely in summer, sparingly in winter. Prune out old growth in spring.
overwintering May need winter protection around the roots in frost-prone areas.
pests & diseases Mildew
special features It can even thrive in a north-facing aspect, although the spring growth may be a little delayed.
decorative ideas Can be trained over hoops and wigwams to create architectural effects.

OLEACEAE
Jasminum
H Up to 3m (10ft) S 3m (10ft)

ZONES 6–9

A large genus of climbers, grown for fragrant, tubular flowers, which open into a five-petalled star, in yellow, white or pale pink. They can be trained over a trellis or fence. The wall shrub *J. humile* 'Revolutum', the yellow jasmine, has fragrant flowers. *J. nudiflorum* can be trained against a wall and is hardy, with whippy, square, green stems and fragrant, yellow flowers throughout winter and early spring; *J. officinale* is frost hardy, with very fragrant, white flowers during summer; *J. o.* 'Argenteovariegatum' has grey-green leaves with cream edges. *J. polyanthum* is ten-

der, with clusters of pink buds, opening into white, highly fragrant flowers. Propagation is by semi-ripe cuttings taken in summer.

hardiness Frost tender to fully hardy
flowering Summer to autumn, or winter
position Full sun to partial shade
cultivation Loam-based compost (J.I. 2) or well-drained soil. Water freely in summer, sparingly in winter. Repot when necessary.
overwintering Frost-tender varieties will need protection during periods of cold weather. Mulch the pot and wrap with insulation material, or move indoors.
pests & diseases Aphids
special features Control growth by regular pruning and pinching out growing tips.
decorative ideas Train over arches and railings for scent and/or flower colour.

Jasminum humile 'Revolutum'

CAPRITOLIACEAE
Lonicera
H 3m (10ft)

ZONES 4–9

Twining, woody climbers, with fragrant, tubular flowers, carried in clusters from spring to autumn, depending on variety. Flower colour ranges from white, pale yellow to gold, pink and scarlet. *Lonicera x brownii* has clusters of orange-scarlet flowers in mid- to late summer: *L. x b.* 'Dropmore Scarlet' has long, scarlet flowers over a long period; *L. x b.* 'Fuchsioides' has orange-scarlet flowers. *L. periclymenum* has oval, mid-green leaves and fragrant, tubular flowers, followed by red berries in autumn: *L. p.* 'Belgica' produces reddish-purple flowers fading to yellow in late spring to early summer (with a second flush in late summer); *L. p.* 'Serotina' flowers mid-summer to mid-autumn, rich reddish-purple fading to yellow. *Lonicera x tellmanniana* has copper-yellow, flushed-scarlet, flowers in late spring to mid-summer. Propagation is by hardwood cuttings taken in autumn.

hardiness Fully hardy
flowering Spring to autumn
position Full sun to partial shade
cultivation Loam-based compost (J.I. 2) or any moist, well-drained soil. Water freely in summer, sparingly in winter and feed monthly with a balanced liquid fertilizer. Prune by removing old wood after flowering.
overwintering Do not allow to become waterlogged.
pests & diseases Aphids and mildew
special features The berries are poisonous.
decorative ideas Grow over a porch for a scented welcome to your home.

Lonicera periclymenum 'Graham Thomas'

Mandevilla xamoena 'Alice du Pont'

APOCYNACEAE
Mandevilla
H 3m (10ft)

ZONES 10

This vigorous woody climber twines around surrounding plants. The young bronze-flushed leaves turn glossy-green as they age and are broadly oval-shaped, finishing with a slender pointed tip. Broad, trumpet-shaped flowers are produced in clusters of between three and five, and are rose pink with a white and yellow throat in the centre. The cultivar *M. splendens* 'Rosacea' has rose-pink flowers, with purple-pink petal margins. *M. xamonena* 'Alice du Pont' is similar with clusters of 20 or more. Propagate by soft-tip cuttings in early summer or semi-ripe cuttings in summer.

hardiness Frost tender
flowering Mid- to late summer
position Full sun
cultivation Loam-based compost (J.I. 2) or well-drained soil. Water freely in summer, sparingly in winter, and feed monthly with a balanced liquid fertilizer. Prune in early spring, if necessary, to control size.
overwintering Take indoors, this plant must be protected from all frosts.
pests & diseases Aphids are often a problem in the summer, and mealy bugs can be a problem throughout the year.
special features This twining climber must have some upright support to cling to. Care must be taken when pruning this plant, as the sap is a skin irritant.
decorative ideas Makes an eye-catching plant to grow around a pillar.

VIRACEAE
Parthenocissus tricuspidata
H 5m (15ft)

ZONES 4–7

The Boston ivy is a vigorous self-clinging climber, ideal for covering walls. Leaves vary according to age, from tiny to 20cm (8in) long, and from three-lobed to three ovate leaflets, but most are deeply toothed. Leaf colour starts mid- to dark green in summer, changing to scarlet and purple. The purple shoots remain stuck to the wall by sucker pads on the ends of tendrils after the leaves have fallen. Small, flowers are produced in summer, followed occasionally by small, black berries. *P. t.* 'Beverley Brook' has small purple leaves in summer, turning red.

P. t. 'Veitchii' has purple leaves turning to reddish-purple. Propagate by taking soft-tip cuttings in spring or hardwood cuttings in winter.

hardiness Fully hardy
flowering Summer
position Sun to partial shade (the autumn colour is better in full sun)
cultivation Loam-based compost (J.I. 2) or moist, well-drained soil. Water freely in summer, sparingly in winter, and feed monthly with a balanced liquid fertilizer.
overwintering No special care
pests & diseases Trouble-free
special features Will grow through a tree or on a fence.
decorative ideas Clothes a wall with brilliant colour in autumn.

Parthenocissus tricuspidata 'Veitchii'

COBAEACEAE
Passiflora
H 3m (10ft)

ZONES 8–10

Perennials which climb using twisting tendrils and die down for the winter, re-emerging in spring. They flower young, producing flowers, up to 10cm (4in). Five white sepals and five white petals of equal length surround blue-purple filaments with a central white band. The flowers are followed in hot summers by egg-shaped, yellow fruits. *P. caerulea* 'Constance Elliot' has fragrant, white flowers, with blue and white filaments. *P. edulis* has white flowers and orange-purple fruit. *P.* 'Amethyst' (zone 9) has purple to purplish-blue flowers with green anthers in late summer.

hardiness Half hardy (*P.* 'Amethyst' is frost tender)
flowering Summer
position Full sun
cultivation Loam-based compost (J.I. 2) or moist, well-drained soil. Water freely in summer, sparingly in winter, feed monthly with a balanced liquid fertilizer. Propagate by taking 8–10cm (3–4in) side shoots with a heel in July/August. Prune if necessary in early spring.
overwintering Protect during severe cold with mulch and insulation, or move indoors.
pests & diseases Virus
special features Tie in young growths until tendrils take hold.
decorative ideas Grow with clematis and roses for maximum effect.

Passiflora 'Amethyst'

COBAEACEAE
Plumbago auriculata
H 2m (6ft)

ZONES 9–10

An evergreen wall shrub, with long, arching stems. The stems need tying to supports to prevent them straggling. Pretty sky blue flowers are borne in clusters of up to 20 throughout summer and autumn amid the long-oval, mid-green leaves. The attractive individual flowers are tubular, flaring out into five petals, each of which is marked with a darker blue central stripe. The form *P.a.* var. *alba* has striking pure white flowers. Propagation is by taking semi-ripe cuttings in summer, layering, or by seed sown in spring.

hardiness Half hardy
flowering Summer to autumn
position Full sun
cultivation Loam-based compost (J.I. 2) or well-drained soil. Water freely in summer, sparingly in winter. Feed every two weeks in spring to summer with a high-potash fertilizer (tomato food). Flowers are produced on current season's growth, so prune in early spring to give the maximum flowering time. Reduce growth by up to two-thirds.
overwintering Move indoors away from any danger of frost.
pests & diseases Red spider mites, whiteflies and mealy bugs
special features Removing fading flowers will encourage more buds.
decorative ideas Underplant with campanula and blue pansies.

Plumbago auriculata

ROSACEAE
Pyracantha
H Up to 3m (10ft)

ZONES 6–8

The firethorn forms a hardy, spreading shrub, but it reacts well to close pruning to create a dense, green wall covering. Small, glossy, ever-green leaves are carried on stout, thorny shoots. Clusters of small, creamy flowers in late spring are followed in autumn by yellow, orange or red berries (which birds love). The cultivar 'Soleil d'Or' has golden-yellow berries; 'Shawnee' has orange-yellow; 'Orange Glow' has bright orange; 'Mohave' has long-lasting red-orange berries; and those of *P.* x *watereri* are bright red. Propagation is by semi-ripe cuttings in summer.

hardiness Fully hardy
flowering Late spring
position Full sun to shade
cultivation Loam-based compost (J.I. 3) or well-drained soil. Water freely in summer, sparingly in winter, and feed monthly with a balanced liquid fertilizer. Tie in framework shoots and prune others back to the main stems regularly to encourage short leafy spurs.
overwintering Do not allow to become waterlogged.
pests & diseases Aphids and scab
special features Once established, the firethorn will support a small climber growing through it for colour in a different season.
decorative ideas Plant chrysanthemums and dahlias in pots at the feet of the firethorn for autumn colour.

Pyracantha 'Orange Glow'

Rhodochiton atrosanguineum

SCROPHULARIACEAE
Rhodochiton atrosanguineum
H Up to 3m (10ft) s 3m (10ft)

ZONES 9–10

This unusual twining climber (formerly known as *R. volubile*) hails from Mexico. In cold areas it is grown as an annual; in warmer climates it can be used to cover a pergola or arch. It has attractive mid-green heart-shaped leaves and curious deep red cup-shaped flowers with a pink or pinkish mauve calyx from summer through to autumn. Propagate from seed sown in warmth in spring. Pot up after frosts have passed.

hardiness Tender
flowering Summer to autumn
position Full sun
cultivation Grow in loam-based compost (J.I. 2) . Water freely in the growing season; sparingly when dormant. Feed regularly with liquid fertilizer until flowering. Provide wires or trellis for support.
overwintering Bring indoors in frost-prone areas.
pests & diseases Trouble-free outdoors; prone to red spider mite indoors
special features None
display ideas Use as a trailer from a large pot, or combine with *Akebia quinata* for late summer effect.

Rosa

Climbing roses have vigorous stiff stems with glossy foliage. The flowers are often scented and borne in clusters; in modern climbers the clusters are of three to seven flowers. Rambling roses are more vigorous, and not really suitable for growing in containers. Some roses flower just once in summer, others flower repeatedly. All roses need plenty of fertilizer and bone meal to flourish. They are prone to a number of pests and diseases, which need to be dealt with speedily.

Rosa 'Albertine'

Rosa 'Albertine'
H 3m (10ft)

ZONES 4–8
Fragrant, salmon pink, open-shaped flowers with a double row of petals and a golden centre, fading to a paler colour as they age.

Rosa 'Mme Alfred Carrière'
H 3m (10ft)

ZONES 4–8
This noisette rose has slender smooth stems, pale green leaves and double pinkish-apricot scented flowers from summer to autumn.

Rosa 'Gloire de Dijon'
H 5m (15ft)

ZONES 4–8
Stiffly branching climbing tea rose with glossy, dark green leaves and highly scented fully double creamy flowers, tightly packed with petals. The flowers are borne from summer through to autumn.

Rosa 'Guinée'
H 5m (15ft)

ZONES 4–8
Vigorous climber with leathery dark green leaves has fully double fragrant dark red double flowers, 8cm (3in) across in summer.

Rosa 'Mme Isaac Periere'
H 2.2m (7ft)

ZONES 4–8
This vigorous Bourbon rose is very highly scented with large double flowers in deep purplish-pink. It flowers from summer to autumn.

Rosa 'Mme Plantier'
H 2.2m (7ft)

ZONES 4–8
This vigorous arching Noisette climbing rose can be trained over pillars and fences. It has smooth green leaves and double white scented flowers.

Rosa 'Variegata di Bologna'
H 2.2m (7ft)

ZONES 4–8
This Bourbon rose has smooth stems and double fragrant pinkflowers that are attractively flushed with purple. It flowers from summer to autumn.

hardiness Fully hardy
flowering Summer
position Full sun, with shelter from winds
cultivation Loam-based compost (J.I. 3) or well-drained soil. Water freely in summer, and feed monthly with a balanced liquid fertilizer. Pruning is done by cutting out some of the old flower-bearing shoots.
pests & diseases Aphids, caterpillars, black spot, rust, mildew and virus
special features 'Suckers' may originate from the rootstock of a grafted plant. These need removing at their base. Roses need a deep container to accommodate the roots if they are to reach a good height.
decorative ideas Grow two or three roses over a wall or fence, and choose those that flower over a long period.

Rosa 'Variegata di Bologna'

Rosa 'Mme Isaac Periere'

HYDRANGEACEAE

Schizophragma hydrangeoides

H 6m (18ft)

ZONES 5–9

A deciduous, woody wall shrub, which is related to the climbing hydrangea, and shares with it the ability to support itself as it grows against a wall by means of small adventitious roots which form along the shoots. It produces pairs of oval-shaped, dark green leaves. Broad, flattened clusters of creamy-white, slightly fragrant flowers are borne in summer, resembling those of the 'lacecap' hydrangea, but with enlarged, petal-like, sterile outer sepals borne on long stems. The clusters can be up to 25cm (10in) across and the outer sepals up to 6cm (2½in) long,

making the flowers extremely showy and attractive. *S. h.* 'Roseum' has outer sepals of white blushed rosy-pink. Propagate by taking semi-ripe cuttings in summer

hardiness Fully hardy
flowering Mid-summer
position Full sun or partial shade
cultivation Loam-based compost (J.I. 3) or moist, well-drained soil. Water freely in summer, sparingly in winter, and feed monthly with a balanced liquid fertilizer.
overwintering Do not allow to become waterlogged.
pests & diseases None
special features Can be used to support a small, spring-flowering clematis.
decorative ideas Good for planting by a shady, cool wall.

Solanum crispum 'Glasnevin'

SOLMACEAE

Solanum

H 3m (10ft)

ZONES 8–9

Evergreen or semi-evergreen wall shrubs, with large clusters of small, star-shaped flowers. Leaves are glossy dark green, turning bright yellow in autumn. The stems are glossy green, even in winter. *S. crispum* is a scrambling climber which needs support. It has dark green leaves, and clusters of fragrant purple flowers, followed by pale yellow fruit. *S. c.* 'Glasnevin' is hardier, with dark purple-blue flowers. *S. jasminoides* is a slender, ever-green climber which produces five-petalled, slate blue flowers with golden anthers from summer to early autumn. *S. j.* 'Album' has

white flowers with yellow anthers. Propagate by taking semi-ripe cuttings in early summer.

hardiness Frost hardy, more hardy against a south-facing wall
flowering Summer to autumn
position Full sun to partial shade
cultivation Loam-based compost (J.I. 2) or well-drained soil. Water freely in summer, sparingly in winter, and feed monthly with a balanced liquid fertilizer. Thin overcrowded, frost-damaged growth in mid-spring.
overwintering Move indoors in frost-prone areas.
pests & diseases Aphids and grey mould
special features Eating the fruits may cause severe stomach upset.
decorative ideas Plant with viticella clematis to prolong the flowering period.

Trachelospermum

APOCYNACEAE

Trachelospermum jasminoides

H Up to 3m (10ft) S 3m (10ft)

ZONES 7–9

This woody, evergreen climber, known as the star jasmine, has twining stems which anchor it to its support. The glossy, oval-shaped leaves are dark green, turning bronzed-red over winter, and up to 10cm (4in) long. In summer, small clusters of fragrant white flowers are produced along the shoots and at the tips. Each has a cylindrical tube, flaring out into five slightly twisted lobes of up to 2.5cm (1in) across. This plant will thrive outdoors against a south-facing wall. It can remain outside as long as it can be protected from frost, otherwise move it indoors.

Propagation is by semi-ripe cuttings taken in summer, or layering in autumn.

hardiness Frost hardy
flowering Mid- to late summer
position Full light indoors (shade from midday sun) or full sun outdoors
cultivation Loam-based compost (J.I. 3) or well-drained soil. Water freely in summer, sparingly in winter, and feed monthly with a balanced liquid fertilizer. Protect from winds.
overwintering Protect from frosts using fleece (or similar) or move indoors.
pests & diseases None
special features The stems contain milky sap which may irritate the skin.
decorative ideas Plant close to a window or door, on a wall or over a support, to benefit from the heady scent.

Vitis coignetiae

VITACEAE
Vitis

H Up to 5m (15ft).

ZONES 5–9

Ornamental vines are ideal for covering a wall, fence or trellis. Some species are grown for their autumn colours of yellow, orange-red and purple-crimson and some produce small bunches of grapes in a hot dry summer. Propagation is by hardwood cuttings taken from October to December, or by vine-eyes taken in mid-winter. *Vitis coignetiae* (Crimson glory vine) is a vigorous species. The tiny blue-black grapes it produces are inedible. *V. vinifera* (Common grape vine) has rough, leathery leaves, oval-round in shape. *V. v.* 'Apiifolia' (syn. 'Ciotat') has finely cut, deeply lobed, fern-like leaves. *V. v.* 'Purpurea' has leaves which are red, fading to deep purple. *V.* 'Brandt' is a hybrid with 3–5-lobed green leaves which turn bronze-red with green veins. It produces blue-black grapes.

hardiness Fully hardy
flowering Late spring to early summer
position Full sun or partial shade
cultivation Loam-based compost (J.I. 3) in a deep container. Water freely in summer, sparingly in winter, and feed monthly in spring with a balanced liquid fertilizer. Thin out old growths in winter, and shorten young growths to 3–4 leaves in late summer.
overwintering Do not allow to become waterlogged.
pests & diseases Brown scale insects, vine weevils, mildew
special features Keep growth restricted by not potting on until it is absolutely necessary.
decorative ideas Grow up a 3m (10ft) pole, and allow to cascade down over the pot.

LEGUMINOSAE/PAPILIONACEAE
Wisteria

H Up to 5m (15ft)

ZONES 5–9

These deciduous climbers support themselves by their stems. Pea-like flowers are white, pink, blue or mauve. It flowers from spring to mid-summer, but some flowers may be produced until autumn. *W. floribunda* produces 30cm (12in) racemes of violet-blue flowers in early summer. *W. f.* 'Alba' has white flowers; 'Macrobotrys' has lilac-blue flowers; and 'Rosea' has pink flowers. *W. sinensis* (Chinese wisteria) produces mauve flowers in early summer from spur-like growths. *W. s.* 'Alba' has white flowers. Take heel or nodal cuttings in late summer, or layer in late spring.

hardiness Fully hardy
flowering Early summer
position Full sun
cultivation Loam-based compost (J.I. 3) or well-drained soil. Water freely in summer, sparingly in winter and feed monthly with a balanced liquid fertilizer. Prune side shoots to two or three buds in February, and whippy growths to 30cm (12in) in July.
overwintering Mulch to protect the roots during periods of severe frost.
pests & diseases Red spider mite, fungal leaf spot, birds may eat flower buds.
special features Hard water may cause lime-induced chlorosis; try to use rain water.
decorative ideas Grow as a weeping standard or against a sunny wall.

Wisteria floribunda 'Macrobotrys'

Heliotrope, Agapanthus

Perennials and annuals These form the backbone of any major flowering display, and vary from tiny mat-forming plants that can be displayed on a table top or windowsill to statuesque plants with tall flower spires or eye-catching large flowers that form a special feature. Bamboos, ferns and grasses are grown for their shape and are listed on pp. 162–165.

Flowering perennials and annuals

Herbaceous perennials are fibrous-rooted plants that reappear every year, but die back, generally, in the colder months. True annuals flower in one season from seed, and biennials do so over a two-season period, flowering in their second year. Other perennials originating in hot climates are treated like annuals in cooler climates, growing them from seed or cuttings for a one-season display only. Summer-flowering displays for hanging baskets make use primarily of annuals and perennials grown as annuals. To create an effective hanging display, you need a proportion of trailing plants.

These carry a symbol (as shown in the key at the start of this section). Perennials will gradually increase in size, and may well need dividing up and repotting every few years, as they grow from the centre out, and this central part will start to die back. The seed of annuals can be collected in autumn and sown for the following year. If creating a mixed display of perennials, make sure that they all have the same sunlight and watering needs (see symbols at top of each entry). When creating colour schemes, limit the colours to two or three, in toning shades or as deliberate contrasts, for maximum impact.

COBAEACEAE
Anemone blanda
H 15cm (6in)

ZONES 6–9

A clump-forming perennial with a low-growing, creeping habit. It grows from tubers, and produces deeply lobed, dark green leaves carried just above the compost on thin, wiry, dark or bluish-green stems. The single flowers are borne in spring, in shades of white, pink and deep blue, above the leaves on stems up to 15cm (6in) high. Forms include: *A. b.* 'Ingramii' which has deep blue flowers with a purple reverse; *A. b.* 'Radar', with white-centred, magenta-pink flowers; and *A. b.* 'White Splendour' which has pure white flowers with a pink reverse. Propagation is by division after flowering.

hardiness Fully hardy
flowering Early spring
position Full sun to partial shade
cultivation Loam-based compost (J.I. 1) with added grit. Keep moist when growing and flowering, then allow to dry through summer, watering sparingly to prevent the compost drying out. Repot every 4–5 years.
overwintering Mulch during severe frost.
pests & diseases Slugs and mildew
special features Plant 5cm (2in) deep during autumn.
decorative ideas Plant up small containers for a spring table-top display. Combine with dwarf iris and crocus.

Anemone blanda 'White Splendour'

RANUNCULACEAE
Anemone x *hybrida*
H Up to 1.5m (5ft)

ZONES 7–9

The Japanese anemone is a hardy perennial with toothed, divided, mid-green leaves. In mid- to late summer produces tall, branching stems bearing open, saucer-shaped flowers in white and shades of pink, with a yellow central tuft of stamens, which persist into autumn. They spread by suckering, and need repotting or dividing every 2–3 years. One of the parents of the hybrids is *A. hupehensis*. *A. h.* 'Hadspen Abundance' is worth growing with bright pink flowers. Cultivars of *A* x *hybrida* include: 'Geante des Blanches' (semi-double with white flowers; 'Honorine Jobert' (single white with pink reverse); 'Konigin Charlotte' (semi-double pink with purple reverse); 'Profusion' (semi-double, rose pink flowers). Propagation is by division in spring.

hardiness Fully hardy
flowering Mid-summer to autumn
position Full sun to partial shade
cultivation Loam-based compost (J.I. 2). Water moderately in summer, very sparingly in winter. Feed monthly with a balanced liquid fertilizer.
overwintering Avoid excess moisture and protect from severe frost.
pests & diseases Caterpillars, slugs, mildew
special features Excellent for providing a glowing display of colour in autumn.
decorative ideas Plant in a large pot to brighten up a shady corner.

Anemone hupehensis 'Hadspen Abundance'

ASTERACEAE/COMPOSITAE

Argyranthemum

H 30–60cm (12–24in)

ZONES 8–10

Formerly known as chrysanthemum, this is an evergreen subshrub with pretty, daisy-like flowers. The foliage is divided and ferny, varying from mid-green to very blue-green. They generally flower from early summer into the autumn, but in milder, frost-free areas, they will often flower continuously, if they are watered, fed and prevented from setting any seed. They flower in a variety of colours, and cultivars include: 'Cornish Gold' (butter yellow); 'Jamaica Primrose' (pale yellow flowers with golden centres); 'Jamaica Snowstorm' (yellow-centred white); 'Mary Cheek' (double, pale pink); 'Petite Pink' (yellow-centred pale pink); and 'Vancouver' (shaded rose to pale pink, anemone-flowered). Propagate from semi-ripe cuttings (non-flowering shoots) in summer.

hardiness Frost tender
flowering Summer to autumn
position Full sun
cultivation Loamless or loam-based (J.I. 1) compost. Water moderately in summer, and feed monthly with a balanced liquid fertilizer. Pinch out growing tips in spring to encourage bushing.
overwintering Protect from frost and water sparingly.
pests & diseases Aphids
special features More vigorous forms, like 'Vancouver' and 'Jamaican Primrose', can be trained as standards.
decorative ideas Plant up several pots using tonal colour schemes – gold and orange, white and yellow – for maximum effect.

Argyranthemum cv.

ROSACEAE

Aruncus dioicus

H 1.5m (5ft)

ZONES 5–8

A hardy herbaceous perennial which has fern-like, light green, deeply veined leaves which are made up of several strap-like leaflets, held on tough, sturdy stems. Large feathery plumes of creamy-white flowers are produced in summer on strong thin reddish-green stems. These are followed by chestnut brown seedheads in the autumn on the female plants, although it is the male plants which produce the most attractive flowers. The form *A. d.* 'Kneiffii' has a more compact growing habit, finely cut leaves and tiny cream flowers. Propagation is by division in spring or autumn or seed sown in spring.

hardiness Fully hardy
flowering Summer
position Partial to full shade
cultivation Loam-based compost (J.I. 3) or moist soil. Water very freely in summer, moderately in winter.
overwintering Do not allow to become waterlogged.
pests & diseases None
special features One of the few plants which will produce flowers in a shady position in the garden.
decorative ideas Plant in a large, deep pot as specimen plant for a shady corner.

Aruncus dioicus

Begonia 'Non-Stop' Series

BEGONIACEAE
Begonia
s Up to 45cm (18in)

ZONES 9–10

Begonias come in many forms, but those most useful for small spaces are the tuberous begonias which divide into several groups, including Multiflora with a shrubby habit and many small single or double flowers, and pendula begonias, which have trailing or pendulous stems. Of the Multiflora begonias, the Non-Stop Series are very popular, with heart-shaped mid-green leaves, up to 15cm (6in) long and double flowers up to 8cm (3in) across in white yellow, apricot, pink or bright red. They flower throughout the summer. They flower in clusters, usually two small females and one showy (often double) male. 'Apricot Cascade' has oval, bright green leaves and apricot-coloured flowers with layers of wide, slightly toothed petals; 'Bridal Cascade' has white flowers, with red-edged petals; the Illumination Series have wide, flat flowers of pink, red or orange; and *B. sutherlandii* has long, slender stems, red-veined leaves and clusters of small, orange flowers. All are ideal for hanging baskets. Propagate by rooting basal cuttings (with a section of tuber) in spring.

hardiness Frost tender
flowering Summer
position Full sun (may need shade at midday)
cultivation Plant tuber hollow-side upwards in spring in loamless or loam-based compost (J.I. 1). Water freely whilst in growth, then reduce in autumn. Feed every two weeks from spring to summer with a balanced liquid fertilizer.
overwintering Tubers become dormant overwinter. Lift and dry.
pests & diseases Aphids, mildew, fungal rot.
special features Pinching out small, female flowers extends the flowering period.
decorative ideas Use the pendula begonias in hanging baskets. The Multiflora begonias make striking feature plants on top of a wall or pillar.

Bellis perennis

ASTERACEAE/COMPOSITAE
Bellis perennis
H Up to 20cm (8in)

ZONES 4–9

This hardy, rosette-forming perennial will grow in most situations and seed itself easily unless regularly deadheaded. It has bright green, spoon-shaped leaves and long-stalked flowers, borne singly throughout the spring and summer. The flowers may be single or double, in white and shades of red, rose and pink with yellow centres. There are many seed mixes available, most producing double flowers, often with two-tone petals, including: Pomponette Series (double flowers); Goliath Mixed and Habanera Mixed (large, spiky flowers); Medicis Mixed (round, tightly-packed flowerheads); and Tasso Series (double flowers). Sow seed in spring (outdoors once the danger of frost has passed).

hardiness Fully hardy
flowering Spring to summer
position Full sun to partial shade
cultivation Loam-based compost (J.I. 1), water moderately and feed monthly with a balanced liquid fertilizer at half strength.
overwintering Protect from severe frost and cold wind.
pests & diseases None
special features They will flower through the winter in mild areas as long as they are prevented from setting seed.
decorative ideas Plant up several small matching pots and line them up on a windowsill.

Brachyscome iberidifolia

ASTERACEAE/COMPOSITAE
Brachyscome iberidifolia
H 30cm (12in) S 60cm (2ft)

ZONES 9–10

The swan river daisy is a pretty, spreading plant, usually grown as an annual, although they are very tolerant plants for a hot, sheltered spot, and may last for a second year in a warm climate. They have finely divided, ferny, grey-green foliage and masses of small, daisy-like flowers in white, blue or purple throughout the whole summer and early autumn. Each has a bright yellow centre of disc florets which fades to brown as it ages. 'Blue Mist' produces bright blue flowers; 'Lemon Mist' has unusual pale yellow flowers; 'Purple Splendour' flowers are a rich, glowing purple; and those of 'White Splendour' are pure white. Propagates easily from seed sown in spring.

hardiness Frost tender
flowering Summer
position Full sun
cultivation Loamless or loam-based compost (J.I. 1). Water freely in spring to summer, sparingly if overwintering. Feed every two weeks spring to summer with a balanced liquid fertilizer.
overwintering Protect from cold.
pests & diseases Slugs and snails
special features Pinch growing tips on young plants to encourage bushing.
decorative ideas Use to relax the planting in window boxes or for hanging baskets as a single display.

Calluna vulgaris 'Gefullt'

ERICACEAE
Calluna vulgaris
H Up to 60cm (2ft)

ZONES 4–8

The heather is a low-growing, acid-loving, subshrub with small hairy leaves borne on thin, woody stems. The foliage may vary in colour from green to grey, yellow, orange and red-brown, with some varieties producing their best display of leaf colour as the temperatures fall during autumn and winter. Small, bell-shaped flowers are carried in spikes on the tips of the shoots, in white and shades of red, pink and purple. Varieties include: 'Beoley Gold' (yellow foliage, white flowers); 'Blazeaway' (golden foliage, turning bright red in winter, mauve flowers); 'Kinlochruel' (green foliage, bronze in winter, double white flowers); and 'Silver Knight' (silver-grey foliage, mauve flowers). Propagation is by semi-ripe cuttings taken in autumn after flowering.

hardiness Fully hardy
flowering Mid-summer to late autumn
position Full sun
cultivation Acid compost, loamless or loam-based (J.I. Ericaceous). Water moderately at all times, as it dislikes excess moisture.
overwintering Do not allow to become waterlogged.
pests & diseases Grey mould and root rot
special features Attractive to bees.
decorative ideas Plant in feature pots on their own, or in window boxes with ornamental cabbages and cyclamens.

CAMPANULACEAE
Campanula
H Up to 1.5m (5ft)

ZONES 3–8

Campanulas vary from tall perennials which need staking to low, ground-covering ones. *C. lactiflora* (milky bellflower) is an upright perennial which will require staking. It has mid-green leaves and bell-shaped flowers in summer and autumn that vary from white to lavender, lilac and violet. 'Loddon Anna' has lilac-pink flowers; 'Prichard's Variety' has purple-blue flowers; 'Pouffe' is compact (30cm/12in) with lavender blue flowers, and 'White Pouffe' is similar, with white. More compact forms include *C. poscharskyana* which is only 15cm (6in) tall with masses of starry mid-blue flowers and *C. portenschlagiana* with large, bluish-purple flowers. Propagation is by seed sown in spring, division in spring or autumn, or basal cuttings in spring.

hardiness Fully hardy
flowering Summer to autumn
position Partial shade
cultivation Loam-based compost (J.I. 2). Water moderately during summer, sparingly over winter. Feed monthly with a balanced liquid fertilizer.
overwintering Protect from severe frost and excess moisture.
pests & diseases Slugs, snails and mildew
special features Regular deadheading as flowers fade will prevent the plant setting seed and encourage more flowers to form.

Campanula poscharskyana

Canna indica 'Purpurea'

CANNACEAE
Canna
H Up to 1.5m (5ft)

ZONES 8–10

Unusual and highly striking rhizomatous herbaceous perennials grown for both their foliage and flowers. The leaves are large and blade-shaped, varying in colour from green to dark bronze, often with marked veins. The flowers are tubular, flaring out as three wide petals, in vibrant reds, oranges and yellows, with long stamens. Many hybrids have arisen, including: 'Black Knight' (dark bronze foliage, red flowers); 'King Midas' (golden-yellow flowers); 'Lucifer' (shorter [60cm/2ft] with yellow-edged red flowers); and 'Wyoming' (bronze-purple foliage, orange flowers). *C. indica* 'Purpurea' has striking dark purple leaves and bright red flowers. Propagation is by seed sown in spring, or division of rhizomes in spring (each piece with a growth bud).

hardiness Frost tender
flowering Summer to autumn
position Full sun
cultivation Loamless or loam-based compost (J.I. 2). Water freely in summer and feed monthly with a balanced liquid fertilizer. As the foliage dies down, reduce watering.
overwintering Protect from frost by moving indoors. In frost-free areas, simply cover the crown with mulch.
pests & diseases Slugs, snails, caterpillars
special features Deadhead regularly to ensure a succession of flowers.

ASTERACEAE/COMPOSITAE
Chrysanthemum
H 45–60cm (18–24in)

ZONES 8–10

There are several annual chrysanthemums with a bushy habit, and producing clusters of daisy-like flowers during late spring, summer and autumn. These are usually single, yellow or white, often with orange or red markings on the petals. *C. carinatum* has purple-eyed flowers with red or white markings (zoning). *C. c.* 'Court Jesters' has white, yellow, orange, red and maroon flowers with red, orange or yellow zoning; *C. c.* 'German Flag' has yellow flowers with dark centres and dark red edges. *C. coronarium* has ferny leaves and single yellow flowers; *C. c.* 'Primrose Gem' has pale

yellow flowers all summer long. Propagate from seed sown in spring (or autumn for early flowering).

hardiness Frost tender to frost hardy
flowering Spring to autumn
position Full sun
cultivation Loam-based compost (J.I. 2). Water moderately in summer and feed monthly with a balanced liquid fertilizer.
overwintering In frost-free areas, water sparingly in winter to keep the plants for a second year.
pests & diseases Leaf miners, grey mould, mildew
special features Provide a glorious display of colour for containers.
decorative ideas Group several pots on a table for an autumn display.

Chrysanthemum cv.

Convolvulus sabatius

CONVOLVULACEAE
Convolvulus
S 50cm (20in)

ZONES 9–10

Unlike the vigorous wild bindweed, the smaller ornamental varieties are pretty, slender, twining plants which produce wide, funnel-shaped flowers in white, pink or blue-purple. *C. althaeoides* is a perennial climber or trailer with slender stems and pink flowers in summer. It can be invasive, unless restricted within a container. *C. sabatius* is perennial (sometimes grown as an annual) with flowers of rich purple-blue, in shades ranging from very pale to quite deep. *C. tricolor* is a bushy annual (or short-lived perennial in warmer areas) which spreads as it ages and bears royal

blue flowers with yellow and white centres; the form *C. t.* 'Royal Ensign' has larger flowers and is good for a hanging basket. Propagate by taking cuttings in late summer to overwinter, or division in spring.

hardiness Frost tender
flowering Summer
position Full sun
cultivation Loamless or loam-based compost (J.I. 1). Water freely in summer, sparingly in winter.
overwintering Protect from frost.
pests & diseases Aphids
special features Not good for mixed planting, as it tends to dominate.
decorative ideas *C. sabiatus* makes an excellent hanging basket plant or to relax the planting in a window box.

Cosmos 'Dwarf Sonata' series

ASTERACEAE/COMPOSITAE
Cosmos
H 75cm (30in)

ZONES 8–10

There are both perennial and annual species. The annual *C. bipinnatus* has bright pink, white or cream flowers. *C. sanguineum* is a perennial and is likely to be killed off by hard winter frost unless given protection. The mid- to dark green foliage is divided and borne on reddish stems. The saucer-shaped, red-brown flowers are produced singly on tall stems throughout the summer and autumn. Propagate perennials by taking basal cuttings in spring. Propagate annuals from seed sown in spring. Dwarf Sonata series cosmos, which are smaller than the perennials, grow up to

45cm/18in tall) come in shades of pink, carmine and white.

hardiness Frost tender
flowering Summer to autumn
position Full sun
cultivation Loam-based compost (J.I. 2 for perennials, J.I. 1 for annuals). Water moderately in summer and feed monthly with a balanced liquid fertilizer.
overwintering In frost-prone areas, lift tuberous perennials and store almost dry in a frost-free place until spring.
pests & diseases Slugs, snails, grey mould
special features Regular deadheading will help ensure a succession of flowers throughout the summer.

Semi-cactus flowered dahlia

ASTERACEAE/COMPOSITAE

Dahlia

H Varies according to variety from 45cm (18in) to 1m
(3ft) or more

ZONES 7–9

There are about 30 species of dahlia and
20,000 cultivars grown for exhibition, cutting
or simply admiring in the garden. They are
attractive and resilient, with an example for
almost every situation, as they range in height
from about 45cm (18in) high to 1m (3ft) or
more. They are classified according to flower
form into: anemone; ball; cactus (and semi-
cactus); collerette; decorative; miscellaneous
(including orchid, peony and star); pompon;
single; and waterlily. Flower width varies from
over 25cm (10in) to under 10cm (4in), and
colours range from pure white to deep
maroon-red through yellow, pink, orange and
red. *D.* 'Bishop of Llandaff' is a peony-flow-
ered variety with dark red leaves and red
blooms with bright yellow anthers, reaching
1m (3ft) high. *D. merckii* is a herbaceous
perennial which can reach 1.5m (5ft), with
big, red-tinted leaves and small flowers with
purplish-white outer florets and yellow inner
florets with purple tips. Sow seed of bedding
dahlias in spring; take basal shoot cuttings
from tubers in spring; or divide tubers into
pieces, each with a shoot.

hardiness Fully hardy (border varieties) to
frost tender (bedding varieties)
flowering Summer to autumn
position Full sun
cultivation Loam-based compost (J.I. 2) or
moist, well-drained soil. Water freely all
summer and feed monthly with a balanced
liquid fertilizer. Taller varieties or those with
large flowers may need staking.
overwintering In frost-free areas, leave
tubers in the pots, cut back foliage in late
autumn and apply a mulch. Where frosts
occur, lift the tuber, cut back stems to 15cm
(6in) and dry, then store packed in dry sand
or peat in a frost-free place. Bedding varieties
are treated as annuals and raised from seed.
pests & diseases Earwigs, aphids and red
spider mite, mildew and fungal rots
special features Pinching out some of the
flower buds on border varieties will result in
larger flowers. Pinch out the growing tip of
bedding varieties to make the plant bushy.
decorative ideas Dahlias look best planted
in single-colour groups, two or three to a pot.

CARYOPHYLLACEAE
Dianthus
H 25–45cm (10–18in)

ZONES 3–8

Dianthus or 'pinks' are attractive, evergreen, sun-loving plants which prefer alkaline conditions and grow to form cushion-like mounds of silver-grey foliage. Silver-grey stems carry narrow, spiky, bluish or grey-green leaves. The flowers, which are produced in flushes, are delicately scented and brightly coloured in white and shades of pink to dark red. They may be single, semi-double or double, with up to six blooms per stem, and may have more than one colour on the petals. 'Gran's Favourite' has clove-scented white flowers with mauve edgings and centres; 'Doris' has fragrant, double flowers of pale pink with darker centres; and 'Mrs Sinkins' has fragrant, double, fringed white flowers. Propagation is by division every three years, or layering in late summer.

hardiness Fully hardy
flowering Summer
position Full sun
cultivation Loam-based compost (J.I. 1). Water regularly, but moderately and apply balanced liquid fertilizer every two weeks spring to summer. Deadhead to prevent seed formation and encourage repeat flowering.
overwintering Protect from severe frost and excess moisture.
pests & diseases Slugs and verticillium wilt
special features Wonderfully fragrant as cut flowers.
decorative ideas Combine with scented plants, such as lavender and heliotrope, using the dianthus to surround the larger plants, or grow with sedums and saxifrages in a trough.

Dianthus

Diascia barberae 'Ruby Field'

SCROPHULARIACEAE
Diascia
H 15cm (6in) S 50cm (20in)

ZONES 8–10

These are mostly mat-forming, spreading perennials, with toothed, mid-green leaves and clusters of tubular, yellow-centred, five-lobed flowers. They are useful plants for providing colour throughout the summer, and will tolerate a hot spot where other plants might struggle, as long as they are kept moist. There are many cultivars with flowers in various shades of pink or pale orange. *D. barberae* 'Blackthorn Apricot' has loose clusters of apricot flowers; *D. b.* 'Ruby Field' has salmon pink flowers on short stems; *D. rigescens* is a trailing perennial, with upright, branching stems and dense spikes of dark pink flowers. Propagation is by seed sown in spring, division of suckering types in spring, or semi-ripe cuttings taken in summer.

hardiness Frost hardy
flowering Summer to autumn
position Full sun
cultivation Loamless (for annuals) or loam-based compost (J.I. 1). Water moderately in summer, sparingly in winter.
overwintering Protect from severe frost. Young plants are best overwintered indoors.
pests & diseases Slugs and snails
special features Regular deadheading will ensure a succession of flowers.
decorative ideas Good for a hanging basket or window box, either as a filler or on its own.

FUMARIACEAE/PAPAVERACEAE
Dicentra spectabilis
H 1m (3ft)

ZONES 6–8

This perennial plant is reliable and attractive with or without its unusual flowers. It forms a dense clump of pale to mid-green leaves up to 40cm (16in) long. During late spring and early summer, long arching stems bear racemes of 3–15 heart-shaped flowers, each up to 3cm (1¼in) long, with pink outer petals and white inner ones in the form of a tiny droplet, which is how the common name of 'Bleeding heart' arises. The form *D. s.* 'Alba' has pure white flowers over a long period. Propagate from seed sown in spring, division in spring, or root cuttings in winter.

hardiness Fully hardy
flowering Late spring to mid-summer
position Full sun (in moist conditions) to partial shade
cultivation Loam-based compost (J.I. 2) or a moist soil, preferably neutral to alkaline. Water freely in summer, sparingly in winter, and feed monthly with a balanced liquid fertilizer. Do not allow to dry out.
overwintering Protect new growth from frost in late winter and early spring.
pests & diseases Slugs may damage young shoots.
special features This plant is one of the few reliable flowerers which will grow well in a shady corner.
decorative ideas
Good for a shady corner, surrounded by ferns and ivies.

Dicentra spectabilis

EUPHORBIACEAE
Euphorbia
H up to 1.2m (4ft)

ZONES 3–7

The spurge is a huge genus of perennials, annuals and biennials, evergreen and deciduous. For growing in containers outdoors those with a neat or distinctive habit are best. *E. characias wulfenii* is a large evergreen with glaucous grey-green leaves and huge flowerheads in a sulphurous yellow-green from late spring to early summer, while *E. polychroma* is much smaller (45cm/18in) and neater, with showy bright yellow clusters of flowers that are smaller and flatter than those of *E. characias*. Propagate by division in spring. *E. cyparissias*, the cypress spurge, is also small (up to 40cm/16in) and has feathery bluish-green leaves and yellow-green flowerheads in summer. *E.c.* 'Clarice Howard' has brownish-tinted flowerheads.

hardiness Fully hardy
flowering Mid-spring to mid-summer
position Full sun
cultivation Plant in multi-purpose compost. Give liquid feed in growing season at regular intervals. Water moderately.
overwintering No special treatment needed.
pests & diseases May be prone to aphids and to grey mould.
special features Sap can be a skin irritant. Wear gloves if cutting stems.
decorative ideas Grow as a pair in large terracotta pots either side of a doorway.

Euphorbia cyparissias 'Clarice Howard'

ASTERACEAE/COMPOSITAE

Felicia

H 25–60cm (10in–2ft) according to variety

ZONES 9–10

The daisy-like flowers are generally blue.
F. amelloides is a subshrub of up to 60cm (2ft) tall, usually grown as an annual and has flower shades from pale to deep blue: 'Read's Blue' is mid-blue; 'Read's White' is pure white; 'Santa Anita' is rich blue, and its variegated form has white-marked leaves. *F. amoena* is also treated as an annual, and has bright blue flowers. *F. a.* 'Variegata' has cream-variegated leaves. *F. bergeriana,* the 'Kingfisher daisy', has blue, yellow-centred flowers and is fairly tolerant of exposure so is a good choice for a balcony. Propagate annuals from seed in spring; take tip cuttings of tender varieties in late summer.

hardiness Tender
flowering Summer to autumn
position Full sun
cultivation Loam-based compost (J.I. 2), multi-purpose loamless compost, or well-drained soil. Water freely in summer and feed fortnightly with a balanced liquid fertilizer at half strength.
overwintering Most varieties are treated as annuals, although subshrub types will live for several years if kept in a frost-free place.
pests & diseases None
special features Pinching back young shoots will encourage the plant to bush.
decorative ideas Excellent choice for window boxes and hanging baskets.

Felicia amelloides

ONAGRACEAE

Gaura lindheimeri

H Up to 1m (3ft)

ZONES 4–8

A bushy perennial, sometimes treated as an annual, which grows to form a dense clump. It has long-oval leaves and tall upright stems bearing long, open spikes of short-lived white flowers. These are pink in bud, open early in the morning, and fade to pink, to be replaced the following morning by others. 'Corrie's Gold' has leaves with golden-yellow edges; 'The Bride' has clouds of white flowers; and 'Whirling Butterflies' has grey-green foliage and flowers profusely. Propagate from seed sown in spring, division in spring, or semi-ripe cuttings in summer.

hardiness Fully hardy
flowering Late spring to autumn
position Full sun to partial shade
cultivation Loamless or loam-based compost (J.I. 1). Water moderately in summer and feed monthly with a balanced liquid fertilizer. Cut down the long stems as flowering finishes and mulch the crown in frost-prone areas.
overwintering Protect from severe frost and excess moisture.
pests & diseases None   .
special features A tall, graceful addition to a collection of container plants, which will provide flowers throughout the summer.
decorative ideas Excellent for softening a display, along with gypsophila, with pastel-coloured flowers.

Gaura lindheimeri

Gazania cv.

ASTERACEAE/COMPOSITAE
Gazania
H Up to 25cm (10in)

ZONES 9–10

Gazanias are reliable and make a fantastic splash of colour. Leaves are usually lance-shaped, but vary between forms, and may be covered with soft silver-grey hairs. The flowers, which close in dull weather, are large and daisy-like with darker centres.
G. 'Chansonette' is a seed mix of vigorous, free-flowering, evergreen perennials up to 20cm (8in) tall, with glossy green leaves and flowers in shades of yellow, orange, bronze, red, pink and white, either single or bicolour.
G. 'Talent' is a seed mix, with the same range of flower colours and attractive silvery foliage. Propagate from seed sown in spring, or basal cuttings taken in late summer and overwintered indoors.

hardiness Tender
flowering Summer
position Full sun
cultivation Loam-based compost (J.I. 1) or sandy, well-drained soil. Water freely in summer, very sparingly in winter, and feed fortnightly with a balanced liquid fertilizer at half strength.
overwintering Take cuttings in late summer to overwinter, or keep pots frost-free.
pests & diseases Grey mould while indoors
special features These plants will tolerate coastal conditions.
decorative ideas Can be planted in a row of single pots or in a pair in window boxes.

GERANIACEAE
Geranium
H 15–60cm (6–24in)

ZONES 4–6

Several of the tolerant, herbaceous perennial geraniums are suitable for container-growing, and all are free-flowering with attractive, divided foliage. They produce saucer-shaped flowers during late spring, summer and into autumn, according to variety. G. 'Johnsons Blue' (densely bushy, blue flowers); G. x *magnificum* (deep blue-mauve flowers); G. x *oxonianum* 'Wargrave Pink' (vigorous, bright pink flowers); G. *macrorrhizum* 'Album' (white flowers); G. *cinereum* (dwarf, rosette-forming, with white- or pink-purple-veined flowers), and the form G. c. 'Ballerina' (purple-red flowers with red veins and a darker eye); G. *himalayense* 'Gravetye' (blue flowers with a white centre surrounded by purple-red); G. *sanguineum* (low-growing, magenta flowers); and G. s. 'Album' (pure white). Propagation is by division in spring or basal cuttings in late spring.

hardiness Fully hardy
flowering Spring to autumn
position Full sun to partial shade
cultivation Loam-based compost (J.I. 1). Water moderately in summer and feed monthly with a balanced liquid fertilizer. Remove old flowerheads to encourage further flowering.
overwintering Avoid waterlogging
pests & diseases Slugs, snails and mildew
special features Many varieties have attractive autumn leaf colours.
decorative ideas Use the attractive foliage as a foil to a brightly coloured flowering display.

Geranium x *magnificum*

Gypsophila repens 'Rose'

CARYOPHYLLACEAE
Gypsophila repens
H 45cm (18in)

ZONES 4–8

A mat-forming, creeping perennial with semi-evergreen, blue-green leaves and clusters of five-petalled flowers in white or pink. The flowers are produced over a long period throughout the summer, giving a long season of interest. It is low-growing and naturally prefers slightly alkaline growing conditions, and is ideal for a low trough, where it can spill over the sides. *G. r.* 'Dorothy Teacher' is compact, with pale pink flowers, and 'Rosea' has flowers of a rich, deep pink. Propagation is by taking root cuttings in late winter, or sowing seed of species in spring.

hardiness Fully hardy
flowering Summer
position Full sun
cultivation Loam-based compost (J.I. 1) with added grit and good drainage in the container. Apply only enough water to keep the compost barely moist at all times. Feed twice during the summer with a balanced liquid fertilizer.
overwintering Protect from waterlogging.
pests & diseases Stem rot
special features Mulch around the plant with gravel, as excess moisture can be fatal to the plant.
decorative ideas Use to soften a planting of taller plants, or plant alone in a tall container, such as an urn.

Helenium cv.

ASTERACEAE/COMPOSITAE
Helenium
H 60–100cm (2–3ft)

ZONES 6–10

These are clump-forming perennials with lance-shaped leaves and daisy-like flowers, borne over a long period. They are ideal for hot spots where other plants might struggle, as long as they have enough moisture. The flowers consist of an inner central circle of disc florets in yellow or brown, and an outer ring of ray florets, of bronze, red, orange or yellow. There are many colourful hybrids, including: 'Bruno' (dark red-brown flowers with brown centres); 'Butterpat' (bright yellow flowers); 'Coppelia' (copper-orange flowers with brown centres); 'Moerheim Beauty' (copper-red flowers, brown centres); and 'Wyndley' (yellow petals marked with dark orange, orange-brown centres). Deadhead regularly to encourage repeat flowering. Propagation is by basal cuttings taken in spring, or division in spring or autumn.

hardiness Fully hardy
flowering Summer to autumn
position Full sun
cultivation Loam-based compost (J.I. 2). Water moderately in summer and feed monthly with a balanced liquid fertilizer.
overwintering Mulch the crowns in frost-prone areas. Water sparingly.
pests & diseases None
special features Good as cut flowers.
decorative ideas Big, bold flowers are best planted alone in large terracotta pots.

ASTERACEAE/COMPOSITAE
Helianthus annuus
H Varies with variety

ZONE 10

There are varieties of the annual sunflower in all shapes, sizes and shades of yellow. Choose smaller-growing ones for a small garden or container. They have heart-shaped leaves, hairy stems and flowers with outer ray florets (usually yellow) and inner disc florets (yellow, brown or purple). 'Teddy Bear' is compact to about 90cm (3ft) with fluffy-looking, deep yellow, double flowers up to 13cm (5in) across. 'Music Box' is a branched variety with flowerheads of 10–12cm (4–5in), ray florets of pale yellow to red, including bicolours, and dark brown disc florets. 'Sunspot' has 25cm (10in) yellow flowers on a plant of 60cm (24in). Propagate from seed in spring.

hardiness Frost tender
flowering Summer
position Full sun
cultivation Loam-based compost (J.I. 1), multi-purpose loamless compost, or well-drained neutral to alkaline soil. Water freely all summer and feed monthly with a balanced liquid fertilizer.
overwintering Seed can be saved, but is unlikely to grow true to type.
pests & diseases Slugs, powdery mildew
special features For container growing, choose varieties of 1.5m (5ft) or less so that they can be staked safely if necessary.
decorative ideas The smaller sunflowers make a good feature in large pots.

Helianthus annuus

Helichrysum petiolare

ASTERACEAE/COMPOSITAE
Helichrysum petiolare
H 15cm (6in) S 60cm (2ft)

ZONE 10

A trailing, evergreen shrub, often treated as an annual and discarded at the end of the summer, but able to grow into a long-lasting mound of colour in warmer areas, especially if the shoots are regularly tipped when it is young to encourage bushiness rather than length initially. It has branching stems and woolly, heart-shaped leaves, and although it is grown mainly for its pretty foliage, it does produce small, whitish flowers in late summer. *H. p.* 'Limelight' has bright, lime green foliage; 'Variegatum' has grey-green leaves, variegated with cream; 'Roundabout' is a sort

of 'Variegatum' and is similarly marked, but in miniature. Propagate by taking semi-ripe or heel cuttings in summer.

hardiness Frost tender
flowering Late summer
position Full sun
cultivation Loamless (for annuals) or loam-based compost (J.I. 1). Water moderately in summer, sparingly in winter. Feed monthly with a balanced liquid fertilizer. Prefers some shelter and tolerates slightly dry conditions.
overwintering Protect from frost. Over-winter young plants indoors.
pests & diseases Mildew
special features Ideal for hanging baskets.
decorative ideas Ideal foil for flowering plants in a hanging basket. Silver-grey leaves look good with blue, mauve and pink flowers.

BORAGINACEAE
Heliotropium
H 30–60cm (12–24in)

ZONES 9–10

The heliotrope is a short-lived shrub, usually treated as an annual in frost-prone areas, which will overwinter in a warm climate. It is also called 'cherry pie' because of the fragrance of its purplish-blue flowers. These are tiny and tubular, borne in large, dense, usually rounded clusters. They are complemented by the rough, deeply veined leaves, which are dark green, often tinted purple. They are ideal plants for containers, and the many forms include: 'Chatsworth' (deep purple, strongly scented); 'Lord Roberts' (compact, light violet); 'Marine' (compact, violet-blue); and

'White Lady' (compact, white flowers, pink in bud). Propagation is by seed sown in spring, or tip cuttings taken in summer and overwintered in a frost-free place.

hardiness Frost tender
flowering Summer
position Full sun
cultivation Loamless (for annuals) or loam-based compost (J.I. 1). Water moderately in summer and feed monthly with a balanced liquid fertilizer.
overwintering Protect from frost and water sparingly.
pests & diseases Whitefly
special features The flowers are highly attractive to butterflies.
decorative ideas Plant with other scented summer-flowering plants, such as lavender.

Heliotropium cv.

SAXIFRAGACEAE
Heuchera
H Up to 60cm (2ft)

ZONES 4–8

This is a clump-forming, semi-evergreen perennial (evergreen in milder climates), grown as much for its foliage as its flowers. As it grows, it forms a mound of attractive, heart-shaped, deeply veined leaves of green, bronze or purple, much prized by flower arrangers. The flowers are tiny and tubular, sometimes petalless, borne in loose clusters on tall upright stems above the foliage. There are many attractive hybrids which will grow well in containers, including: 'Firebird' (scarlet flowers); 'Green Ivory' (mid-green foliage, greenish flowers); 'Red Spangles' (green

foliage, larger crimson flowers); and *H. micrantha* var. *diversifolia* 'Palace Purple' (metallic bronze foliage, cream flowers with red anthers). Propagation of hybrids is by division in autumn.

hardiness Fully hardy
flowering Summer
position Full sun to partial shade
cultivation Loam-based compost (J.I. 2). Water moderately in summer and feed monthly with a balanced liquid fertilizer.
overwintering Protect the crown from severe frost and water sparingly.
pests & diseases Leaf eelworms and vine weevil
special features The flowers attract bees.
decorative ideas The bronze-purple 'Palace Purple' looks good alone in a tall container.

Heuchera micrantha var. *diversifolia* 'Palace Purple'

HOSTACEAE/LILIACEAE
Hosta
H Up to 1m (3ft)

ZONES 4–8

A long-lived, hardy perennial which forms a clump of attractive long, rounded or heart-shaped leaves in a range of colours from dark green to golden or bluish, often with splashes or stripes of white, cream or yellow. Tall, upright stems carry trumpet-shaped, pendulous flowers in white or mauve, sometimes with a delicate fragrance. There are many forms, including: *H. fortunei* var. *albopicta* (thin, creamy-gold leaves with dark green edges); *H. f.* var. *aureomarginata* (olive green leaves with yellow edges); *H. sieboldiana* var. *elegans* (thick, ribbed, blue-green leaves). The slightly smaller variety *H.* 'Frances Williams' has thick, puckered, blue-green leaves with a lighter, yellow-green edge, and grey-white flowers. Propagation is by division in early spring,but replant immediately.

hardiness Fully hardy
flowering Summer
position Partial shade, especially from mid-day sun
cultivation Loam-based compost (J.I. 2). Water freely in summer and feed monthly with a balanced liquid fertilizer.
overwintering Protect from severe frost and water moderately.
pests & diseases Slugs and snails
special features Golden-leaved forms need some sun to maintain their colour.
decorative ideas Plant two or three different forms in a group in a shady corner.

Hosta fortunei var. *albopicta*

Impatiens cv.

BALSAMINACEAE
Impatiens
H Up to 35cm (14in)

ZONE 10

A busy lizzie will flower throughout the summer, preferring shelter, partial shade and moist conditions. It produces spurred, five-petalled blooms, and fleshy foliage. Propagation is by seed sown in spring or tip cuttings rooted in water or compost in spring or summer. *I. balsamina* is tall bearing purple, red, pink or white flowers. The Camellia-flowered Group have large, double flowers; the Tom Thumb Group are dwarf with large, double flowers. *I.* New Guinea hybrids are perennial, and almost shrubby in habit. Leaves may be green, green with yellow, or bronze-red and flowers are generally single. *I. walleriana* is the traditional form; 'Starbright' (coloured petals marked with a white star); Super Elfin Series (compact plants with a wide range of colours).

hardiness Frost tender
flowering Summer to autumn
position Full sun to partial shade
cultivation Loamless (for annuals) or loam-based compost (J.I. 1). Water freely in summer and feed every two weeks with a standard liquid fertilizer. Deadhead regularly.
overwintering Protect from frost and water moderately.
pests & diseases Aphids and grey mould
special features One of the best groups of plants for colour in containers.
decorative ideas An excellent shade plant. Use a bigger 'New Guinea' hybrid as a feature.

ASTERACEAE/COMPOSITAE
Inula
H 60cm–1.8m (2–6ft)

ZONES 5–9

This genus comprises a range of daisy-like perennials. Some, such as *I. ensifolia* are low-growing and shrubby, others, such as *I. magnifica* are handsome clump-forming plants. *I. magnifica* has long, oval dark green leaves and bears corymbs of large bright yellow daisy-like flowers in late summer. *I. ensifolia* spreads by rhizomes. It can be invasive if it is not confined within a container or kept under control. Its erect, slender stems bear lance-shaped, mid-green leaves up to 9cm (3½in) long with fine-haired edges. Masses of flat, daisy-like, golden flowers are produced singly

or in small clusters in mid- to late summer. *I. e.* 'Gold Star' is smaller, reaching only 30cm (12in) high, with flowers of a deep golden-yellow. Propagate by division in spring.

hardiness Fully hardy
flowering Mid- to late summer
position Full sun
cultivation Loam-based compost (J.I. 2) or any moist, well-drained soil. Water freely in summer, sparingly in winter, and feed monthly with a balanced liquid fertilizer.
overwintering Do not allow to become waterlogged.
pests & diseases Mildew
special features Divide in spring or autumn if it is outgrowing its situation.
decorative ideas Plant in a large terracotta pot with other golden flowers.

Inula magnifica

ASTERACEAE/COMPOSITAE
Leucanthemum
H 45–90cm (18–36in)

ZONES 5–9

The Shasta daisy is an attractive and tolerant clump-forming perennial with strap-like, dark green leaves with deeply toothed edges. Throughout the summer, it produces solitary, daisy-like flowers on tall, green stems, which are good for cutting. These may be single or double, and are white with golden- or pale yellow disc florets in the centre. There are many hybrids, including: 'Aglaia' (fringed, semi-double); 'Esther Read' (double, pure white); 'Snowcap' (compact, single white); and 'Wirral Supreme' (double, short ray florets). Propagation is by division in

spring or late summer, or basal softwood cuttings taken in spring.

hardiness Fully hardy
flowering Summer to autumn
position Full sun to partial shade
cultivation Loam-based compost (J.I. 2) with some added grit or sharp sand. Water moderately in summer and feed monthly with a balanced liquid fertilizer.
overwintering Protect the crown from excess moisture and severe frost. Water sparingly.
pests & diseases Aphids, slugs, earwigs and leaf spot
special features Some of the taller varieties will need support for the flowers.
decorative ideas Create a white and yellow display with argyranthemums and gazanias.

Leucanthemum cv

PORTULACACEAE
Lewisia
H Up to 30cm (12in)

ZONES 8–10

This evergreen perennial plant is grown for its colourful, funnel-shaped flowers. It grows as a broad, flat rosette of thick, fleshy, dark green leaves with toothed margins, spreading slowly to form a clump. The Cotyledon Hybrids produce flowers in late spring or early summer, in white and bright shades of purple, magenta, pink, orange and yellow, on slender green stems up to 30cm (1ft) high. These tolerant plants are ideal for growing in a container as long as the compost is very free-draining and a mulch of grit is laid over the surface.

Propagation is by seed sown in the autumn or by division of rosettes after flowering.

hardiness Half hardy
flowering Early summer
position Full sun to partial shade
cultivation Loam-based compost (J.I. 1) with added sharp sand. Water moderately in summer and feed monthly with a balanced liquid fertilizer.
overwintering Protect from excess moisture and severe frost.
pests & diseases Slugs, snails and rotting
special features These plants must have a free-draining soil or they will rot.
decorative ideas Use with other small sun lovers, such as sedums and sempervivens, in a dry corner.

Lewisia Cotyledon Hybrid

Ligularia dentata

ASLERACEAE/COMPOSITAE

Ligularia dentata 'Desdemona'

H 1.2m (4ft)

ZONES 4–8

A perennial member of the daisy family which prefers a moist, but sunny position. It will slowly form a clump of heart-shaped, purple-green leaves with toothed edges and a maroon-red underside. These contrast with the big, orange, daisy-like flowers which appear in summer, carried on 1m (3ft) tall orange-brown stems. It makes a bold splash of colour, and would blend well amongst green-leaved plants, whether deciduous or evergreen. Intense midday sun and cold, drying winds can cause scorch on the leaves, so some protection may be necessary to

overcome this. Propagation is by division in spring or autumn, or seed sown in spring.

hardiness Fully hardy
flowering Mid-summer to autumn
position Full sun
cultivation Loam-based compost (J.I. 2) or any soil, but must be moist at all times. Water very freely in summer, sparingly in winter, and feed monthly with a balanced liquid fertilizer.
overwintering Protect crowns from frost.
pests & diseases Young shoots are often damaged by slugs.
special features Seedlings may come true to type, despite being a hybrid, especially if the parent was seed-raised.
decorative ideas Surround with purple heliotrope and orange tagetes for colour.

Lobelia 'Minstrel'

CAMPANULACEAE/LOBELIACEAE

Lobelia

S 20–30cm (8–12in)

ZONE 10

This is the popular lobelia used in bedding schemes and baskets everywhere. It is a bushy perennial, usually grown as an annual and discarded at the end of the season, but it will overwinter if placed in a warm place. The small leaves are long-oval, toothed and mid-green or bronze. The lobelia flowers are two-lipped and borne in small clusters, in shades of purple, blue, red, pink or white. The darker colours often have a white eye. Cultivars which trail include the Cascade Series, Regatta Series, 'Lilac Fountain' (lilac-pink flowers), and 'Sapphire' (white-eyed,

bright blue flowers). Propagation is by seed sown in late winter.

hardiness Frost tender
flowering Summer to autumn
position Full sun to partial shade
cultivation Loamless or loam-based compost (J.I. 1). Water freely in summer, sparingly if overwintering. Feed every two weeks in spring with a balanced liquid fertilizer, in summer with high-potash fertilizer (tomato food).
overwintering Keep in a frost-free place.
pests & diseases Slugs
special features Regular watering and feeding will ensure masses of flowers all summer long.
decorative ideas Use for window boxes or hanging baskets. Combine with orange pansies or tagetes, or pink cosmos and petunias.

Nemesia strumosa

SCROPHULARIACEAE

Nemesia strumosa

H Up to 30cm (12in)

ZONE 10

A group of colourful annuals raised from seed or cuttings each year. They form bushy plants which branch from low down, with lance-shaped, mid-green leaves, sometimes toothed and slightly hairy. The flowers are produced during mid- and late summer, and are two-lipped, in purple, blue, pink, red, yellow or white – either single colour or a combination of two. They have a yellow throat, and may show outer purple veins. *N. s.* 'KLM' has bi-coloured flowers in blue and white with a yellow throat; the Carnival Series are dwarf with pink, orange, yellow, bronze and white

flowers; 'Danish Flag' is a striking bicolour of red and white. Sow seed in autumn for spring flowering, or in spring for summer.

hardiness Frost tender
flowering Mid- to late summer
position Full sun
cultivation Loam-based compost (J.I. 1), multi-purpose loamless compost, or well-drained soil, preferably neutral to acid. Water freely in summer and feed monthly with a balanced liquid fertilizer.
overwintering Will not usually survive.
pests & diseases Susceptible to fungal attack in very moist conditions.
special features The flowers are good for cutting, for use indoors.
decorative ideas
Plant in wall pots or as a table-top display.

LABIATAE/LAMIACEAE

Nepeta

H 45–90cm (18–36in)

ZONES 3–8

Catmint is a clump-forming perennial with long-oval leaves which may have a silvery appearance due to a covering of fine hairs. Two-lipped flowers are produced in loose spikes in summer, in purple, blue or white. *N. x faasseni* has scalloped, aromatic, silvery leaves and lavender blue flowers. *N. sibirica* is taller, with larger deep purple-blue flowers. The hybrid 'Six Hills Giant' has grey-green leaves and lavender-blue flowers. *N. nervosa* is small with blue spiky flowers and leaves with a dark purple cross-shaped band. Trim during the season to encourage repeat flowering and keep plants neat. Propagation is by seed in autumn or soft-tip cuttings in summer.

hardiness Fully hardy
flowering Early summer to autumn
position Full sun to partial shade
cultivation Loam-based compost (J.I. 2). Water moderately in summer and feed monthly with a balanced liquid fertilizer. Taller varieties will need staking to support the stems as they grow.
overwintering Protect the crown from severe frost and waterlogging, water sparingly.
Pests & diseases Slugs and mildew
special features Cats and bees are both attracted to these plants.
decorative ideas Makes an attractive base level planting for standards, such as roses and fuschia, or in pots with purple lavender.

Nepeta nervosa

SOLANACEAE

Nicotiana

H Up to 1.5m (5ft)

ZONES 8–10

This ornamental relative of the tobacco plant grows as an annual, a biennial or a short-lived perennial, according to conditions. The two most commonly grown are *N. alata* and *N. sylvestris*. Generally, the warmer the situation, the longer it will live. The wrinkled, blue-grey leaves can reach 30cm (12in). The flowering stems can reach 1.5m (5ft) tall in *N. sylvestris* and have dense clusters of white, green, pink or mauve scented flowers during the summer. The individual flowers have a tube up to 9cm (3½in) long, flaring out into a trumpet shape with five lobes. They tend to open during the evening and close in bright sunlight. Propagation is by seed in spring.

hardiness Half hardy
flowering Summer
position Full sun to partial shade
cultivation Grow in loam-based compost (J.I. 1), multi-purpose loamless compost, or moist, well-drained soil. Water freely in summer, sparingly in winter, and feed monthly with a balanced liquid fertilizer.
overwintering Move indoors if the temperature drops below freezing.
pests & diseases Aphids, whitefly and grey mould.
special features Contact with the foliage may irritate the skin.
decorative ideas Plant near windows so scent drifts in at night.

Nicotiana alata

OXALIDACEAE

Oxalis

H 8–10cm (3–4in)

ZONES 5-9

The shamrock is a tolerant perennial which produces palmate leaves of green or bronze, sometimes with a darker centre. The flowers are furled like a rolled umbrella when in bud, opening into a cup or bowl shape. *O. adenophylla* grows from a bulb, producing greyish-green leaves with up to 22 leaflets, and purple-pink flowers with darker veins and throats, and whitish centres. *O. enneaphylla* is clump-forming, with blue-grey leaves divided into up to 20 leaflets and deep pink funnel-shaped, fragrant flowers; *O. e.* 'Minutifolia' has smaller leaflets, on more compact plants, and white flowers; and *O. e.* 'Rosea' has lighter pink flowers. *O. tetraphylla* 'Iron Cross' has reddish-purple flowers and leaves with a dark purple cross-shaped band. Propagate by sowing seed in early spring, or division in spring.

hardiness Fully hardy
flowering Spring to early summer
position Full sun
cultivation Loam-based compost (J.I. 2). Water moderately in summer and feed monthly with a balanced liquid fertilizer.
overwintering Protect from severe frost and waterlogging.
pests & diseases Slugs and snails
special features Flowers open in sunlight and close at night and in dull conditions.
decorative ideas Plant in a group with diascia and pink cosmos.

Oxalis tetraphylla 'Iron Cross'

Pelargonium

This wide-ranging genus includes species and hybrids. They are frost tender and are grown in cold climates as annuals, flowering from mid-summer to early autumn. Species pelargoniums are smaller-flowered, some with scented leaves; hybrids tend to be larger-flowered and are divided into three main groups: ivy-leaved, zonals and regals. Zonals have interesting leaves and a range of flower types, such as rosebuds and stellars; regals make bushier plants with attractive flowers.

Pelargonium peltatum

Pelargonium 'L'Elegante'

H 1.2m (4ft)

ZONES 9–10

This trailing ivy-leaved pelargonium has thick fleshy leaves with cream edges (that become pink flushed if the plant is dry) and small white flowers in summer. Makes a good hanging basket plant.

Pelargonium 'Frank Headley'

H 60cm (2ft)

ZONES 9–10

This attractive zonal has coral pink flowers and variegated leaves splashed with cream.

Pelargonium graveolens

H 90cm (3ft)

ZONES 9–10

Species pelargonium known as the rose gernaium, or sweet-scented geranium, grown mainly for its highly aromatic, slightly hairy green leaves. Small mauve flowers in clusters.

Pelargonium 'Mme Fournier'

H 15cm (6in)

ZONES 9–10

Miniature single-flowered zonal with dark leaves and scarlet flowers borne in clusters.

Pelargonium peltatum

H Up to 2m (6ft)

ZONES 9–10

Trailing species pelargonium with clusters of bright salmon-pink flowers and rounded leaves. It can be trained to climb up a pillar or trellis.

Pelargonium 'Rouletta'

H 60cm (2ft)

ZONES 9–10

Vigorous ivy-leaved trailing pelargonium, with fleshy green leaves. It has strikingly striped crimson and white semi-double flowers. It makes an excellent subject for hanging baskets.

Pelargonium tomentosum

H 90cm (3ft)

ZONES 9–10

Vigorous bushy pelargonium, with peppermint-scented mid-green leaves and small white flowers from late spring to early summer

hardiness Frost tender
flowering Summer
position Full sun to partial shade
cultivation Loamless or loam-based compost (J.I.1). Water freely in summer and feed every two weeks with a balanced liquid fertilizer in spring, then high-potash fertilizer (tomato food) in summer.
overwintering Keep frost-free and water sparingly.
pests and diseases Aphids and vine weevil.
special needs Needs protection from frost and a sunny wall. Deadhead regularly. Support trailers on wires or trellis or grow them in hanging baskets.
decorative ideas Create a pelargonium-clad wall by training vigorous trailing pelargoniums upwards over wires.

Pelargonium 'Frank Headley'

Pelargonium 'Mme Fournier'

SOLANACEAE
Petunia
H 15cm (6in) S 90cm (3ft)

ZONES 9–10

Wonderfully reliable flowering plants which produce a colourful display throughout the summer. They have long-oval, grey- or mid-green leaves and showy, wide trumpet-shaped flowers from late spring to autumn. Most of the trailing cultivars have been raised as seed series, including the prolific Surfinia Series, which are large-flowered, with a vigorous, branching habit and flowers in shades of blue-purple, red, magenta, pink and white; and Supercascade Mixed, which flower early in shades of blue, red, pink, salmon and white. Both are quite tolerant of damp weather, and need deadheading regularly to ensure a succession of flowers. Propagate from seed in autumn or spring, or tip cuttings in summer.

hardiness Frost tender
flowering Late spring to autumn
position Full sun with shelter from cold winds
cultivation Loamless or loam-based compost (J.I. 1). Water freely in summer, sparingly if overwintering. Feed every two weeks with a high-potash fertilizer (tomato food) whilst in growth.
overwintering Keep frost-free.
pests & diseases Aphids, slugs and virus
special features Contact with the foliage may cause skin irritation.
decorative ideas Trailing petunias are hanging basket plants, *par excellence*, creating exciting displays when matched with lobelia and helichrysum. Alternatively, plant single colour petunias in matching wall pots.

Petunia cv.

Phlox 'Chattahoochee'

POLEMONIACEAE
Phlox
H Up to 1.2m (4ft)

ZONES 6–9

This genus comprises more than 60 species of evergreen or herbaceous perennials and annuals, some low-growing and mat-forming, others stately perennials. The flowers, which come in a range of colours, have five petals and the leaves are simple, oval and often in opposite pairs. P. 'Chattahoochee' is a low-growing semi-evergreen with purple-tinted stems and lavender blue flowers with reddish-purple eyes. They flower from mid-summer to early autumn. The annual phlox, *P. drummondii*, has many cultivars in a range of colours, varying from tiny to medium sized (45cm/18in). *P. paniculata*, a perennial, is one of the tallest, growing to 1.2m (4ft) tall. Large panicles of flowers in white, lilac or purple are borne from summer to autumn.

hardiness Fully hardy to half hardy
position Full sun or partial shade
cultivation Grow perennial phlox in J.I. 2 compost. Water moderately in growing season, more sparingly in winter. Cut back in autumn.
overwintering No special needs
pests & diseases Susceptible to mildews and leaf spot.
special features Stake tall perennials, such as *P. paniculata*.
decorative ideas Line up repeating pots of small annuals. Use larger perennials as a feature plant.

Primula 'Wanda Supreme' (Polyanthus hybrid)

PRIMULACEAE
Primula
H 20cm (8in)

ZONES 3–6

A large genus of mostly perennial plants, including auricula, primrose and polyanthus. All have a basal rosette of rough leaves and wide-flaring, funnel-shaped flowers. They are grouped according to botanical characteristics: *P. auricula* (auricula) has flowers in a cluster (umbel) on a stout stem above the foliage; *P. vulgaris* (primrose) bears solitary flowers on short, slender stems amid the foliage; Polyanthus hybrids (from *P. elatior*, *P. juliae*, *P. veris* and *P. vulgaris*) bear primrose-shaped flowers, but in umbels above the foliage. Years of inter-breeding mean that some

characteristics may cross from one species to another. Many colours have been bred, particularly with polyanthus, which are extremely popular for containers due to their reliability. Shades of maroon, red, orange, yellow, pink, white and blue are common, often with a yellow eye. Propagate by sowing seed in spring, or division in autumn. *P. auricula* produces fragrant, deep yellow flowers. Other forms have red or purple flowers with a yellow centre, such as *P. a.* 'Mark' (wine red and yellow), and *P. a.* 'Adrian' (purple-blue and pale yellow). *P. vulgaris* produces pale yellow flowers. Forms include: *P. v.* subsp. *sibthorpii* which has purple, lilac, red, rose or white flowers. Polyanthus hybrids include several seed mixtures: Crescendo Series (yellow-eyed flowers); and Gold Laced Group (dark

mahogany-red flowers with golden-yellow eye and petal edge).

hardiness Fully hardy to frost tender
flowering Early to mid-spring
position Full sun to partial shade
cultivation Loam-based compost (J.I. 1). Water freely during the spring, moderately in summer, autumn and winter. Feed every two weeks in spring with a balanced liquid fertilizer at half strength. Repot every 2–3 years.
overwintering Protect during periods of severe frost.
pests & diseases Slugs, red spider mite and grey mould
special features Plants are quite fragrant, and many varieties are grown for showing.
decorative ideas Plant rows of single pots with auricula primulas or display on shelves.

RANUNCULACEAE
Pulsatilla
H 20–30cm (8–12in)

ZONES 4–8

Clump-forming, deciduous perennials with ferny leaves covered with silky hairs. The flowers are saucer- or bell-shaped in purple or white with yellow centres. Pulsatillas are related to clematis, and they bear spherical seedheads, with feather-like styles. *P. alpina* (30cm/12in) has hairy mid-green leaves and white flowers with a blue tint, and the sub-species *P. a. apiifolia* is unusual in that it has pale yellow flowers; *P. halleri* has large, silver-hairy, bell-shaped violet to lavender flowers; *P. vernalis* has white flowers with a violet flush; and the purple-flowered *P. vulgaris* has

given rise to forms which range from white (*P. v.* alba) to deep red (*P. a.* 'Rode Klokke'). Propagate by sowing the seed as soon as it is ripe or taking root cuttings in winter.

hardiness Fully hardy
flowering Spring to early summer
position Full sun
cultivation Loam-based compost (J.I. 1) with added grit or well-drained soil. Water freely in summer, sparingly in winter, and feed monthly with a balanced liquid fertilizer.
overwintering Do not allow to become waterlogged.
pests & diseases Slugs and snails
special features Pulsatillas do not like root disturbance, so only repot when necessary.
decorative ideas Display on a small table near a window to appreciate the flowers.

Pulsatilla vulgaris 'Gotlandica'

SAXIFRAGACEAE
Saxifraga
H Up to 15cm (6in)

ZONES 2–8

A diverse genus, with many low-growing species for containers. The 'alpine' types are ideal for well-drained troughs, and are ever-green perennials, often mossy-looking. They produce cup-shaped pink, yellow or white flowers in spring and early summer. They include *S. x apiculata* (cushion-forming, with yellow flowers); 'Cloth of Gold' (cushion-forming, with rosettes of golden foliage and cream flowers); 'Jenkinsiae' (mound-forming with lime-encrusted foliage and pale pink flowers); and 'Tumbling Waters' (rosettes of silver-green foliage, long, arching spike of

white flowers). *S. x urbium* (London Pride) has spires of pink-flushed white flowers in early summer. Propagate by division, or removal of offsets, in spring.

hardiness Fully hardy
flowering Spring
position Full sun to partial shade
cultivation Loam-based compost (J.I. 1) with added grit. Water moderately in summer, feed monthly with balanced liquid fertilizer.
overwintering They cannot tolerate wet, so keep well-drained
pests & diseases Slugs and vine weevils
special features Rosette types: the rosette which produces the flower dies off, so remove offsets regularly and pot separately.
decorative ideas Grow saxifrages with other mat-forming plants in an old clay tile.

Saxifraga x urbium

GOODENIACEAE
Scaevola
H up to 3m (10ft) s 1.5m (5ft)

ZONE 10

This is a short-lived, slightly shrubby ever-green perennial commonly known as the 'fairy fan flower'. It is usually grown as an annual and discarded at the end of the season, but will overwinter if given protection from frost and cold, drying winds. It has slightly hairy, scrambling stems, rounded leaves and fan-shaped purple or blue flowers. 'Blue Wonder' has vigorous, trailing stems and a profusion of lilac-blue flowers all summer. 'Mauve Clusters' also has a trailing habit, and lilac-mauve flowers during summer and early autumn. Propagate from soft-tip

cuttings taken in late spring or early summer, or seed sown in spring.

hardiness Frost tender
flowering Summer
position Full sun or partial shade
cultivation Loamless or loam-based compost (J.I. 1). Water freely in summer, and feed monthly with a balanced liquid fertilizer.
overwintering Keep in a frost-free place and water sparingly.
pests & diseases None
special features This is an ideal plant for a raised container or hanging basket where the long stems can cascade down.
decorative ideas Useful for hanging baskets with other blue/mauve flowers, such as pansies and petunias, and small-leaved foliage, such as helichrysum.

Scaevola 'Mauve Clusters'

Sedum acre var. 'Aureum'

GRASSULACEAE

Sedum

H Up to 1m (36in)

ZONES 4–8

Most of the plants in the *Sedum* genus are tolerant of slightly dry conditions and are ideal for growing in containers. One of the most attractive and reliable is *S. spectabile,* which is a clump-forming deciduous herbaceous perennial with thick, fleshy, broadly oval leaves on thick, upright stems. Throughout late summer and early autumn it produces broad, flat clusters of star-shaped pink- or mauve-tinted flowers with prominent stamens, up to 15cm (6in) across. *S. s.* 'Brilliant' is an outstanding hybrid with large pink flowerheads, and 'Iceberg' has pale green leaves and pure white flowers. *Sedum acre* 'Aureum' is mat-forming with golden leaves. Propagation is by division in spring.

hardiness Fully hardy
flowering Summer to autumn
position Full sun
cultivation Loam-based compost (J.I. 2). Water moderately and feed monthly with a balanced liquid fertilizer. Prune off the dead flowerheads in spring.
overwintering Do not allow to become waterlogged, as they cannot tolerate excessive moisture.
pests & diseases Slugs
special features *S. spectabile* is highly attractive to butterflies and bees.
decorative ideas Plant several forms in small pots for a table-top display.

GRASSULACEAE

Sempervivum

H 5–10cm (2–4in)

ZONES 4–8

Hardy, evergreen, spreading perennials which grow to form rosettes of narrowly oval, succulent leaves with pointed tips, sometimes tinted reddish-purple or covered with fine white webbing. Each rosette eventually produces a flat head of star-shaped flowers, of yellow, white, red or purple, and then dies off. *S. arachnoideum* (cobweb houseleek) has small rosettes of green leaves, flushed red, with their tips woven together by fine white hairs, giving a cobweb appearance, and bright rose-red flowers. *S. giuseppii* has bright green leaves with red tips, and red flowers. *S. tectorum* has open rosettes of blue-green to red-purple leaves and reddish flowers. Propagation is by division of offsets in spring.

hardiness Fully hardy
flowering Summer
position Full sun
cultivation Loam-based compost (J.I. 2) with added grit to ensure good drainage. Water sparingly in summer, as they cannot tolerate excess moisture. No extra feeding is required.
overwintering Protect from waterlogging and severe frost.
pests & diseases Birds may uproot newly-planted rosettes. Rust.
special features Ideal for low containers, troughs, or even a crevice in a wall.
decorative ideas Combine the different forms, each in its own shallow dish, on a table top. Alternatively, display one large shallow container on a plinth or pedestal, or mark each step with a single pot.

Mixed *sempervivums*

Tagetes patula

ASTERACEAE/COMPOSITAE

Tagetes

H Up to 60cm (2ft)

ZONES 9–10

Most marigolds grown for their flowers of hot yellow, gold, orange and mahogany-red are half-hardy annuals which set seed as the flowers fade. Single and double varieties are available, the singles being daisy-like, sometimes with a darker eye or coloured splash on the petals. *T. erecta* (African marigold) is tall, with spherical, double flowers in yellow and orange: seed mixes include Marvel (compact, all colours); and 'Vanilla' (large cream flowers). *T. patula* (French marigold) is shorter and bushy, with smaller flowers: seed mixes include: 'Mischief' (single, all colours); and

'Juliette' (golden-yellow, flecked flame red). Propagate by sowing seed in spring.

hardiness Frost tender
flowering Summer to autumn
position Full sun
cultivation Loamless or loam-based compost (J.I. 1). Water freely in summer and feed every two weeks with a balanced liquid fertilizer at half strength. Deadhead regularly unless saving seed in late summer.
overwintering May continue flowering in mild areas if fed and deadheaded. Water moderately and keep sheltered.
pests & diseases Grey mould
special features F1 seed mixes give consistent results, but saved seed will not be as good.
decorative ideas Combine with blue-purple flowers in a window box.

TROPAEOLACEAE

Tropaeolum majus

H 15cm (6in) S 1.5m (5ft)

ZONES 9–10

The nasturtium is a climbing or trailing hardy annual with rounded, light green leaves and long-spurred, broadly trumpet-shaped flowers about 5cm (2in) across throughout summer and autumn, in shades of yellow, orange and red. The leaves may be marked with white splashes. There are many seed mixes available, some of which are more bushy than trailing, and suitable where there is less space. Seed mixes include: 'Trailing Mixed', 'Out of Africa' (white-marbled leaves), and 'Gleam Mixed' (less vigorous, to 38cm/15in). Propagation is by seed sown in spring (indoors, or outdoors once the risk of frost has passed).

hardiness Frost tender to hardy
flowering Early summer to autumn
position Annuals, full sun; perennials, full sun to partial shade
cultivation Loamless or loam-based compost (J.I. 1) for annuals, loam-based (J.I. 2) for perennials. Water moderately in summer, very sparingly in winter (perennials). Feed monthly with a balanced liquid fertilizer (all).
overwintering Protect perennials from excess moisture.
pests & diseases Caterpillars, blackfly
special features The flowers of *T. majus* are edible, looking wonderful in a salad.
decorative ideas Nasturtiums can be employed either to provide a screen, by training up wires, or equally to cascade from a high-level hanging basket, or over the edges of a tall container.

Tropaeolum majus

Verbascum chaixii

SCROPHULARIACEA
Verbascum chaixii
H 1m (3ft)

ZONES 5–9

The Nettle-leaved mullein is a perennial which forms a low rosette of oval, mid-green leaves with greyish hairs. They can grow to reach 25cm (10in) and are semi-evergreen, so the plant retains some colour during the winter. Upright, white woolly stems bear open, saucer-shaped flowers. These are 2.5cm (1in) wide and pale yellow with violet centres in panicles up to 40cm (16in) long. The individual flowers are short-lived, but appear in a succession from mid- to late summer, giving a long period of interest. *V.c.* 'Album' has similar growth, but bears attractive white flowers with mauve centres. Sow seed or divide in spring, take root cuttings in winter.

hardiness Fully hardy
flowering Mid- to late summer
position Full sun
cultivation Grow in loam-based compost (J.I. 2) with added grit, or poor, preferably alkaline, well-drained soil. Water freely in summer, sparingly in winter, and feed monthly with a balanced liquid fertilizer.
overwintering Do not allow to become waterlogged.
pests & diseases Mildew
special features This plant will grow in a hot, dry corner where other plants might struggle.
decorative ideas Combine with similar plants, such as phlox and taller campanulas.

Verbena bonariensis

VERBENACEAE
Verbena
H 25cm (10in)

ZONES 9–10

The trailing verbenas are cultivars of *V. x hybrida* and usually grown as annuals, although they will overwinter in milder areas or a frost-free greenhouse to form spreading, shrubby perennials. They have a branching habit and coarse, toothed leaves. The tiny flowers are produced in rounded clusters, opening from the outside inwards over a long period, in shades of white, pink, red or purple. The darker colours often have a white eye, and some varieties are fragrant. 'Romance Lavender' produces lilac flowers; 'Romance Pastels Mixed' has flowers of red, magenta, apricot, purple and pink; 'Imagination' is wide-spreading, with flowers of deep violet-blue. Verbenas include perennials and annuals. *Verbena bonariensis* is a tall perennial (1.2/4ft) with mauve flowers, attractive to bees, which looks good in large containers. Propagation is by seed in autumn or spring.

hardiness Frost tender
flowering Summer to autumn
position Full sun
cultivation Loamless or loam-based compost (J.I. 1). Water freely in summer and feed monthly with a balanced liquid fertilizer.
overwintering Protect annuals from frost and water sparingly.
pests & diseases Aphids and mildew
special features Will flower profusely and continuously throughout the summer and until the first frosts of autumn.
decorative ideas Annuals make good window box plant, or as the central feature in a hanging basket.

VIOLACEAE
Viola

s 20–30cm (8–12in)

ZONES 4–9

This is a large genus, which contains several evergreen or semi-evergreen perennials as well as the cultivars referred to as garden pansies. Of the perennials, *V. labradorica* makes an attractive plant for a small container, with dark leaves and light muave flowers. Pansies are reliable, hardy plants which will provide colour throughout the year as long as they have shelter from cold, drying winds. They have heart-shaped, mid-green leaves and two-lipped flowers in white and shades of purple, blue, bronze, maroon, pink, orange and yellow. The flowers may have a darker-coloured eye, colour splashes or petals of different colours. There are many seed mixes available, including: 'Contessa' (wavy-edged petals, dark-eyed flowers); and 'Orchi' (full, ruffled petals of pale violet with a darker centre and yellow eye). Sow seed any time except mid-summer.

hardiness Fully hardy
flowering All year round
position Full sun to partial shade
cultivation Loamless or loam-based compost (J.I. 1). Water moderately at all times and feed monthly with a balanced liquid fertilizer. **overwintering** Protect from severe frost, cold winds and excess moisture.
pests & diseases Slugs, snails and mildew
special features Deadhead regularly to prevent seed being set, and ensure a succession of flowers.
decorative ideas Use for window boxes or hanging baskets, or plant single pots of matching colours to line up along a shelf or ledge.

Viola labradorica cv.

Zinnia cv.

ASTERACEAE/COMPOSITAE
Zinnia
H 25–60cm (10–24in) according to variety

ZONES 9–10

Tender, bushy plants with branched stems, mid-green lance-shaped leaves and daisy-like flowers. *Z. elegans* is a bushy annual 60cm (2ft) tall with broad-petalled purple flowers. Its forms include the Thumbellina Series, dwarf (15cm/6in) with single or semi-double flowers of magenta, red, pink or yellow, and 'Envy' (60cm/2ft) which has lime green flowers. *Z. haageana* is also about 60cm (2ft) tall, an annual with orange flowers. Forms include 'Persian Carpet', with semi-double and double flowers in single and bicolours, in purple, red, brown, orange and yellow. *Z.*

'Profusion Cherry' is a dwarf (25cm/10in) with cherry red, dahlia-like flowers. Sow seed in spring for summer flowering.

hardiness Tender
flowering Summer
position Full sun
cultivation Loam-based compost (J.I. 1), multi-purpose loamless compost, or well-drained soil. Water freely in summer and feed fortnightly with a balanced liquid fertilizer. Deadhead to prolong the flowering period.
overwintering Sow from seed each spring.
pests & diseases Mildew, if conditions are particularly moist.
special features The taller zinnias are excellent for cutting.
decorative ideas Pack a metal window box with clashing colours of zinnia together.

Bamboos, grasses and ferns

Although these are not botanically in the same group, they are all grown principally for their foliage, rather than their flowers. They are useful plants for adding shape and form to a planting scheme, and ferns, in particular, are excellent for shade, as indeed are most bamboos. Some grasses and bamboos, which can be rampant in the open, are ideal for containers, which control their potential spread. Some of these plants have very different needs in terms of sunshine and water, so make sure you pay attention to this when selecting those that you would like to put together in a display. Bamboos make excellent screening plants and can be grown in a long deep trough. While some grasses make handsome feature plants in pots, others are small enough to provide foliage interest in a window box, throwing the brighter coloured flowers into relief. *Poa* and *Festuca* are both excellent for this purpose. Grasses make equally handsome feature plants in their own right. Grow the bigger ones in a large terracotta planter, for example, and position the pot where the sunlight will catch the seedheads of the grass. Create a foliage display in a shady corner mixing ferns and bamboos with other shade lovers.

Adiantum pedatum

ADIANTACEAE/PTERIDACEAE
Adiantum pedatum
H 30cm (12 in) with a similar spread

ZONES 5–9

This is a hardy, low-growing, deciduous fern, known as the five-fingered or American maidenhair fern, with creeping rhizomes. The pale green leaves are palmate, with 30cm (12in) leaf blades on a glossy dark brown or black stem. Each has two opposite rows of pale green, triangular or oblong leaflets. The whole leaf can be up to 50cm (20in) long. The form *A. p.* 'Japonicum', or the "early red maidenhair', has fronds which are 30cm (12in) long and tinted purple-pink when they first emerge. This fern must be grown in shade or it will scorch very badly.

Propagation is by division in the spring, or by sowing spores, also in spring.

hardiness Fully hardy
flowering None
position Partial shade
cultivation Grow in fern compost, one part loam-based compost (J.I. 2): one part sharp sand: two parts shredded bark, or moist, well-drained soil. Water moderately in summer, sparingly in winter, and feed monthly with a balanced liquid fertilizer at half strength.
overwintering Do not allow to become waterlogged.
pests & diseases None
special features This fern will grow well in a shady corner.
decorative ideas Plant in a hanging basket for a shady spot.

Arundo donax var. *versicolor*

GRAMINCEAE/POACEAE
Arundo donax
H 3m (10ft)

ZONES 7–9

This giant grass, known as the giant reed, is grown for its bamboo-like leaves which are long and grey-green, splaying out from broad stems reaching to 3m (10ft) or more in height. Spikes of feathery, greenish-purple flowers, up to 60cm (2ft) long, are produced in mid- to late autumn on 3m (10ft) tall stems, making it an ideal choice for hiding an eyesore or providing a screen. The form *A. d.* var. *versicolor* is slower-growing, with attractive white striping on the leaves and reaches 1.8m (6ft), although it is slightly less hardy. Propagation is by division in the spring.

hardiness Half hardy
flowering Mid- to late autumn
position Full sun to partial shade.
cultivation Loam-based compost (J.I. 2) or any moist soil. The variegated form can be grown in loamless compost for ease of movement, taking it inside in winter. Water freely in summer, sparingly in winter.
overwintering The variegated form will need protection.
pests & diseases None
special features Prune for foliage by cutting all shoots to ground level in the spring. For flowers, prune out only two-year-old shoots (which have flowered).
decorative ideas This sizeable plant needs a special place as a feature plant in a tall, handsome container.

CYPERACEAE

Carex hachijoensis 'Evergold'

H 30cm (12in) s About 35cm (14in).

ZONES 7–9

This is a beautiful grass, of Japanese origin, which forms a tufted, evergreen clump of long arching leaves. The leaves are narrow, soft, and up to 25cm (10in) long. Each is dark green with wide, creamy-yellow striped markings, making it a very striking plant, and one which is well worth growing for itís foliage, especially in a container near a seating area where the sound of the rustling leaves can be appreciated. The brown flower spikes are 1–3cm (½–1¼in) long on 15cm (6in) tall stems, and are produced in mid- to late spring, although they are unremarkable, and very much secondary to the attractive foliage. Propagate by division in spring.

hardiness Fully hardy
flowering Mid- to late spring
position Full sun or light shade
cultivation Loam-based compost (J.I. 2) or moist, well-drained soil. Water freely in summer, sparingly in winter.
overwintering Do not allow to become waterlogged.
pests & diseases None
special features Planting this grass into a container means that it can be raised above ground level, on a wall or on blocks, so that the foliage can be fully appreciated.
decorative ideas This can be planted singly in pots, to provide foliage interest along a balcony, interspersed with troughs of flowers.

Carex hachijoensis 'Evergold'

DRYOPTERIDACEAE

Dryopteris filix-mas

H 1m (3ft)

ZONES 2–8

This attractive deciduous or sometimes semi-evergreen male fern thrives in shade, but will tolerate a certain degree of bright sunlight. It forms a shuttlecock-shaped clump of lance-shaped, deeply cut fronds reaching up to 1m (3ft) high. Cultivated forms include: *D. f-m.* 'Grandiceps Wills' which is a truly striking plant with a broad, heavy crest at the tip of each frond; and *D. f-m.* 'Cristata' which has crested fronds and pinnae. Propagation is by division in the spring, or by sowing spores as soon as they are ripe.

hardiness Fully hardy
flowering Foliage plant
position Prefers shade, but will tolerate some bright light.
cultivation Loam-based compost (J.I. 2) with added bark, or moist soil. Water freely in summer, sparingly in winter, and feed monthly with a balanced liquid fertilizer at half strength.
overwintering Do not allow to become waterlogged.
pests & diseases None
special features Tolerates a range of conditions, but prefers to be sheltered from cold winds.
decorative ideas Makes a good hanging basket or feature plant for a shady corner.

Dryopteris filix-mas

GRAMINACEAE/POACEAE

Festuca glauca

H up to 3m (10ft) s 3m (10ft)

ZONES 6–9

The blue fescue is a tough rhizomatous evergreen grass. The fine strappy foliage, which varies in colour from quite a bright blue to a bluish-green, forms a neat upstanding clump that arches at the tips. During the summer it has short panicles of mauvish-green flowers. There are a number of named cultivars including *F.g.* 'Blaufuchs' with blue leaves, and 'Seeigel' with very fine blue leaves. Since this is a plant that prefers dry soil, it does well in containers that are prone to neglect! Propagate by division in spring.

hardiness Fully hardy
flowering Summer
position Full sun
cultivation Grow in multi-purpose compost to which some grit has been added. The base leaves will turn brown if left unwatered over a long periods, but it will recover once watering starts again. Feed occasionally with a liquid fertilizer, but do not overfeed.
overwintering No special care
pests & diseases None
special features Good permanent display plant.
decorative ideas This bluish-green foliage looks good with white, green and pale blue. Combine with silver-leaved plants and blue flowers in a verdigris-effect metal container.

Festuca glauca

Milium effusum 'Aureum'

GRAMiNACEAE/POACEAE

Milium effusum 'Aureum'

H 60cm (24in)

ZONES 5–9

This is a semi-evergreen, perennial grass, which forms a loose mound up to 60cm (2ft) high, and spreads only slowly within the garden or container. Every part of the plant is a rich, golden yellow, from the soft, smooth leaves through to the flowers and seedheads, but the colour pales to a lime green if the plant is grown in shade. The leaves are strap-like in shape and up to 30cm (12in) long. Flowering starts in mid-spring and continues until late summer, with delicate golden spikelets growing up to 30cm (12in) long, so light that the tiny flowers dance in the most gentle of breezes. Propagate by division in spring or seed sown in spring.

hardiness Fully hardy
flowering Late spring to late summer
position Full sun (although beware scorch in very intense heat) to light shade
cultivation Loam-based compost (J.I. 2) or moist, well-drained soil. Water freely in summer, sparingly in winter.
overwintering Do not allow to become waterlogged.
pests & diseases None
special features This is a pretty grass to keep near the house where it can be seen throughout the year.
decorative ideas This delicate grass looks good as a feature plant if positioned where it catches the light.

Molinia caerula 'Variegata'

GRAMINACEAE/POACEAE

Molinia caerulea

H 1m (3ft)

ZONES 5–8

A slender, tufted perennial grass which grows slowly to form a dense clump in the garden or container. It occurs naturally in damp moorland, and so prefers to be kept moist at all times. The narrow, mid-green leaves are long and flat, with purple bases, reaching to a length of 45cm (18in). Narrow purple flowerheads are produced from spring to autumn on 40cm (16in) yellow stems. The leaves turn to an attractive bronze-yellow in autumn. The spiky, sunburst form of this grass blends well with round-leaved plants, acting to accentuate and contrast with their foliage.

There are several forms available, including *M. c.* 'Variegata', which is more compact, with dark green, cream-striped leaves, ochre-yellow stems and purple spikelets. Propagate by division in spring.

hardiness Fully hardy
flowering Spring to autumn
position Full sun to partial shade
cultivation Loam-based compost (J.I. 2) or moist, well-drained soil. Water freely in summer, sparingly in winter.
overwintering Do not allow to become waterlogged.
pests & diseases None
special features Use this plant as a filler to contrast with different types of foliage.
decorative ideas Combine with *Choisya* and *Pittosporum* to create a foliage display.

GRAMINACEAE/POACEAE

Phyllostachys nigra

H Up to 5m (15ft)

ZONES 7–9

The compact, clump-forming 'black bamboo' has tall, hollow canes up to 5m (15ft) tall, although this will be restricted by the size of container it is growing in. The canes are green at first, turning to a shining black as they age, with a groove to one side and a white waxy powder below the nodes. The leaves are lance-shaped and dark green, up to 13cm (5in) long. This is an elegant plant which occurs in the wild in the forests of China, so it will tolerate a shady position. It grows well in a container, when it is useful as a screen, blocking the wind from other plants or a seating area. Propagate by division in spring.

hardiness Fully hardy
flowering Foliage plant
position Sun or partial shade
cultivation Loam-based compost (J.I. 3) or moist, well-drained soil. Water freely in summer, sparingly in winter.
overwintering Do not allow to become waterlogged.
pests & diseases Young shoots may be damaged by slugs.
special features By putting castors on the container, this can become a mobile windbreak, moved around according to the wind direction.
decorative ideas Makes an excellent screening plant in a long deep trough.

Phyllostachys nigra

Poa alpina

GRAMIMACEAE/POACEAE
Poa alpina
H Up to 45cm (18in)

ZONES 4–8

One of a large range of perennial and some grasses, this dwarf perennial grass makes an attractive densely tufted mound of flat, linear, short-pointed mid-green leaves. From early to mid-summer it produces panicles of purplish-green flowers, roughly 8cm (3in) long. A naturally occurring variety, *P.a. vivipara*, has little plantlets in the flower tips which can be pegged down to propagate new plants. *P. chaixii* is larger, up to 45cm (18in), tall with pale green flowers in spring and early summer held well above the leaves.

hardiness Fully hardy
position Full sun or partial shade
cultivation Plant in J.I. 2. Remove flowering stems in late autumn. Cut back any dead foliage in early spring. Water well during the growing season.
pests and disease Trouble-free
special features Can be used to create a turf-like effect in a container.
decorative ideas Plant as the central feature in a window box with flowering plants on either side.

GRAMINACEAE/POACEAE
Sasa
H 2m (6ft)

ZONES 8–9

This genus contains more than 40 species of small or medium-sized bamboos. *S. palmata f. nebulosa* grows up to 1.8m (6ft) with broad glossy green leaves with yellow midribs. *S. veitchii* is a low-growing bamboo which is tolerant of a wide range of conditions, including deep shade, but can be quite invasive when not restricted within a container. It spreads by means of rhizomes, from which the smooth, purple canes emerge. The glossy, mid-green leaves are a broad, oval, lance shape and make a wonderful rustling sound as the wind disturbs them. The leaf edges tend to wither during the winter, giving each leaf the effect of a beige variegation. Propagation is by division in spring, keeping the youngest parts of the rhizome and discarding the oldest.

hardiness Fully hardy
flowering Foliage plant
position Full sun to deep shade
cultivation Loam-based compost (J.I. 2) or any moist, well-drained soil. Water freely in summer, sparingly in winter. Rather than increase the container size each time you repot, divide the plant and keep the youngest section.
overwintering Do not allow to become waterlogged.
pests & diseases Slugs may attack shoots.
special features Do not overfeed this plant, or it will quickly outgrow its container.
decorative ideas This plant makes a good foil for flowering displays and an effective screen for a balcony or terrace.

Sasa palmata f. nebulosa

Crocus

Bulbs and bulb-like plants
These are valuable plants for containers. Although spring is the season that most people associate with bulbs, there are, in fact, bulbs for summer and autumn too. Although true bulbs are those with a swollen stem, perennials with root tubers and corms are treated in much the same way and are also included in this section.

Bulbous plants (or those treated like bulbs) make particularly good container plants, as their food system is stored within the bulb itself, leaving you with little work, and they have particularly attractive, slightly waxy flowers in jewel-like colours. In the garden, they are prone to get eaten or may well rot in overly damp conditions, but containers provide an ideal environment, and also allow you to create the kind of drainage needed for the smaller alpine bulbs. To get a good result from bulbs you need to do no more than plant the bulbs in the right conditions, at the right depth (usually twice the depth of the bulb itself) at the appropriate season (generally around four to six months before flowering)

and ensure that they have adequate supplies of water together with supports for the taller bulbs, like lilies and the big fritillaries. Feeding is only necessary after the flowers have died down to ensure next year's food supply is built up. Bulbs make excellent subjects for spring window boxes, dwarf tulips, crocuses and narcissus being ideal. Summer bulbs tend to be large, and the big, scented 'Regale' lilies can be used in pairs to flank a doorway, their scent drifting indoors on the breeze. There are a few bulbs that flower in autumn, including nerines (*Nerine bowdenii*) and colchicums. Both have spectacular flowers. They should be displayed where their beauty can be best appreciated, such as on a window ledge.

Agapanthus 'Blue Giant'

ALLIACEAE/LILIACEAE
Agapanthus
H Up to 1.2m (4ft)

ZONES 9–10
This is a genus of large, often evergreen perennials, some of which are hardy, some half hardy, known as the African blue lily. They are notable for their large clumps of leathery, strap-like deep green leaves, that arch gracefully. Arising from the centre of these clumps on long stems are umbels of trumpet-shaped flowers in blue or white. *A.* 'Blue Giant' is hardy with mid-blue flowers; *A.* 'Snowy Owl' is also hardy but with white flowers. This plant is best propagated by division in spring.

hardiness Half hardy to fully hardy, depending on type
flowering Mid-summer to early autumn
position Full sun
cultivation Grow in loam-based compost (J.I. 3). Feed regularly from late winter until flowering. Water freely when growing; sparingly when dormant.
overwintering Mulch less hardy forms.
pests & diseases Fairly trouble-free in containers
special features None
decorative ideas Plant in pairs in big terracotta pots to flank a doorway or steps.

Allium cristophii

COBAEACEAE
Allium cristophii
H 60cm (2ft)

ZONES 6–9

This bulbous perennial plant, known as the 'star of Persia', is a member of the extensive onion family. It has grey-green, strap-like, basal leaves of up to 40cm (16in) in length with small, stiff hairs along the edges. These surround a ribbed flowering stem which can grow up to 60cm (2ft) tall, although they are usually dying off as the stem grows. The flowers are produced in groups of up to 50 in a loose, globe-shaped umbel 10–20cm (4–8in) in diameter. Each individual star-shaped flower is 2–3cm (1in) across and coloured pinkish-purple with a shiny metallic sheen. Propagate from seed sown in spring or removing offsets in autumn.

hardiness Frost hardy
flowering Early summer
position Full sun
cultivation Loam-based compost (J.I. 1) with extra sand, or well-drained soil. Water freely in summer, sparingly in winter, and feed monthly with a balanced liquid fertilizer.
overwintering Protect if temperatures fall below -5°C (-40°F).
pests & diseases Onion fly, white rot and downy mildew
special features The flowerheads dry well.
decorative ideas For a dramatic indoor arrangement, spray the dried flowerhead gold or silver.

COBAEACEAE
Colchicum
H 23cm (9in)

ZONES 5–8

The crocus-like colchicums are cormous perennials which produce long, strap-like leaves and large, showy, goblet-shaped flowers. There are many species, which flower during every season of the year. Of these, the autumn-flowering varieties and cultivars are particularly attractive, producing their blooms as other plants are starting to die down. They flower without leaves, which appear in spring. *C. agrippinum* has 1–2 deep, purple-pink flowers; *C. speciosum* 'Album' has 2–3 pure white flowers; *C.* 'The Giant' has up to five violet flowers with white centres; and *C.* 'Waterlily' has up to five double lilac-pink flowers. Propagation is by dividing dormant corms (in summer for autumn-flowering types).

hardiness Fully hardy
flowering Autumn
position Full sun
cultivation Loam-based compost (J.I. 2). Keep moist during the growing and flowering period, and allow to dry almost completely during the summer (dormant period). Repot every 4–5 years during summer, dividing if they become congested.
overwintering Protect during severe frost, and do not allow to become waterlogged.
pests & diseases Slugs
special features Plant 10cm (4in) deep in late summer or early autumn.
decorative ideas Plant on their own in 15cm (6in) deep terracotta pots. Combine in a display with pink chrysanthemums.

Colchicum speciosum

Crocus x *luteus* 'Dutch Yellow'

IRIDACEAE
Crocus
H 10–20cm (4–8in)

ZONES 4–8

These small, spring- or autumn-flowering perennials grow from individual corms, producing long, slender leaves, often with a white-striped upper surface. The flowers are goblet-shaped, four or more produced per corm, in shades of white, yellow, blue or purple, and plain or striped. Propagate by dividing the plants during the summer dormant period. *C. chrysanthus* flowers are golden-yellow with a striped maroon reverse (late winter to early spring). *C. minimus* has rich purple blooms, feathered on the reverse with a deeper shade (late spring). *C. nudiflorus*

produces solitary purple blooms without leaves (autumn). *C. vernus* and its hybrids flower in shades of white ('Jeanne d'Arc'), lilac ('Queen of the Blues') or purple ('Purpureus Grandiflorus') in late spring to early summer. *Crocus* x *luteus* 'Dutch Yellow' is a vigorous spring-flowering crocus with 2–5 bright yellow flowers, roughly 5cm (2in) long.

hardiness Fully hardy
flowering Early to mid-spring
position Full sun to partial shade
cultivation Loam-based compost (J.I. 2). Keep moist during the growing and flowering period, then allow to dry slightly. Repot every 4–5 years, or more frequently if they are becoming congested.
overwintering Protect during severe frosts,

and do not allow to become waterlogged.
pests & diseases Squirrels, birds and slugs. Fungal rot on corms in storage.
special features Plant 8–10cm (3–4in) deep in autumn.
decorative ideas Small and delicate bulbs are best planted with a few to a pot. To create a more impressive display, line up several pots along a windowsill or by the railings of a balcony. Their delicate waxy flowers and fine strappy leaves look good in silvery metallic pots.

Cyclamen

PRIMULACEAE
Cyclamen
H 10cm (4in)

ZONES 6–9
A genus of several species of tuberous
perennial, normally found in woodland. The
rounded to heart-shaped leaves have attractive markings. The small flowers with reflexed
petals in white or pink are borne in autumn,
winter and early spring. The most commonly
grown types in containers are the hardy *C.
coum*, with deep green leaves marked with silver and flowers in shades of white through
pink to carmine, and *C. hederifolium* with
darker leaves and bright pink flowers.
Propagate from seed in late winter/early
spring, having soaked seed thoroughly first.

hardiness Fully hardy
flowering Late winter to early spring
position Light shade
cultivation Multi-purpose compost. Water
and feed moderately.
overwintering Do not allow to become
waterlogged.
pests & diseases Generally trouble-free
special features Deadhead to prolong
flowering.
decorative ideas Good for underplanting
deciduous trees and shrubs that cast shade
only in winter.

Fritillaria imperialis

LILIACEAE
Fritillaria
H 20–100cm (8–39in)

ZONES 4–9
A varied group of bulbous perennials, bearing
lance-like leaves and bell-shaped flowers.
Small species include *F. michailovskyi*, at 20cm
(8in) with up to seven brownish-purple
flowers in late spring. The 'snake's head'
fritillary, *F. meleagris*, produces purple, mauve
or white flowers with darker patterning on
the reverse, 30cm (12in) tall, in spring.
F. imperialis reaches around 1m (3ft), with up
to eight flowers in a cluster, topped by a tuft
of narrow bracts, in late spring. They may be
orange ('Prolifera'), yellow ('Maxima Lutea')
or red ('Rubra'). Propagate by sowing seed in

autumn, dividing offsets or collecting and
sowing bulbils in late summer.

hardiness Fully hardy
flowering Mid- to late spring
position Full sun
cultivation Loam-based compost (J.I. 2)
with added grit. Keep moist during growth
and flowering, and almost dry during
dormancy. Repot every 4–5 years.
overwintering Tend to be very intolerant of
excess moisture (except *F. meleagris*) and may
need protecting from severe frost.
pests & diseases Lily beetles and slugs
special features Plant in autumn at four
times the depth of the bulb.
decorative ideas Large plants like fritillaria
deserve a prominent position. Plant in a deep
terracotta pot and surround with narcissus.

Galanthus 'Ophelia'

AMARYLLIDACEAE
Galanthus nivalis
H 22cm (9in)

ZONES 4–9
The 'snowdrop' is a hardy, clump-forming,
low-growing perennial which produces flat,
strap-shaped leaves of a dull mid- or bluish-
green, arranged in pairs, usually one on each
side of the flower stalk. They are grown for
their drooping white flowers, often marked
with green on the inner tepals, produced in
the early spring before the plant dies down
and becomes dormant during the summer,
and autumn. Forms include: *G. n.* 'Flore
Pleno' (honey-scented, double white flowers);
the unusual *G. n.* 'Lady Elphinstone' (yellow
markings on the inner tepals on established

plants); and *G. n.* 'Pusey Green Tip' (double
with green markings on the outer petals).
Propagation is by division immediately
after flowering.

hardiness Fully hardy
flowering Spring
position Partial shade
cultivation Loam-based compost (J.I. 2),
kept constantly moist at all times, not just
during the growing and flowering period.
Repot every 4–5 years.
overwintering No problems
pests & diseases Narcissus bulb fly, and
grey mould
special features Lift and divide 'in the
green' after flowering, before the leaves die.
decorative ideas Place pots on a windowsill
or around a clipped box plant on a table.

HYACINTHACEAE/LILIACEAE
Hyacinthus orientalis
H 20–30cm (8–12in)

ZONES 6–9

Hyacinths are perennials grown for their bright, scented waxy flowers. These are bell-shaped, single or double, and come in white, yellow, pink, orange, red and blue, in clusters of up to 40 on a single stem amid bright green strap-like leaves. 'Blue Jacket' (single, navy-blue); 'City of Haarlem' (single, prim-rose yellow); 'Delft Blue' (single, powder blue); 'Gipsy Queen' (single, orange-pink); 'Hollyhock' (double, crimson); 'L'Innocence' (single, white); and 'Pink Pearl' (single, pink). Propagation is by removing small offsets in summer when the bulb is dormant.

hardiness Fully hardy
flowering Spring
position Full sun to partial shade
cultivation Loam-based compost (J.I. 1) with added grit. Water moderately during growth period, very sparingly during dormancy. Feeding is not necessary. Repot when dormant in late summer or autumn.
overwintering Mulch to prevent frost damaging the growing tip and do not allow to become too wet, or the bulb will rot.
pests & diseases Slugs
special features Plant with the tip of the bulb 2-3cm (1in) below the surface of the compost in autumn.
decorative ideas Plant five to a 30cm (12in) diameter pot, and support with a willow cage to prevent the flowering heads from keeling over (see page 30).

Hyacinthus 'L'Innocence'

IRIDACEAE
Iris
H Up to 1m (3ft)

ZONES 5–6

Bulbous irises have deciduous, lance-shaped leaves and beardless flowers. They all have a dormant period during the summer. There are three groups: Reticulata, with blue, white or red-purple flowers; Juno, with colourful 'fall' petals and small 'standard' petals; and Xiphium (including Dutch, English and Spanish irises), with blue, lavender, yellow or white flowers. *I. danfordiae* (yellow) and *I. reticulata* (violet-blue) are small, winter- or early spring flowering species; *I. magnifica* (Juno, pale lilac); *I.* 'Golden Harvest' (Dutch, golden-yellow); *I. latifolia* (English, blue, violet or white); *I. xiphium* (Spanish, blue, white or yellow). Propagate by separating offsets in late summer.

hardiness Fully hardy
flowering Late winter to mid-summer
position Full sun to partial shade
cultivation Loam-based compost (J.I. 2) with added grit. Water moderately during the period of growth and very sparingly when dormant. Feed every two weeks after flowering with high-potash fertilizer (tomato food) until the leaves die down.
overwintering Protect during periods of severe frost and do not allow to become waterlogged.
pests & diseases Slugs and snails
special features Plant (or lift and divide) in autumn at twice the depth of the bulb.
decorative ideas Plant about six irises in a 25cm (10in) diameter clay pot for an attractive group.

Iris reticulata

Lilium regale

LILIACAEA
Lilium
H Up to 1.5m (5ft)

ZONES 7–9

The lily family is large, comprising around 100 bulbous perennial plants which vary in height and flower size, shape and colour. The bulb is made up of fleshy white or yellow scales (which may turn purple when exposed to light). The flowers are trumpet-shaped and very fragrant, with six petals which curl into an open star shape, varying from 2.5cm (1in) to 25cm (10in) across depending upon variety. The leaves are pale to dark green, some narrow, almost grass-like and grouped at the base of the plant, others in clusters (whorls) at intervals along stems

which often reach 1m (3ft) tall. Propagate the plant from scales before planting. *Lilium regale* (Regal lily) has large, highly fragrant flowers in clusters of up to 25 at the top of the stem. Pink in bud, opening white with a pinkish-purple reverse and yellow centre with golden anthers. *L. speciosum* (Japanese lily) has bowl-shaped flowers, white with red markings, highly scented, and 8–12cm (3–5in) across.

hardiness Fully hardy
flowering Mid-summer to early autumn
position Full sun to partial shade (depends on species)
cultivation Loam-based compost (J.I. 2). Keep thoroughly moist during the growing period. After flowering, reduce watering to keep compost just moist and apply high

potash fertilizer (tomato feed) every two weeks from when the flower begins to fade until the leaves die down. Repot in autumn. Mulch the container with organic matter.
overwintering Do not allow to become waterlogged and protect from severe frost.
pests & diseases Lily beetles, slugs
special features Choose bulbs which are plump and glossy, not shrivelled or dry-looking. Plant immediately, keeping the 'nose' or tip of the bulb just under the surface of the compost.
decorative ideas Unless you stake lilies, they will flop, so provide cane and wire supports in a circle around the lower third of the stems. Plant up two big pots to flank a doorway.

HYACINTHACEAE/LILIACEAE
Muscari armeniacum
H 20cm (8in)

ZONES 4–8

The 'grape hyacinth' is a hardy, dwarf, bulbous perennial with long, narrow, fleshy leaves which begin to grow in autumn, then spread and separate as flower buds appear. The spiky flowerheads are densely packed with tiny, bell-shaped, deep blue flowers, produced in late spring, over a period of several weeks. Forms include: *M. a.* 'Argaei Album' (white flowers); *M. a.* 'Blue Spike' (large, double, blue flowers); *M. a.* 'Cantab' (paler blue than the species); and *M. a.* 'Heavenly Blue' (a much brighter blue). Propagation is by division of large clumps in mid-summer when they are dormant. This should be done on a regular basis to keep the plants healthy and prevent congestion.

hardiness Fully hardy
flowering Spring
position Full sun to partial shade
cultivation Loam-based compost (J.I. 1). Water moderately in spring, there is no need to feed. Repot every 2–3 years or when the container becomes congested.
overwintering Do not allow to become waterlogged
pests & diseases Virus (occasional)
special features Plant 10cm (4in) deep in autumn.
decorative ideas These small but brightly coloured bulbs look good massed together in a very large pot. Alternatively, use them to create a topiary-style pyramid with chicken wire and moss, pushing individual pots of muscari into the chicken wire to create a pyramid shape.

Muscari armeniacum

Narcissus 'Paper White'

AMARYLLIDACEAE
Narcissus
H Up to 60cm (2ft)

ZONES 6–9

Hardy, perennial, spring-flowering bulbs with narrow strap-like leaves, and flowers with an inner trumpet, and outer row of petals. They range from 10cm (4in) to tall varieties 60cm (2ft). Flowers include yellow, white, orange, cream, and pink; single or clustered, with single or double petals, and varying lengths and shapes of trumpet. *N.* 'Cheerfulness', 40cm (16in) is creamy-white and highly scented; *N.* 'Tete-a-Tete', 15cm (6in) is yellow and multi-headed; and *N.* 'Paper White', 40cm (16in) has white flowers. Propagation is by division when bulbs are lifted after flowering.

hardiness Fully hardy
flowering Spring
position Full sun to partial shade
cultivation Loam-based compost (J.I. 1). Water moderately during spring and feed with a balanced liquid fertilizer every week for four weeks after flowering. Deadhead after flowering and remove foliage during mid-summer. Lift and divide every 3–5 years, six weeks after flowering.
overwintering Protect containers from frost and excessive moisture.
pests & diseases Stem and bulb eelworm, narcissus fly, narcissus yellow stripe virus
special features Plant at 1.5 times their own depth in autumn.
decorative ideas Insert twigs of twisted hazel or willow at intervals to provide a support for the bulbs, which tend to flop. over.

Nerine bowdenii

AMARYLLIDACEAE

Nerine

H 45–60cm (18–24in)

ZONES 6–9

This genus of striking bulbous perennials is found in the wild on the mountain screes of southern Africa. Their exotic-looking waxy flowers are borne, in many cases, before the leaves, in the autumn. *N. bowdenii* is a robust species with strap-shaped leaves and umbles of pink, funnel-shaped flowers up to 8cm (3in) across. The hybrids *N.* 'Snow Queen' has pure white flowers; *N.* 'Radiant Queen' has rose pink flowers; and *N.* 'Salmon Supreme' has salmon pink flowers. Propagate by dividing clumps after flowering or sow seed in warmth when ripe.

hardiness Fully hardy to half hardy
flowering Autumn
position Full sun
cultivation Plant in loam-based compost (J.I. 2) with the tips of the bulbs level with the surface of the compost. Water freely while growing, but keep dry when dormant. Apply a low-nitrogen liquid fertilizer after flowering.
overwintering No special care needed.
pests & diseases Prone to attacks by slugs.
special features Do not eat any part of the plant; can cause stomach upsets.
decorative ideas Display nerines on a table or place the pot on a pedestal for maximum impact.

Nymphaea 'Chromatella'

NYMPHAEACEAE

Nymphaea

H 90cm–120cm (3–4ft)

ZONES 6–8

The water lily belongs to a genus of aquatic tuberous perennials with large rounded mid-green leaves and exotic-looking waxy flowers in white, yellow- pink or red. The smaller hardy varieties are best for water pots. *N.* 'Albida' has fragrant cup-shaped white flowers with yellow stamens. *N.* 'Chromatella' has large canary yellow flowers. *N.* 'Firecrest' has deep pink star-shaped flowers and purplish leaves when young.

hardiness Fully hardy to frost tender hardy
flowering Summer
position Full sun
cultivation Plant in an aquatic planting basket with J.I. 2 compost, covered with pea gravel. Cover with 25cm (10in) of water until the crowns are established, then fill up the water pot. Propagate by dividing older plants in autumn.
overwintering No special care needed of hardy varieities. Bring frost-tender ones indoors.
pests & diseases Prone to various leaf spot type diseases.
special features Divide established plants regularly to improve flowering.
decorative ideas Plant water lilies in a 60cm (24in) deep watertight glazed pot.

HYACINTHACEAE/LILIACEAE

Scilla siberica

H 15–20cm (6–8in)

ZONES 5–8

The 'Siberian squill' is a low-growing, delicate-looking perennial bulb. It is grown for it's nodding, wide bell- or bowl-shaped flowers 1.5cm (½in) across, which are carried in clusters of 4–5 on dark green stems. The flower buds emerge along with the long, slender leaves in early spring, and flowering normally continues for several weeks. The flowers are bright-blue, but forms with different flower colours include: *S. s.* 'Alba' which has white flowers; and *S. s.* 'Spring Beauty' which has deep blue flowers. Flowering performance is better if the bulbs are not disturbed too

often. Propagation is by dividing up the new bulb offsets when repotting.

hardiness Fully hardy
flowering Spring
position Full sun to partial shade
cultivation Loam-based compost (J.I. 1). Water moderately during the growing period but allow to dry almost completely during the summer dormancy. Repot every 3–4 years. There is no need to apply fertilizer.
overwintering Protect the container from frost and excessive moisture.
pests & diseases Virus
special features Plant bulbs 8–10cm (3–4in) deep in autumn.
decorative ideas Plant up a small trug or basket with these delicate little baskets and display on a table.

Scilla siberica

Parrot tulips

Tulipa 'Queen of Night'

Tulipa tarda

LILIACEAE
Tulipa
H Up to 1.2m (4ft)

○ ⊛

ZONES 5–9

Tulips are perennial, spring-flowering bulbs classified according to botanical character-istics and time of flowering. The flowers may be single, double, goblet- or star-shaped, fringed, or long and slender. Flower shades include white, yellow, pink, red, orange and purple to almost black. *T. kaufmanniana* hybrids (water-lily tulip), such as 'Giuseppe Verdi' (yellow/red striped flowers) and *T. greigii* 'Red Riding Hood' (red flowers) are low-growing. *T. praestans* bears clusters of up to 5 orange-red flowers. Propagation is by division when the bulbs are lifted after

flowering. *T.* 'Queen of Night' has single dark maroon flowers in late spring. *T.* 'White Parrot' has pure white parrot-form flowers in late spring. *T. tarda* is a small species tulip with white and golden flowers in early or mid-spring.

hardiness Fully hardy
flowering Spring
position Full sun, sheltered from strong wind
cultivation Loam-based (J.I. 1) or loamless compost. Keep the plant moist in the growth period and feed weekly with a balanced liquid fertilizer for four weeks after flower-ing. Deadhead after flowering and allow to die down. Leave the bulbs in the container or lift and store in a cool place. Replant larger ones together to flower, and new bulbs together to grow larger.

overwintering Protect pots from frost and excessive moisture.
pests & diseases Slugs, stem and bulb eelworm, fungal rots and tulip fire
special features Discard any plants showing distortion (leaves or flowers).
decorative ideas It is best to confine displays to one colour only. Plant up matching large pots with the same kind of tulip, and display either side of a door. Plant up shallow troughs of the smaller tulips for windowsills, with just trailing ivy for company. Grow the tall, dark red or almost black tulips in square metal containers and underplant with the black grass, *Ophiopogon planiscapus* 'Nigrescens'.

Parsley, lettuce, ruby chard

Vegetables, fruits and herbs A small selection of edible plants is worth

growing, even in a limited space. Even a few really delicious cherry tomatoes, a few pots of culinary herbs,

like thyme, basil and parsley, and perhaps a dwarf fruit tree, such as the 'Ballerina' apple, will create some

of the pleasures of a country garden in a small city apartment with just a tiny balcony.

Vegetables

Although vegetables need a good supply of nutrients to produce a healthy crop, most of them can manage on quite restricted quantities of compost. You can buy 'grow-bags' in which the nutrients have already been added for tomatoes, for example, and then disguise these unattractive bags by making a wooden trough for them. At the end of the season, you simply lift the grow-bag out, and start again. Potatoes can be grown successfully in deep barrels, which do not take up a lot of room, so are ideal if space is limited. With a bit more space, you can train beans up a supporting trellis, as indeed you can with cucumbers in warmer climates. Smaller vegetables, like lettuce, rocket or radishes can be grown in window-box sized troughs, or large terracotta pots if you prefer. Most vegetables need copious supplies of water and nutrients during critical points of the growing season, so you will have to spend time looking after them in order to harvest a worthwhile crop. However, being so close to hand and under supervision, you can arrest any attacks by pests in the early stages, and, if you garden on a balcony or rooftop, you do not have to worry about slugs and snails!

CHENOPODIACEAE
Beta vulgaris
H 60cm (24in)

ZONES 5–9

This hardy vegetable, known as Swiss chard, is grown for its glossy succulent leaves which are up to 45cm (18in) long and 23cm (8in) wide. The leaf stalks are red or white, and the leaves range in colour from deep green to a coppery-green. There are several cultivars, including 'Fordhook Giant' with dark green leaves, and 'Rhubarb' or 'Ruby Chard' with bright scarlet stalks. The latter is very popular.

hardiness Fully hardy
position Full sun
propagation Sow seed thinly 2cm (¾in) deep from early spring to mid-summer in a large deep pot.
cultivation Swiss chard prefers well-drained, loam-based compost (J.I. 2). When the seedlings are about 5cm (2in) high, thin them out to 30cm (12in) diameter pots. If you want a cut-and-come-again crop, thin them instead to 8cm (3in) apart. Water thoroughly in growing season to prevent bolting.
cropping Harvest Swiss chard in individual pots by cutting off stems at the base. The plants will be ready to harvest within 12 weeks from sowing, but remain throughout the winter. For a cut-and-come-again crop, harvest leaves to within 2.5cm (1in) above soil level, and let the leaves resprout from the base.

Swiss chard with radicchio

SOLANACEAE
Capsicum
H Up to 2m (6ft)

ZONE 9

Sweet peppers are annuals, grown for their fruits. They reach 90cm (3ft) high and 75cm (2.5ft) across and need average temperatures of around 21°C (70°F) and fairly high humidity. Fruits can be red, yellow, orange or bluish-black. Flavour can range from mild to hot, with strength increasing as the fruit ripens.

hardiness Frost tender
position Full sun
propagation Sow seed in individual pots mid-spring, and place in a frost-proof structure at 18°C (64°F). Germination takes 10–14 days, and young plants are ready to transplant ten weeks after germination.
cultivation Loamless or loam-based compost (J.I. 2). Allow each plant a minimum of a 30cm (12in) pot and stake to provide support. Pinch out the growing point to make the plants bushy. As fruits develop, apply high-potash feed every two weeks (tomato feed applied through a watering can is ideal). Spray regularly with water to keep the humidity high.
cropping For most easy-to-grow cultivars, such as 'Bell Boy' and 'Yellow Bell', start harvesting green fruits about 14 weeks after planting out, three weeks later for the coloured ripened fruits, which have higher vitamin levels. Harvest when ripe by cutting the stalk about 2cm (¾in) from the fruit top.

Green pepper

CURCUBITACEAE
Cucumis
H Up to 2m (6ft)

ZONE 10

Outdoor cucumbers, smaller and more rough-skinned than greenhouse cucumbers, can be grown in a grow-bag or large pot, once frosts are over. They are ready to harvest about 12 weeks after sowing, when about 15cm (6in) long. Cucumbers transplant badly, so sow in biodegradable jiffy pots.

hardiness Frost tender
position Full sun
propagation Sow seed individually into 7.5cm (3in) pots under cover in mid-spring. Germination will take about ten days and the seedlings are ready for planting out when they are 30cm (12in) high.

cultivation Will not tolerate temperatures below 10°C (50°F), so protect from frost. They will grow well in loamless compost such as a grow-bag, or loam-based compost (J.I. 2). Water freely and feed every two weeks with high-potash fertilizer (tomato feed). To save space, train vertically as a cordon with support strings twisted around the plants to hold them upright. The main stem is kept growing upwards and the side shoots trimmed back to 2–3 leaves. Allow 40–45cm (16–18in) per plant to allow sunlight to reach the plant.

cropping Harvesting can start about 16 weeks after germination. Cut the fruit leaving a short stalk of about 2.5cm (1in). Good cropping cultivars include; 'Birgit' and 'Petita'.

Cucumber

CURCUBITACEAE
Cucurbita
H Up to 2m (6ft)

ZONE 10

Courgettes (zucchini) are small cultivars of marrow, harvested when they are immature, usually 10–15cm (4–6in) long, while the skin is smoooth and shiny. Fruit colours range from dark green 'Ambassador', through to lighter shades and even yellow 'Taxi'.

hardiness Frost tender
position Full sun
propagation Prefers warm temperatures for seed germination, and resents root disturbance, so are usually raised indoors in spring and hardened off before being transplanted outside. For rapid germination, soak the seed overnight, and sow individually into 7.5cm (3in) pots the following day. Provided they are kept warm, germination will take about ten days.

cultivation Protect from overnight frost after planting out. Loamless or loam-based compost (J.I. 2) or grow-bags. Allow bush types 90cm (3ft) and trailing cultivars 2m (6ft). Water freely and feed every two weeks with high-potash fertilizer (tomato feed). Cut away any leaves which shade the fruit, and as the fruits start to swell, remove any male flowers close by to prevent the fruit tasting bitter.

cropping Although they can become much larger, courgettes are usually harvested when the fruits are about 10–15cm (4–6in) or so long.

Courgette

COMPOSITAE
Eruca sativa
H Up to 3m (10ft) S 3m (10ft)

ZONES 7–9

Rocket is a tender-looking plant which is actually quite hardy and will survive most winters outdoors as long as it has some shelter and does not get waterlogged. The leaves have a sharp, spicy flavour which increases in strength when the plant matures, or is kept too dry. It is a versatile vegetable which can be eaten raw in salads or cooked like spinach. It can be grown as individual plants or harvested regularly as a cut-and-come-again crop throughout the season.

hardiness Frost hardy
position Full sun
propagation Seed sown in succession at three week intervals from mid-spring through to early summer.

cultivation Loamless or loam-based compost (J.I. 1) or grow-bags. This crop must be kept well-watered to promote very rapid growth, so apply freely and feed every week with high-nitrogen fertilizer at half strength.

cropping Harvesting is mainly from early summer until mid-autumn, and can consist of either removing individual leaves from the outside of the plants, or cutting whole plants down to about 2.5cm (1in) above ground-level in rotation, and waiting for them to resprout before cutting them again.

Rocket (*Eruca sativa*)

COMPOSITAE

Lactuca

H Up to 30cm (12in)

ZONES 6–8

The main categories of lettuce are butter-head, loose-leaf and cos, and all can be grown in containers as long as they are well-fed and given sufficient water. Butterhead varieties are quick to mature, with soft, smooth leaves and a loose heart. Loose-leaf varieties, such as 'Lollo Bionda', 'Lollo Rosso' and 'Salad Bowl' do not form a heart as such, so leaves can be removed on a cut-and-come-again basis. 'Bubbles' and 'Little Gem' are small cos types, so are ideal for containers. The loose-leaf varieties make attractive edging for a trough of plants.

hardiness Frost tender

position Full sun

propagation Seed sown in succession from early spring to mid-summer to ensure continued cropping. The earliest sowings will need to be protected from frost and cold, the later ones from excess heat.

cultivation Grow in loamless or loam-based compost (J.I. 1), or grow-bags (even used ones in the season following a crop of tomatoes). Water freely throughout the growing season and feed weekly with high nitrogen fertilizer at half strength.

cropping From early summer onwards, harvest whole plants by pulling them up, or loose-leaved varieties by removing just the outer leaves so that the rest of the plant can continue to grow.

Oak-leaved lettuce

SOLANACEAE

Lycopersicon esculentum

H Up to 1.2 m (4ft)

ZONES 9–10

Tomatoes are versatile and reliable, and may be grown in grow-bags or in containers, undercover or outdoors (depending on the variety), and still give a good yield. Outdoors, the crop will depend on the weather, but a variety such as 'Gardener's Delight' is usually reliable. Some varieties, such as the sweet orange 'Sun Gold' will need staking, as they are best cordon-grown with the side shoots removed. 'Yellow Pear' and 'Red Pear' have unusual pear-shaped fruit, ideal in salads. 'Tumbler' and 'Tiny Tim' are cherry varieties, ideal for pots, window boxes and hanging baskets.

hardiness Frost tender

position Full sun

propagation Sow seed at 16°C (60°F) from early spring, depending on when they are to be planted outside (allow 6–8 weeks from sowing to planting).

cultivation Harden off before finally planting out, and allow each plant 30cm (12in). Grow in loamless or loam-based compost, (J.I. 1) or grow-bags. Keep moist at all times. Feed weekly with tomato food once trusses start to form. Remove side shoots on cordon varieties and 'stop' (remove growing tip) after four trusses to keep the plants small if space is limited.

cropping Harvest fruit as it ripens (7–8 weeks after planting for bush types, 10–12 for cordons). Use fresh or store by drying, freezing or bottling.

Tomato (*Lycopersicon esculentum*)

LEGUMINOSAE
Phaseolus
H Up to 3m (10ft)

ZONE 10

Dwarf varieties of both runner and French beans are suitable for growing in small gardens, in containers or grow-bags. With their bright, colourful flowers and long pods, they can be ornamental as well as extremely tasty. Staking should not be necessary as long as the varieties chosen are dwarfing. Varieties of runner bean include; 'Hestia' (a new compact, bushy variety with red and white flowers and stringless pods) and 'Pickwick' (red flowers, long pods). Dwarf French varieties include; 'Atlanta', 'Ferrari', 'Montano', and 'Sunray'.

hardiness Frost tender
position Full sun
propagation Sow seed in modules or small pots, in late spring. Plant out in early summer for harvesting from late summer through to early utumn.
cultivation Grow in a sheltered, sunny position for best results, in loamless or loam-based compost (J.I. 2). Allow each plant 20cm (8in). Keep moist at all times and water plentifully in the groing season. Apply high-potash fertilizer (tomato food) periodically as a boost.
cropping Start to harvest the beans as they reach about 10cm (4in) long, and pick regularly to ensure a continued supply and to prevent them becoming stringy. Runner beans freeze well.

Runner bean 'Armstrong'

'Second early' potato

SOLANACEAE
Solanum tuberosum
H Up to 60cm (24in)

ZONES 7–9

Potatoes come in a huge range of shapes, sizes, colours and textures. Their shape may be round, oval or knobbly; their size anything from large marble to tennis ball. Skin colour may be white, red, yellow or purple, and the flesh either white, cream, yellow or blue. In texture, they vary from waxy to floury. They also mature at different times, leading to classification as First Early, Second Early (or Mid-crop) or Maincrop. The first two are better for smaller gardens, as they mature more quickly and do not take up as much space for as long as Maincrop types.

hardiness Fully hardy to frost tender
position Full sun
propagation Use 'seed' potatoes and lay them in a shallow tray in a cool, frost-free place for about six weeks to allow them to sprout ('chit'). When the shoots reach 2.5cm (1in) long, plant out. Handle with care to avoid breaking off the brittle new shoots.
cultivation Potatoes will grow in any container which is at least 30cm (12in) wide and deep, with drainage holes in the base, in a sunny position. Lay 2–3 chitted potatoes on 10–12.5cm (4–5in) of compost/soil in the container and cover with a similar depth of compost/soil. Cover with another similar depth once the shoots are about 15cm (6in) tall, leaving the tips showing. Repeat until the shoots are within 5cm (2in) of the rim.
cropping Harvest as required from early summer onwards, and use when they reach the size of a hen's egg. Check a few at the edge before lifting the whole plant.

Fruit

The nurseries breeding fruit trees have been concentrating on smaller, dwarf stocks for easier picking. As a consequence, it is now relatively easy to find fruit trees small enough to grow on a balcony or roof terrace. Apples, in particular, are now to be found in dwarf forms, like 'Ballerina'. Fig trees do best with their roots in a confined space, and it is also possible to grow a vine in a pot. Strawberries can be grown in special tall pots with planting pockets, to ensure a decent-sized crop from very little actual floor space. A thornless blackberry can be trained along a railing, to produce a good-sized crop.

The disadvantage of growing fruit is that some of the tree fruit are prone to a variety of pests and diseases and you may need to resort to chemical sprays in order to ensure a crop. You will also need to prune the plants to ensure a good crop. Strawberries, however, are relatively easy to grow, although a great attraction for slugs and snails. Blackberries are tough survivors but strong growers, and will need keeping in check with hard pruning. A fig tree, whether or not it produces fruit, is still a singularly beautiful ornamental plant and if fan-trained against a wall, will take up relatively little space.

COBAEACEAE
Ficus carica
H Up to 3m (10ft) S 3m (10ft)

ZONES 7–9
Figs are among the oldest fruits in cultivation, and they will grow and crop well in a warm, sheltered position. Allowed to grow unchecked, they can become large and unproductive, so they thrive in a large container when they are well-watered and well-fed. They can be fan-trained against a wall or fence. 'Brown Turkey' is a reliable cropping variety, which does not require a poy well in containers or grow-bags.

hardiness Half hardy
position Full sun
cultivation Plant young plants in loam-based compost (J.I. 3) in a deep container. Feed in spring with an organic mulch. Water freely in summer. Remove any runners (or peg them down in pots of compost to increase stock).
cropping Harvest in summer. Figs are ready to pick when flesh yields to gentle pressure.
pruning Cut out old fruited wood in early spring, and prune weak young shoots to a single bud. Cut out dead or diseased wood. If fan-trained, cut back new growth by one-third, and tie in new shoots.

Ficus 'Rouge de Bordeaux'

ROSACEAE
Fragaria
H Up to 23cm (8in)

ZONES 5–9

Many varieties of strawberry produce all their fruit in one month during the summer, and may crop early ('Elvira'), mid-season ('Cambridge Favourite') or late ('Florence'). The cropping season can be extended by a mixture of all three, or choosing a perpetual variety (such as 'Mara des Bois') which will crop less heavily, but throughout the summer. Container-growing allows control over the runners. Cut them off, or root the new plants by pegging into pots of compost to increase stock or replace older plants and ensure continued fruit.

hardiness Frost hardy
position Full sun
cultivation Grow in loam-based compost (J.I. 2) in a container or grow-bag. Keep watered until well established. Keep moist and feed every week with high-potash fertilizer (tomato food) as they fruit. Mulch the compost surface (with straw).
cropping Pick berries with stalks when red over three-quarters of their surface. Handle as little as possible. Pick every other day.
pruning Cut off runners not needed for replacement plants, and cut the foliage down to 10cm (4in) in autumn after picking.
propagation Strawberries are particularly easy to propagate. Small plantlets will be produced at the end of long runners in late summer/early autumn. Simply snip these off when rooted and replant in small pots.

Fragaria

Malus 'Gala'

ROSACEAE
Malus
H Up to 3m (10ft)

ZONES 4–8

Apples have a wide variety of flavours and uses, and a long cropping and storing season from late summer to mid-spring. They grow in containers if well-fed and watered. Choose a variety on a dwarfing rootstock so that it does not grow too big. M27 is the smallest, and will restrict the tree to under 1.5m (5ft). Family trees produce several varieties of apple on one plant. Apples can also be trained as cordons, fans or espaliers, which is ideal for limited space. The young plants are trained against wires set roughly 40cm (16in) apart. Most cultivars need cross-pollinating to produce fruit, so grow varieties with overlapping flowering periods.

hardiness Fully hardy
position Full sun
cultivation Grow in loam-based compost (J.I. 3) in a deep container. Feed in spring with balanced granular fertilizer, and in summer with high-potash fertilizer (tomato food) every two weeks. Keep moist, but not wet.
cropping To test, lift one of the fruits up in the palm of the hand and twist gently. If apple and stalk come away from the spur easily, it is ready for picking. Handle with care as they bruise easily and will deteriorate rapidly when stored. This may cause surrounding apples to rot. Early season apples which are ready for harvest between late summer and early autumn will not store and should be used within a few days of being picked. Middle season cultivars are picked from early to mid-autumn before they are fully ripe to continue ripening in store, and are ready for use from mid-autumn into early winter. Late season apples picked from mid- to late autumn continue to ripen in store, and are ready from mid-winter until late spring.
pruning Tree and bush forms of apple require moderate pruning in winter to stimulate growth so that they crop well on a regular basis and maintain an open, well-balanced structure. Strong shoots and leaders are reduced by one-third of their length, and laterals cut back to four or five buds. The habit of the tree affects the pruning: spur-bearing trees need spur-thinning and pruning; tip-bearing cultivars (such as 'Worcester Pearmain') need renewal pruning. These cultivars differ because they produce most fruit on the tips of branches, and need pruning back to a growth bud to remove areas of bare, unproductive wood.

On spur-bearers, fruit is produced on shoots of two years old or more, in clusters on short growths (spurs). Branches will carry two types of bud; large swollen buds (flowers) and smaller, pointed buds (growths). Spur systems become overcrowded and can be thinned or removed entirely.

To train cordons and espaliers, trim back the leading shoot and secure two vigorous shoots to the horizontal wires, trimming back to a couple of healthy buds. Continue to trim the leading shoot and the side shoots, as they emerge, in late summer.

Thornless blackberry

ROSACEAE
Rubus
H Up to 1.8m (6ft)

ZONES 5–9

Most blackberry cultivars produce heavy crops of large, well-flavoured glossy black fruits. Although the species plants are notoriously prickly, there are several thornless cultivars which are ideal for balconies and terraces, such as *R.f.* 'Oregon Thornless' or 'Thornfree'. The pricklier forms can prove a useful deterrent to intruders. Blackberries can be cropped for the first time two years after planting. Being vigorous, they will need to be kept under control and grown in a fan-shape against posts and wires, or railings. Most blackberries do best in full sun, but they will also cope with partial shade, cropping slightly later as a result.

hardiness Hardy
position Full sun
cultivation Grow in loam-based compost (J.I. 3). After planting, cut back to 25cm (10in) above ground level, to encourage strong stems to grow. Keep the plant well watered in dry periods and mulch with organic matter in spring and feed in summer with a high-potash fertilizer (tomato food). Tie new shoots into wires or onto posts, ideally in a fan-shape against wires roughly 30cm (12in) apart vertically.
cropping From mid- to late summer.
pruning Blackberries are vigorous plants, so cut back new shoots by one-third or more after fruiting or in autumn.

ROSACEAE
Vitis vinifera
H Up to 3m (10ft)

ZONES 7–10

Grapes are both attractive and versatile in a small garden. They can be trained to cover a sunny wall or over a pergola to provide shade. The fruit can be eaten fresh, processed for juice or used in wine making, and can be blackish-purple, greenish-white or yellow in colour depending on the cultivar.

hardiness Fully hardy to frost tender
position Full sun
cultivation Grow in loam-based compost (J.I. 3). Keep moderately moist, never wet, especially as the fruit swells. Feed in spring with a balanced granular fertilizer and every two weeks all summer with high-potash fertilizer (tomato food). Drape the plant with netting to protect the fruits from birds. Some fruit thinning may be required if the bunches are very heavy, and should be done when the grapes are about the size of peas.
cropping Cut ripe bunches of grapes with a short section of stalk and place them in a container lined with tissue paper. If not bruised, grapes will keep for up to two months in a cool dry store.
pruning Winter pruning of established vines (Guyot system) involves cutting out all old fruited wood leaving only three replacement shoots. Tie two shoots down, one on either side of the centre and tip prune as for the third winter. Prune the third shoot to three strong buds. For summer pruning and training of replacement shoots, cut out shoots obscuring the fruits, completely removing any leaves shading the grapes about six weeks before they are expected to ripen.

Vitis vinifera

Herbs

With limited space at your disposal, the culinary herbs are worth concentrating on, as just a few fresh herbs transform almost any dish, from simple grilled food to salads, soups and stews, or a couple of leaves can be added to summer drinks and deserts. All herbs need sunshine, with the exception of mint, which will do fine in partial shade. While some are herbaceous perennials, others are tender and are treated as annuals – basil (*Ocimum basilicum*) and coriander (*Coriandrum sativum*), for example. Most herbs can be harvested by plucking a few sprigs, but you can also cut them, hang them up and dry them for winter use. Thyme, rosemary and sage are excellent dried, as is bay (*Laurus nobilis*, see page 120). Most herbs come from around the Mediterranean, and are ideal for containers. They thrive in poor soil and with relatively little water. There is a wide range grown for medicinal properties and culinary value. Many of them are also attractive plants in their own right, particularly those such as rosemary and sage, which have a range of cultivars to choose from. The purple-leaved sage (*Salvia officinalis* 'Purpurascens') makes an attractive foil for ornamental flowering displays.

Chives

ALLIACEAE
Allium
H 30–60cm (12–24in)

ZONES 5–8

The Allium family includes both garlic (*Allium sativum*) and chives (*Allium schoenoprasum*). Garlic is a good source of vitamins and minerals and is mildly antibiotic. It can be used to reduce blood pressure, help ease hardened arteries and rheumatism, and as an aid to clearing catarrh (including hay fever in summer). It can also be taken as protection against illnesses such as colds. Chives are hardy, bulbous perennials, which are grown for their edible, hollow, dark green leaves, which have a mild onion flavour and complement many dishes, especially those containing cheese and eggs. They produce dense, round heads of purple or white flowers in summer. Propagation is by seed sown in spring.

hardiness Fully hardy
flowering Summer
position Full sun
cultivation Loam-based compost (J.I. 2) or well-drained soil. Water freely in summer, very sparingly in winter, and feed with a balanced liquid fertilizer every two weeks in spring, once a month in summer.
overwintering Do not allow to become waterlogged.
pests & diseases Slugs may attack new shoots.
special features The flowerheads are an attractive bonus on these tasty plants.

Coriander

APIACEAE

Coriandrum sativum

H 50cm (1½ft)

ZONE 10

Coriander is an aromatic annual, with toothed, flat leaflets at its base, and finely divided upper leaves. White or pale purple flowers are produced in summer, followed by golden-brown seeds. The flavour resembles strong parsley, and all parts of the plant can be used, seed, leaf, stem and root. Seed is used in curry, chutney, soup, apple pies, cakes and biscuits. The leaves are added to curry, salad, and used as a garnish. Fresh roots can be cooked as a vegetable or added to curries, and the stem can be cooked with beans and soups. Propagate by sowing seed in spring

(in mild climates, it can be sown in autumn to overwinter outdoors).

hardiness Fully hardy
flowering Mid-summer to autumn
position Full sun (for seed) to partial shade (for leaf growth)
cultivation Loam-based compost (J.I. 2) or well-drained soil. Water freely in summer, sparingly if overwintering. Apply a balanced liquid fertilizer every two weeks in spring, monthly in summer. Harvest leaves regularly.
overwintering Protect from frost (self-seeds easily).
pests & diseases Fungal wilt
special features Aniseed grows better near coriander; fennel suffers.

LAMBICEAE

Melissa officinalis

H 60cm (2ft)

ZONES 4–8

A hardy herbaceous perennial plant, the lemon balm has scented, toothed, oval-shaped leaves with uses from the aromatic (pillows and pot-pourri) to the medicinal. It can ease tension, bronchial catarrh, nausea, high temperature and headaches, acts as a mild sedative, and has a tonic effect on the digestive system. Fresh leaves can be applied directly to insect bites. Culinary uses include infusing the leaves to make herbal tea, adding them to vinegars, and in both sweet and savoury dishes. *M. o.* 'Aurea' has gold-splashed leaves. Propagate by sowing seed in spring.

hardiness Fully hardy
flowering Summer
position Light shade (the scent becomes harsh if the leaves have too much hot sun).
cultivation Loam-based compost (J.I. 2) or well-drained soil. Water freely in summer, very sparingly in winter, and feed with a balanced liquid fertilizer every two weeks in spring, monthly in summer.
overwintering Do not allow to become waterlogged.
pests & diseases None
special features Cut back every spring to encourage new growth.

Lemon balm

LAMIACEAE

Mentha

H 60cm (2ft)

ZONES 3–7

The mint family is large, and includes a wide range of hardy, spreading, aromatic perennials. Forms include: *M.* x *gracilis* 'Variegata' (ginger mint); *M.* x *piperita f. citrata* (eau-de-Cologne mint); *M. pulegium* (pennyroyal); *M. requienii* (Corsican mint); *M. spicata* (spearmint); M. suaveolens 'Variegata' (pineapple mint); and *M.* x *villosa f. alopecuroides* (Bowles mint). *M. spicata* will flavour peas and potatoes, and make mint sauce. Peppermint leaves (*M. piperita*) can be infused to make a soothing and relaxing drink (hot in winter, iced in summer). It is good for relieving

indigestion and heavy colds, and for promoting good sleep. Propagate by division in spring, rooting tip cuttings in summer or sowing seed in spring.

hardiness Fully hardy
flowering Summer
position Full sun
cultivation Loam-based compost (J.I. 2) or well-drained soil. Water freely in summer, very sparingly in winter.
overwintering Do not allow to become waterlogged.
pests & diseases Rust, if the plant dries out
special features Pick the leaves before flowering and use fresh, dried, frozen, or chopped finely and infused in vinegar.

Apple mint

LAMIACEAE
Ocimum basilicum
H 30–60cm (1–2ft)

ZONE 10

Basil is usually grown as a half-hardy annual (positioned outdoors after the danger of frost has passed) or a short-lived perennial in frost-free areas. It needs a warm, sheltered position to grow well. The aromatic, bright green leaves are delicious and can be used in tomato dishes, pasta dishes, salads, vinegars and pesto. Spikes of two-lipped, pinkish-white flowers are produced in summer. *O. b.* 'Dark Opal' has red-purple leaves. *O. b.* var. *minimum* is smaller and more compact. Propagation is by seed sown in spring and early summer.

hardiness Frost tender
flowering Summer
position Full sun (protect from scorching midday sun)
cultivation Loam-based compost (J.I. 2) or well-drained soil. Water freely in summer, very sparingly in winter, and feed with a balanced liquid fertilizer every two weeks in spring, monthly in summer. Pinch out the flowers to keep a succession of leaves.
overwintering Protect from frost and do not allow to become too wet.
pests & diseases Aphids
special features Young leaves can either be picked and used fresh, or frozen, dried or bottled in oil for future use.

Basil

Marjoram

LAMIACEAE
Origanum vulgare
H 30–60cm (1–2ft)

ZONES 5–9

The name *Origanum* covers oregano and marjoram, which are both hardy herbaceous perennials with aromatic, oval leaves. They will tolerate a hot, sunny position, preferring alkaline conditions. They produce loose spikes of small pink or white flowers in summer and need warmth and bright light in order to grow well. The leaves can be used in Italian, egg and cheese dishes. Forms include: *O. v.* 'Aureum' which has golden-yellow foliage and pink flowers; *O. v.* 'Compactum' which is smaller and dome-shaped; and *O. v.* 'Variegatum' which has yellow tips to the leaves. Propagate by rooting tip cuttings in summer.

hardiness Fully hardy
flowering Summer
position Full sun (gold-leaved forms need shading from midday sun)
cultivation Loam-based compost (J.I. 2) or well-drained soil. Water freely in summer, sparingly in winter, and feed with a balanced liquid fertilizer every two weeks in spring and monthly in summer.
overwintering Do not allow to become waterlogged.
pests & diseases None
special features Leaves can be used fresh, dried or frozen.

Parsley

APIACEAE
Petroselinum crispum
H 60cm (2ft)

ZONES 6–8

Parsley is a hardy biennial, which is commonly grown as an annual, and related to carrot and celery. The edible, mid-green leaves are popular in cooking and as a garnish. Green-yellow flowers are produced in summer. There are two main types; curly- and flat-leaved. *P. crispum* has densely curled, moss-like leaves, carried on hollow stems. French or Italian parsley (*P. c.* var. *neapolitanum*) has flat leaves and a stronger flavour. Forms include: *P. c.* 'Darki' with very dark green, tightly curled leaves; *P. c.* 'Clivi' is compact; and *P. c.* var. *tuberosum* (Hamburg parsley) has edible roots. Propagate from seed sown in spring.

hardiness Fully hardy
flowering Summer
position Full sun to partial shade
cultivation Loam-based compost (J. I. 2) or well-drained soil. Water freely in summer, sparingly in winter, and feed monthly with a balanced liquid fertilizer. Cannot tolerate waterlogging.
overwintering Protect from frost in order to maintain a good supply of leaves.
pests & diseases Celery maggot fly. Celery canker may cause root rot.
special features Use the leaves in their first year, fresh, dried or frozen.

LAMIACEAE
Rosmarinus officinalis
H Up to 1.5m (5ft)

ZONES 6–9

A hardy, lax shrub with narrow, aromatic, evergreen leaves which can be used fresh or dried to flavour hot and cold food dishes, especially lamb, pork and baked potatoes. Small, two-lipped flowers are produced in spring and summer, in shades of purple-blue to mauve and white. Forms include: *R. o.* var. *albiflorus* (white flowers); *R. o.* 'Aureus' (yellow variegated leaves); 'Benenden Blue' (bright blue flowers); 'Roseus' (pink flowers); 'Severn Sea' (compact, with bright blue flowers on arching shoots); and 'Tuscan Blue' (upright, blue flowers). Propagation is by

semi-ripe cuttings taken in late summer and early autumn.

hardiness Hardy
flowering Spring to late summer
position Full sun
cultivation Loam-based compost (J.I. 2) or well-drained soil. Water freely in summer, very sparingly in winter, and apply a balanced liquid fertilizer monthly.
overwintering Mulch in prolonged periods of frost. Do not allow to become water-logged.
pests & diseases None
special features Tip regularly to trim back straggling shoots and encourage bushing. These plants do not respond well to hard pruning.

Rosemary

LAMIACEAE
Salvia officinalis
H 60cm (2ft)

ZONES 5–8

Sage is a woody subshrub with aromatic, woolly, evergreen leaves on erect, square stems (often with a reddish tinge). Two-lipped, lilac-blue flowers are produced in summer, in spikes at the tips of the stems. The leaves are cooked with fatty meats to aid digestion. Medicinally, they have an antiseptic effect, and an infusion will help soothe a sore throat. Forms include: *S. o.* 'Purpurascens' (reddish-purple leaves); *S. o.* 'Ictarina' (yellow variegated leaves); 'Kew Gold' (golden-yellow leaves and mauve flowers); and *S. o.* 'Tricolor' (cream and pinkish markings on grey-green

leaves). Propagation is by soft-tip cuttings in spring or semi-ripe cuttings in summer.

hardiness Fully hardy
flowering Summer
position Full sun to partial shade
cultivation Loam-based compost (J.I. 2) or well-drained soil. Keep slightly dry, watering regularly in summer, sparingly in winter. Apply a balanced liquid fertilizer monthly in summer.
overwintering Do not allow to become waterlogged. Protect from cold winds.
pests & diseases Caterpillars may eat the leaves.
special features Do not take during pregnancy, as the leaves contain oestrogen.

Sage (*Salvia officinalis* 'Tricolor')

Thyme

LAMIACEAE
Thymus x *citriodorus*
H 30cm (12in)

ZONES 7–9

The thymes are small, shrubby perennials with thin, twiggy stems and small, oval, grey-green, lemon-scented leaves. Clusters of tiny pale lavender flowers appear from mid- to late summer on the tips of the shoots and attract bees. Use leaves in stocks and soup, or with chicken and fish. Aids sore throats, coughs and headaches. Forms include: *T.* x *c.* 'Aureus' (golden leaves, tinged green); *T.* x *c.* 'Bertram Anderson' (golden-variegated green leaves); and *T.* x *c.* 'Silver Queen' (cream-variegated leaves). Propagation is by semi-ripe cuttings, with a heel, taken in late summer.

hardiness Fully hardy
flowering Mid- to late summer
position Full sun to partial shade (variegated forms lose their colour in shade)
cultivation Loam-based compost (J.I. 2) or well-drained soil, preferably neutral to alka-line. Water moderately in summer, sparingly in winter, and feed monthly with a balanced liquid fertilizer.
overwintering Protect from cold winds and do not allow to become waterlogged.
pests & diseases None
special features Prune frequently, including flowerheads (after flowering) to keep the plant dense and bushy.
decorative ideas Grow in low pots close to pathways, so the aroma is released as people brush past the plants.

INDEX

PLANT LISTS

Plants for aromatic foliage and/or scented flowers

Buxus sempervirens
Chimonanthus praecox
Choisya ternata
Dianthus cv.
Eucalyptus gunnii
Geranium (species)
Heliotropium cv.
Hyacinthus cv.
Jasminum officinale
Lavandula sp.
Lilium 'Regale'
Lonicera sp.
Marjoram sp.
Mentha sp.
Narcissus (some, such as 'Pheasant's Eye')
Nicotiana sp.
Pelargonium (species)
Philadelphus 'Beauclerk'
Primula
Rosmarinus officinalis
Salvia officinalis
Trachelospermum jasminoides
Thymus sp.
Verbena x *hybrida*
Viola cv.

Plants for foliage effect

Acer palmatum
Agave americana
Buxus sempervirens
Chamaecyparis sp.
Cordyline australis
Cyclamen
Erica gracilis
Eucalyptus gunnii
Euphorbia sp.
Hebe sp.
Hedera helix
Helichrysum petiolare
Heuchera micrantha 'Palace Purple'

Hosta sieboldii 'Elegans', *H.* 'Halcyon'
Humulus lupulus 'Aurea'
Laurus nobilis
Parthenocissus
Pinus sp.
Phormium tenax
Saxifraga sp.
Sedum sp.
Vitis coignetiae

Plants for shade

Anemone blanda, A. x *hybrida*
Astilbe
Athyrium filix-femina
Convallaria majus
Cyclamen coum, C. hederifolium
Dryopteris filix-mas
Galanthus nivalis
Helleborus corsicus
Heuchera micrantha
Hosta sp.
Impatiens cv.
Oxalis sp.
Polypodium sp.
Primula sp.
Rhododendron sp.
Viola sp.

Hanging basket plants

Ageratum
Argyranthemum
Begonia (trailing)
Brachyscome iberidifolia
Diascia
Felicia amelloides
Fuchsia (trailing)
Glechoma hederacea 'Variegata'
Impatiens
Lobelia
Lotus berthelottii
Pelargonium (ivy-leaved trailing)
Petunia (trailing)

Primula
Senecio cineraria
Scaevola
Tagetes
Tropaeolum majus
Verbena x *hybrida*
Viola

Silver/grey/blue foliage

Artemisia sp.
Cerastium tomentosum
Convolvulus cneorum
Elaegnus 'Quicksilver'
Festuca glauca
Hebe pingifolia 'Pagei'
Hosta 'Halcyon'
Pyrus salicifolia 'Pendula'
Santolina chamaecyparisus
Tanacetum haradjanii

Purple/dark foliage

Acer palmatum 'Atropurpureum'
Berberis thunbergii 'Atropurpurea'
Clematis recta 'Purpurea'
Cordyline australis 'Atropurpurea'
Dahlia 'Bishop of Llandaff'
Foeniculum vulgare 'Purpureum'
Heuchera micrantha 'Palace Purple'
Rosa glauca
Salvia officinalis 'Purpurascens'
Viola labradorica
Vitis vinifera 'Purpurea'

Hot-coloured flowers

Achillea 'Cerise Queen'
Astrantia major 'Ruby Wedding'
Cosmos atrosantuineus (red)
Begonia 'Non-Stop' series cvs (reds, oranges)
Dahlia 'Bishop of Llandaff' (red)
Dianthum 'Brympton Red'
Geum ' Mrs Bradshaw' (orange)
Lobelia 'Cherry Ripe' (red)

Lychnis chalcedonica (pink)
Paeonia (pink, red)
Papaver orientale (pink, red)
Pelargonium cvs (reds, pinks)
Penstemon 'Cherry Ripe' (red)
Potentilla 'Gibson's Scarlet'
Primula cvs (yellow, orange and red cvs)
Tagetes (yellow and orange)

Cool coloured flowers

Agapanthus (blue)
Anemone x *hybrida* 'Honorine Jobert'
Campanula (white and blue)
Cyclamen (white cvs)
Geranium 'Johnson's Blue'
Gypsophila paniculata (white and pale pink)
Hosta spp (white and mauve)
Hyacinthus 'L'Innocence' (white)
Hydrangea (blue)
Leucanthemum 'Everest' (white)
Lobelia (blue)
Nepeta nervosa (blue)
Primula (blue and white cvs)
Scilla siberica (blue)

Plants for autumn foliage colour and/or fruit

Acer palmatum
Capsicum
Chaenomeles
Cotoneaster horizontalis
Gaultheria
Ilex
Mahonia
Pyracantha sp.
Rosa
Rubus
Skimmia
Solanum
Vitis coignetiae

ZONE CHART

Zones designate the lowest range of temperatures in which a plant will normally survive. Thus a plant in Zone 8 will normally survive between -12°C and -6°C (10°F and 20°F).

Zone	1	2	3	4	5	6	7	7.5	8	9	10
°Centigrade	Below -45	-45 to -40	-40 to -34	-34 to -29	-29 to -23	-23 to -18	-18 to -15	-15 to -12	-12 to -6	-6 to -1	-1 to 5
°Fahrenheit	Below -50	-50 to -40	-40 to -30	-30 to -20	-20 to -10	-10 to 0	0 to 5	5 to 10	10 to 20	20 to 30	30 to 40

ACKNOWLEDGMENTS The authors and publishers would like to thank the following for their help in producing this book: Ruth Hope *for the design*; Corinne Asghar *for editorial work*; Steven Wooster *for his photography*; Edward Berry Wooster *for help at photography shoots*; Kate Simunek *for her artwork*; Andrew Lord *at the Garden Picture Library for picture research assistance*; Kate Kirby and Niamh Hatton *at Collins & Brown for editorial help. Plants and materials supplied by:* Granville Garden Centre, Granville Road, London NW2 *and* Clifton Nurseries, Maida Vale, London W9.

PICTURE CREDITS

T *top;* B *bottom;* C *centre;* L *left;* R *right*

1 Steven Wooster; C & B; 2-3 Steven Wooster/Wichford Pottery, Chelsea Flower Show; 4-5 Steven Wooster/C & B; 6-7 Steven Wooster/C & B; 8-9 Steven Wooster/C & B ; 10-11 Steven Wooster, Chelsea Flower Show 199l; 12-13 C & B except for 13B Steven Wooster/C & B; 14-15 C & B; 16-17 C & B except for 17B Michelle Garret/C & B; 18-19 C & B except for 18B, 19T Steven Wooster/C & B; 20-21 C & B; 22T Steven Wooster/C & B; 23 C & B; 24 C & B; 24B Steven Wooster/C & B; 25T Steven Wooster/C & B; 25B C & B; 26-27 Michelle Garrett/C & B except for 26BL and BR Steven Wooster/C & B; 28-29 Michelle Garrett/C & B; 30-31 Steve Wooster/C & B; 32-33 Steven Wooster/C & B; 32BR, 33 Steven Wooster; 34-35 C & B; 35T Steven Wooster; 36-37 C & B; 38-39 C & B; 40-41 C & B; 42-3 Steven Wooster/ Glebe Cottage Plants; 44 Steven Wooster; designer Susan Bennett & Earl Hyde; 45 Friedrich Strauss/GPL; 46-47 Steven Wooster; 47T Steven Wooster/Hampton Court Flower Show, Beachcomber Trading Co; 47B Steven Wooster; 48 Zara McCalmont/GPL; 49 Lamontagne/GPL; 50-51 C & B, except for 51B Steven Wooster/designer Ian Sidaway; 52-53 Steven Wooster/C & B except for 53B Michelle Garrett; 54-55 C & B; 56-57 C & B except for 57T Steven Wooster/designer Tony Noel; 57B Steven Wooster/ designers Ross and Paula Greenville; 58-59 Michelle Garrett/C & B except for 59TR Steven Wooster/Ranui Road, NZ; 60T Michelle Garrett/C & B; 60-61 Steven Wooster/C & B; 62-63 Mayer/Le Scanff/ GPL; 64B and R Steven Wooster/C & B; 65BL and BR Michelle Garrett/C & B; 66T Steven Wooster/C & B; 66B Steven Wooster/ Anthony Nolan; 67 Steven Wooster; 68 B and C Steven Wooster; 69T Steven Wooster/C & B; 69 BL, BC and BR C & B; 70A Steven Wooster/C & B; 71 John Ferro Sims/GPL; 72C John Glover/GPL; 72T Lynn Brotchie/GPL; 72B Marijke Heuff/GPL, 73 Friedrich Strauss/GPL; 74-5 Steven Wooster/C & B; 76 and 77B Michelle Garret/C & B; 77T Steven Wooster/C & B; 78B and T Michelle Garrett/C & B; 79 Steven Wooster; 80-81 Steven Wooster/C & B; 82 Gareth Sambidge/C & B; 83 Michelle Garrett/C & B; 84-85 Steven Wooster/C & B; 86B, 87T and R Steven Wooster; 88T and B Steven Wooster; 90T and B Steven Wooster; 92T Steven Wooster/C & B; 93 C & B; 94L Steven Wooster/designer Terence Conran, Chelsea Flower Show; 95T Steven Wooster/designer Terence Conran, Chelsea Flower Show; 95B and C C & B; 95R Friedrich Strauss/GPL; 96T Steven Wooster/C & B ; 96BL Steven Wooster; 96BR Steven Wooster; 97 Steven Wooster/designer Terence Conran, Chelsea Flower Show; 98T Brian Carter/GPL; 98B David Cavagnaro/GPL; 98C Vaughan Fleming/GPL; 99T Linda Burgess/GPL; 99R Linda Burgess/GPL; 100-101 Steven Wooster/C & B; 102 Steven Wooster/C & B; 104 Friedrich Strauss/GPL; 105T Andrew Lawson/C & B; 105B Juliette Wade/GPL; 106T Friedrich Strauss/GPL; 106B Brigitte Thomas/GPL; 107T Steven Wooster; 107B Michelle Garrett/C & B; 108T Mel Watson/GPL; 108B Lynne Brotchie/GPL; 109T Christopher Fairweather/GPL; 109B Steven Woosten (Beth Chatto Gardens); 110T Lynne Brotchie/GPL; 110B Neil Holmes/GPL; 111L Friedrich Strauss/GPL; 111TR and BR Steven Wooster/C & B; 112T Juliette Wade/GPL; 112B Friedrich Strauss/GPL; 113T Steven Wooster/C & B; 113C Steven Wooster/GPL; 113B Densey Clyne/GPL; 114T Lynne Brotchie/ GPL; 114B Steven Wooster/C & B; 115TR Steven Wooster/ C & B; 115C Steven Wooster/Duane Paul Design Team/ GPL; 115B Friedrich Strauss/GPL; 116T Andrew Lawson/C & B; 116B Steven Wooster/C & B; 117T Ron Sutherland/GPL; 117B Steven Wooster/C & B; 118T John Glover/GPL; 118C Andrew Lawson/C & B; 118B Clive Nichols/GPL; 119T Steven Wooster/C & B; 119C Steven Wooster/C & B; 119B Sunniva Harte/GPL; 120T Steven Wooster/

C & B; 120C Eric Crichton/GPL; 120B Steven Wooster/C & B; 121T Friedrich Strauss/GPL; Andrew Lawons/C & B; 121B Steven Wooster/C & B; 122T Steven Wooster/C & B; 122B Lamontagne/ GPL; 123T Philipe Bondue; 124 Friedrich Strauss/ GPL; 125T Howard Rice/C & B; 125B John Glover/GPL; 126T JS Sira/GPL; 126C Steven Wooster/C & B; 126B Howard Rice/C & B; 127BL Steven Wooster/ C & B; 127BR John Glover/GPL; 128T Steven Wooster/C & B; 128C Brian Carter/GPL; BR Steven Wooster/C & B; 129T Steven Wooster/ C & B; 129C Howard Rice/C & B; 129B Howard Rice/C & B; 130T Jane Legate/GPL; 130B Steven Wooster/C & B; 131T Howard Rice/C & B; 131C Howard Rice/C & B; 131B Steven Wooster/C & B; 132T John Glover/GPL; 132B John Glover/GPL; 133T JS Sira/GPL; 133BL Howard Rice/C & B; 133BR John Glover/ GPL; 134T Jerry Pavia/ GPL; 134C Howard Rice/C & B; 134B Steven Wooster/C & B; 135T Steven Wooster/GPL; BR Howard Rice/C & B; 136 Georgia Glyn-Smith/GPL; 137T Juliette Wade/ GPL; 137B Steven Wooster/C & B; 138T Steven Wooster/C & B; 138B Howard Rice/C & B; 139 Andrew Lawson/C & B; 140T Howard Rice/C & B; 140C Andrew Lawson/C & B; 140B Friedrich Strauss/GPL; 141T Steven Wooster/C & B; 141B Andrew Lawson/C & B; 142T Friedrich Strauss/ GPl; 142C Steven Wooster/C & B; 142B Steven Wooster/C & B; 143 Brian Carter/GPL; 144T Janet Sorrell/GPL; 144B Andrew Lawson/C & B; 145T Janet Sorrell/GPL; 145B Steven Wooster/C & B; 146T Howard Rice/C & B; 146B Mark Bolton/GPL; 147T Steven Wooster/C & B; 147B Howard Rice/C & B; 148T Andrew Lawson/C & B; 148C Howard Rice/C & B; 148B Steven Wooster/C & B; 149T Howard Rice/C & B; 149C Steven Wooster/C & B; 149B Howard Rice/C & B; 150T Andrew Lawson/C & B; 150B Andrew Lawson/C & B; 151T Howard Rice/ C & B; 151C Howard Rice/C & B; 151B Sunniva Harte/GPL; 152T Howard Rice/C & B; 152C Steven Wooster/C & B; 152B Eric Crichton/GPL; 153T Steven Wooster/ C & B; 153C Howard Rice/C & B; 153B Andew Lawson/C & B; 154T Friedrich Strauss/GPL; 154BL Andrew Lawson/C & B; 154BR Friedrich Strauss/ GPL; 155T Mayer/Le Scanff/GPL; 155B Andrew Lawson/C & B; 156 Steven Wooster/C & B; 157T Vaughan Fleming/ GPL; 157C Howard Rice/C & B; 157B Ron Sutherland/GPL; 158T Andrew Lawson/ C & B; 158B Steven Wooster/Cheneys Manor Garden; 159T Steven Wooster; 159B Howard Rice/C & B; 160T Howard Rice/C & B; 160B Christopher Fairweather/GPL; 161T Andrew Lawson/C & B; 162B Steven Wooster/C & B; 162T Andrew Lawson/C & B; 162B David Cavagnaro/GPL; 163T Lamontagne/GPL; 163C Howard Rice/ C & B; 164B Steven Wooster/C & B; 164T Christopher Fairweather/ GPL; 164C John Glover/GPL; 164B Neil Holmes/GPL; 165T Steven Wooster/C & B; 165B Didier Willery/GPL; 166 Steven Wooster/C & B; 167 Howard Rice/C & B; 168T John Glover/GPL; 168B JS Sira/GPL; 169 Howard Rice/C & B; 170T Michelle Garrett/C & B; 170C Howard Rice/C & B; 170B Steven Wooster; 171T & B Steven Wooster/ C & B; 172 Howard Rice/C & B; 173T and B Andrew Lawson/C & B; 174T Howard Rice/C & B; 174C Steven Wooster/C & B; 174B Friedrich Strauss/GPL; 175TL Andrew Lawson/C & B; 175TR John Glover/GPL; 175BR Howard Rice/C & B; 176 Steven Wooster/GPL; 177T Sunniva Harte/GPL; 177B Janet Sorrell/GPL; 178T David Cavagnaro/GPL; 178C and B Howard Rice/C & B; 179T Elizabeth Crowe/GPL; 179B John Glover/GPL; 180T Michael Howes/ GPL; 180B Mel Watson/GPL; 181 Howard Rice/GPL; 182T Steven Wooster/ C & B; 182B John Glover/GPL; 183T Neil Holmes/ GPL; John Glover/ Chelsea Flower Show/GPL; 184 Steven Wooster; 185T Mel Watson/ GPL; 185C A Lord/GPL; 185B A Lord/ GPL; 186T Friedrich Strauss/ GPL; 186C A Lord/GPL; 186B Andrew Lawson; 187T Friedrich Strauss/ GPL; 187C Andrew Lawson/C & B; 187B Howard Rice/C & B.